W9-DFL-414

Paedophiles in Society

Paedophiles in Society

Reflecting on Sexuality, Abuse and Hope

Sarah D. Goode
University of Winchester, UK

Foreword by Deborah Donovan Rice
Executive Director of Stop It Now! USA

First published 2011 by
PALGRAVE MACMILLAN

Palgrave Macmillan in the UK is an imprint of Macmillan Publishers Limited,
registered in England, company number 785998, of Houndmills, Basingstoke,
Hampshire RG21 6XS.

Palgrave Macmillan in the US is a division of St Martin's Press LLC,
175 Fifth Avenue, New York, NY 10010.

Palgrave Macmillan is the global academic imprint of the above companies
and has companies and representatives throughout the world.

Palgrave® and Macmillan® are registered trademarks in the United States,
the United Kingdom, Europe and other countries.

ISBN 978–0–230–27188–3

This book is printed on paper suitable for recycling and made from fully
managed and sustained forest sources. Logging, pulping and manufacturing
processes are expected to conform to the environmental regulations of the
country of origin.

A catalogue record for this book is available from the British Library.

Library of Congress Cataloging-in-Publication Data
Goode, Sarah D.
    Paedophiles in society : reflecting on sexuality,
    abuse and hope / Sarah Goode.
       p.   cm.
    Includes index.
    ISBN 978–0–230–27188–3 (hardback)
    1. Pedophilia.   2. Child sexual abuse.   I. Title.
    HQ71.G654 2011
    306.77—dc22   2011001479

10   9   8   7   6   5   4   3   2   1
20 19 18 17 16 15 14 13 12 11

Transferred to Digital Printing in 2012

To all those who have helped; to all those with the courage and vision to make things better; to all those who have the guts to stand up and speak out and to call it as they see it; to all those who put children first and who remember that children are not little adults, they need our protection; to all those disparate voices speaking out different truths but working together for good sense, integrity, maturity and compassion; to all those who may not even agree with each other but who fundamentally are pointing in the same loving direction; to Andrew Blake, Andrea Driver, Emily Droisen, Judith Golberg, Fran Henry, Judith Herman, Liz Kelly, Jim Kincaid, Tink Palmer, Judith Reisman, John Stoltenberg; to children – mine, yours, all our children in the future and all the children we once were.

Contents

Foreword

Prepare to move beyond accepted notions about the sexual abuse of children in evidence in the media, in the classroom and in the halls of government. The author calls on her reader to grapple with the underpinnings of our current framework for thinking about this social problem. Much like an investigative reporter, she sorts out the threads of scientific research, ideological and religious history and cultural discourses which have influenced and continue to shape our response to what is a pervasive threat to the wellbeing of our children.

Not shy about calling out the disconnections between our espoused views of valuing children and our actions which indicate otherwise, she challenges us on a personal and professional level to be more careful about how we proceed in considering how best to prevent sexual abuse of children. Focusing on protecting children and punishing those who abuse them, as she states, can leave out the point of view of the child. Often the policies and laws which are enacted privilege the adult needs over those of the child.

There is plenty for the mind to grapple with here and there are stories that speak directly to the heart. This blend of cited research juxtaposed with observations of the culture and reports of direct experience by individuals makes for a compelling read. Not something you find very often or necessarily expect in professional literature. In my work in the prevention of sexual abuse of children, I find this more holistic approach refreshing.

At the same time, the author adds new dimensions to our thinking with her bold assertions, carefully researched and deeply considered. Creating the space for numerous difficult questions to be brought to light gives the reader a chance to safely question and come to her or his own conclusions. How does our use of language impact on our understanding of the subject? How far are we willing to go to be open to new concepts that may challenge our supposed ethical point of view? I found myself welcoming the challenge and adding some of my own previously unconsidered questions.

The author successfully dispels some of the confusion so prevalent in our cultural responses to sexual abuse of children. As one example, in discussing pedophiles, she asks that we de-link adult sexual attraction to children from adult sexual contact with children. This will be seen as a radical concept by some. However, this clarification based on her research points to a way forward beyond the 'us and them' polarity. It is this place of fear and paralysis that so many people find themselves in when faced with everyday situations where a child may be at risk – caring but not knowing what to do, as reported in Stop It Now!'s report: *What Do U.S. Adults Think about Child Sexual Abuse? Measures of Knowledge and Attitudes among Six States* (online, June 2010).

I find myself in a hopeful frame of mind, with potent recommendations made by the author which I will continue to consider and discuss with colleagues, friends and family. Above all, are we as individuals willing to work to create the communities which value children enough to make every effort to prevent and stop the abuse? Embracing the depth of empathy espoused within these pages is one way forward.

Deborah Donovan Rice
Executive Director of Stop It Now! USA

Preface

This book is not like any other book you may have read on paedophiles, or adult sexual attraction to children, or child protection. It is not about the medical, forensic, psychological, psychiatric, legal or criminological aspects of these phenomena. Those issues are adequately dealt with in other texts. Instead, this book is about ordinariness, about culture and society around us and about how people in everyday life think about and make sense of men being sexually attracted to children (the book says something too about women sexually attracted to children but the focus is predominantly on men).

We know that paedophiles exist, although we don't yet have a clear idea of how many there may be. As far as we can tell from the small number of studies so far, in every group of a hundred men there will be at least a few – maybe two or three, maybe more – whose main or only sexual interest is in children. In addition, around one in five of all men find themselves, at least sometimes, sexually aroused to children.

How does society respond? This book argues that we respond with confusion and bafflement. There is little consensus on how to react when, for example, Michael Jackson is accused of sexually molesting boys, or Roman Polanski is arrested for the statutory rape of a minor. The massive public distress when 3-year-old Madeleine McCann disappeared from a holiday resort in Portugal in 2007 shows us, however, that our confusion is not caused by indifference. We care deeply. The protection of children matters to us, but we are just not sure how to make sense of it or what to do about it.

One of the most important innovations of the last few decades has been the internet. The internet has both been shaped by paedophiles (through, for example, 'darknet' sites for the dissemination of child sexual abuse images) and has itself profoundly shaped the experience of being a paedophile in contemporary society. The internet is capable of acting as an amplifier for the 'paedophile voice', and this book, through a study of the online editing of the term 'child grooming' by paedophile activists, illustrates the ways in which knowledge is socially constructed and technical terms such as 'paedophilia' or 'grooming' become absorbed into popular culture.

Popular culture comprises all the ways in which a society shares and shapes its understanding. As the book argues, popular culture reflects the confusion felt over paedophiles. Newspapers, internet jokes, popular cartoon series, Hollywood films – all provide examples of different and conflicting responses to paedophilia. Drawing on history, anthropology and biology provide insights but leave us not much clearer.

Academic and cultural understandings of paedophilia tend to diverge into a 'sexual liberation' discourse and a 'child protection' discourse. In order to understand why this might be so, the book discusses the most influential text on human sexuality in the twentieth century, Alfred Kinsey's Report on *Sexual Behavior in the Human Male*, and examines in detail what Kinsey actually said about 'childhood sexuality'. Kinsey's work is of central importance in understanding contemporary views on paedophilia and adult sexual contact with children and his views have continued to be put forward in numerous books and articles. This book provides an overview of a selection of works (academic, lay and professional) which advocate a tolerant or positive view of adult sexual contact with children. The influence of such books is little-recognized but, I argue, has fundamentally shaped the perception of paedophiles in society.

A central thesis of this book is that paedophiles are not 'outside' culture or society. Rather, it is argued that they are part of our everyday human existence and that sexual attraction to children is part of human sexuality. This may help to explain both the powerful rage and fear we feel at the very word 'paedophile' and, at the same time, the paradoxical prevalence and tolerance of 'pro-paedophile' arguments within society – and thus our cultural bewilderment over how to respond. I propose that what is needed is to disaggregate the discourse on 'sexual liberation' (the acceptance of sexualities alternative to penetrative heterosexuality) from the acceptance of child sexual abuse. This, in turn, requires us to make a careful distinction between the two phenomena of 'adult sexual attraction to children' and 'adult sexual contact with children' and, in order to do that, we need a more sophisticated understanding of normative adult male sexuality and the ways in which it has historically and culturally been constructed to be abusive and non-empathic.

This book is written to be a challenging and thought-provoking response to contemporary anxieties over paedophilia and child sexual abuse. It is written primarily for students and academics studying aspects of the phenomenon of paedophiles in contemporary society, but it will also be of value to others; for example, to adults who are themselves experiencing sexual attraction to children; to those who, as children, had sexual contact with an adult and now seek to understand that experience more clearly; and those who live with, care about or work with paedophiles. It aims to satisfy a need for information on paedophiles which does not assume that they are monsters, mad, evil or 'other', and which seeks to locate paedophiles in their everyday context, in society.

Acknowledgements

Aspects of this book are based on the *Minor-Attracted Adults Daily Lives Project*, an internet-based survey conducted during 2006 to 2008. My analysis and writing-up of this research was supported with periods of funded and unfunded research leave from the University of Winchester and with funded research leave from the Arts and Humanities Research Council. I express my profound gratitude for this support.

 **Arts & Humanities Research Council**

I would like to acknowledge the kind encouragement of Lisa Isherwood, Philip Jenkins, Jim Kincaid, Jeffrey Masson, Linda Watson-Brown and Ethel Quayle while this book was being written; Judith Reisman for corresponding so helpfully on the Kinsey material; Tim Tate for providing a copy of *Kinsey's Paedophiles* (Tate, 1998); Adam Stapleton for drawing my attention to the recent work of Patrick Califia; John Ross for generously permitting me to use quotations from his book *Formosan Odyssey: Taiwan Past and Present*; The British Psychological Society for kindly granting permission to quote from their definition of sexual grooming; David for continuing to provide information and advice from his own perspective as a paedophile, the anonymous reviewer at Palgrave for advice and encouragement, Jill Lake and Jo Wilkinson for helping get this book into print, plus all the other dear people who have been there when I needed them!

A few aspects of this discussion have been previously published in my book *Understanding and Addressing Adult Sexual Attraction to Children: A Study of Paedophiles in Contemporary Society* (2009). This book builds on and extends the arguments presented in my earlier work.

Every effort has been made to contact copyright holders, but in the event that any have inadvertently been overlooked, the publisher will make amends at the earliest opportunity.

1
Encountering Paedophiles in Society

Introduction

This book is about paedophiles; that is, it is about adults who are sexually attracted to children or minors below the legal age of sexual consent. This sexual attraction may be to children who are moving through the changes of puberty, or who have just emerged from puberty, or it may involve much younger children, in some cases even toddlers or babies. The sexual attraction to children may be the only sexual interest experienced or it may be part of a much wider sexual desire, including for people in other age-ranges as well, so that a 'paedophile' may also be sexually attracted to adults and may be married, but nevertheless still maintain a sexual interest in children. Paedophiles may be sexually attracted to girls, to boys or to both sexes. While the great majority of adults who self-define as 'paedophile' are men, some women also may be paedophiles. The identification or diagnosis of paedophilia is dependent on the social context, on the definition of 'adult', of 'minor' and of 'sex'. In this book, the state of 'being a paedophile' is taken not as a medical, clinical or forensic condition but primarily as a social fact, a sexual attraction which the individual experiences and which – whether it is acted on or not, whether it is shouted from the rooftops or kept entirely hidden – will profoundly shape the sense of self, relations with others, and place in the world.

Paedophiles do not exist in isolation: they exist, as we all must, in relation to those around them. Their experiences, and our experiences as we attempt a deeper understanding of this phenomenon, are shaped by the prevailing social and cultural environment. This book is therefore also about society. It is about how people individually, in groups and in societies, attempt to make sense of and address this particular sexual desire.

1

For example, how does contemporary Western society make sense of 'the paedophile' and the phenomena of adult sexual attraction to children and adult sexual abuse of children? Within just one generation, awareness of child sexual abuse has been transformed. Up until the 1970s, popular awareness of child sexual abuse was all but non-existent. Similarly, until the 1990s, the word 'paedophile' was almost unknown outside the medical profession: it was an obscure technical term describing a condition most people had never even imagined. All that changed radically in just a few years. The concept of a 'paedophile' is now embedded in everyday life at the level of popular culture – how ordinary people think about, talk about and share stories about adults behaving sexually with children.

In order to understand paedophilia in contemporary society, it is essential to grasp how deeply, and how rapidly, this medical diagnosis has moved from obscurity into the heart of Western thinking and Western culture. The term 'paedophilia', although originally derived from a medical textbook on sexual pathology first published in 1886 (Krafft-Ebing, 1998), is by no means simply a clinical definition as, for example, is 'urolagnia' (sexual interest in urination). Over the last two decades, this term has moved out of the medical texts and into daily life in an extraordinary way. For cultural observers and laypeople alike, paedophilia has become not simply a description of an individualized sexual disorder but a way of thinking about, talking about, and worrying about huge issues of our culture, our sexuality, and our children. Alongside fears over drugs, terrorism, urban gun crime and other manifestations of social breakdown, fears over paedophilia point beyond any one specific example or situation to a wider social malaise.

Sociologists and cultural theorists employ the term 'discourse' to describe how a society uses language to think about and develop shared meanings. The concept 'paedophile' has become part of this public discourse within contemporary Western culture in which we think about and construct meanings for our shared sense of confusion and unease – and also, perhaps underlying that, our shared fascination. It is a cliché that 'sex sells', as newspaper editors know only too well, and sex combined with taboo, risk and horror sells even better. It is not merely the 'paedophile' but the 'evil paedophile' who features routinely in news stories. Sound-bites about 'stranger danger', 'paedophile sex rings', 'monsters', 'sex fiends' and 'beasts' spring to mind as soon as a child is harmed or disappears. For example, one three-month review of Britain's highest-selling daily paper, *The Sun*, together with its stable-mate, *The News of the World*, in 2005, found only two articles referring to 'child sexual abuse' but an astonishing 94 articles using the word 'paedophile', including a stream of references to 'perverts', 'pervs', 'nasty pervs', 'sickest', 'vile', 'nauseating', 'outrage' and 'horror' (Goode, 2008a: 221).

Alongside, and buttressed by, these articles on evil paedophiles and sadistic child-murderers in the newspapers are fundraising appeals from children's charities, drawing on stock images from this same terrifying public discourse in order to urge people to dig deeply into their pockets for the sake of child protection. These portrayals reached a crescendo during the first decade of the twenty-first century, at the same time as the publishing world witnessed the rise of a new phenomenon: 'misery lit', a entire genre of books devoted to agonising portrayals of tormented childhoods, many of them involving sexual abuse. During the heyday of these tearjerkers, whole supermarket shelves were stocked with nothing but 'misery lit' and entire sections of bookshops were set aside just for them. Within a few brief decades at the end of the twentieth and beginning of the twenty-first centuries, a new public discourse had been shaped, combining a complex and potent blend of childhood, sex and evil; a discourse expressed most violently in the 'anti-paedophile riots' in Portsmouth in southern England during the hot and febrile summer of 2001, when mobs of people – many of them working-class mothers – spontaneously demonstrated in the streets, chanting, waving banners, daubing slogans, and terrorising local residents known or suspected of sexually abusing children.

Thus, from the 1970s onwards, a particular mix of ingredients has formed the cultural discourse around paedophilia: a mix including courageous and pathbreaking accounts – initially by women and more recently by men – of the profound damage caused by child sexual abuse, first through a political analysis of women's position within society and subsequently through more individualized and sentimentalized narratives within the genre of 'misery lit'; an increasing tendency by newspapers to report sexual crimes against children; awareness-raising by children's charities; and a sense of overwhelming, even hysterical, fear and rage which briefly expressed itself, in Britain especially, through street-activism and organized mob violence. The British Government responded, much as the United States and other countries also responded, with an increased emphasis on surveillance and bureaucracy, for example by establishing a sexual offenders' database and setting up systems to vet and bar offenders from working with children.

What this discourse suggests is that there is now a consensus, a shared social understanding, of what a 'paedophile' might be and how society should respond. The rhetoric of fear and hatred which has been prominent over the last decade or so, and the heavy-handed legal and statutory policies put in place, all give the impression that society is united in its loathing of paedophiles and the sexual abuse of children. This book argues, however, that such a consensus is illusory and in reality there are multiple competing discourses both on adult sexual attraction to children and on adult sexual contact with children. Examples of this come into play most acutely when 'the paedophile' is someone well-known to the public.

In many newspaper reports, 'the paedophile' is faceless and obscure, and all the more terrifying for that. At other times, however, the face is already famous, so that when a member of the public thinks of the word 'paedophile', the first image which springs to mind is likely to be of a recent celebrity scandal. Almost every month such examples will change, as more well-known individuals are caught downloading child pornography or are accused of having behaved inappropriately with an under-age child. These examples obscure as much as they inform. They leave us still puzzled, bewildered even, about what paedophilia is, what it means to 'be a paedophile', what adult sexual attraction to children means in real life and in everyday experience. The example of the film director Roman Polanski epitomizes the confusion felt by many people. In Polanski's case, the facts are clear. In 1978, he pleaded guilty to sex with a minor, a 13-year-old girl whom he had photographed with the consent of her mother (*New York Post*, 2009). It appears that, after the photographic shoot, Polanski gave the child champagne and a sedative drug and then orally, vaginally and anally raped her (*The Smoking Gun*, 2003). After the trial and before sentencing, Polanski escaped justice by fleeing from the United States to France. There is no doubt, therefore, about whether Polanski sexually abused a child. He did. He should therefore, according to the public discourse on paedophiles, be universally reviled. However, when the Swiss authorities cooperated with the United States to arrest and extradite Polanski in 2009 so that he could finally be made to face the consequences of his actions, there was a public outcry led by some of the most senior figures in France and by many of Polanski's fellow celebrities in the United States (Knegt, 2009). This example demonstrates some of the many tensions and ambiguities surrounding this topic, and the ways in which adult sexual contact with children is both condemned and condoned.

In order to begin to grasp some of these issues, and investigate some of the confusion we have as a society about adults sexually attracted to children, in this chapter I would like to introduce you to three people who each exemplify an aspect of paedophilia, helping us in the process of exploring what paedophilia means and how we respond to it in contemporary society.

In Section 1 is the first of these three people, the world-famous singer and celebrity, the late Michael Jackson. In Section 2 is a discussion of the disappearance of Madeleine McCann, a little girl, and in Section 3 we meet Kevin Brown, a self-confessed paedophile and an activist for paedophile rights. Section 4 then provides a brief overview of the structure and contents of the book.

1. Michael Jackson

For many people around the world, the case that has exemplified questions around 'paedophilia' or 'child molesting' – and one that has hit the global headlines the most in the past few years – has been that of Michael Jackson, known to his many fans as 'The King of Pop' and to others, less star-struck, as 'Wacko Jacko'. Jackson, who was born 29 August 1958 and died 25 June 2009, began his career in popular music at the age of 5. His album, *Thriller*, released in 1982, has sold well over 100 million copies and is the best-selling album in the world. By the time he reached his 40s, Jackson had achieved the status of 'The Most Successful Entertainer of All Time', according to the *Guinness Book of Records*. To many people, he was a hero, an icon, someone who represented beauty, talent, genius... and wounded vulnerability. Often appearing frail, childlike and even victimized himself, Jackson – with his curious, surgically altered face and fragile cross-gendered beauty – aroused emotions of staunch protectiveness and fierce loyalty among his many fans. Among those less enamoured, his quirky behaviour and sexual ambiguity appeared less as the sign of genius and more as pathological, perhaps even 'creepy'. When allegations of sexual abuse of children first began emerging, therefore, popular interest was both intense and prolonged.

Jackson allegedly was first accused of child molestation in 1990, when he paid $2 million to the son of an employee at his Neverland Ranch after the 12-year-old had accused Jackson of fondling him (Rashbaum, 2004). This initial allegation and payoff did not emerge publicly, however, until much later, after further allegations had been made. The next accusations appear to have been made in December 1993, when Jackson was accused of having shared his bed with a 13-year-old boy, Jordan Chandler, and having initiated sexual contact with him. Like the earlier complaint, this case too was settled out of court, in January 1994, for a sum believed to be in the region of $25 million (Vineyard, 2004).

Subsequently, the 'Michael Jackson molestation case', as it came to be known, began in earnest with a search of his property, Neverland, and his high-profile arrest in November 2003. In April 2004, the singer was indicted on ten criminal counts, alleging 28 acts involving child abduction, false imprisonment and extortion, against a 13-year-old boy, Gavin Arvizo and his family. The trial centred on Jackson's behaviour towards this child and another boy. It seemed indisputable that Jackson indeed sought out pubescent boys for company and spent considerable time with them, including in his bedroom and also in his bed. It also seemed plausible that certain individuals wished to trade on Jackson's dubious, even 'creepy', reputation and make money out of him by receiving huge sums in compensation for alleged crimes. The jury were asked to decide, on the evidence, whether Jackson had in fact committed sexual abuse. In January 2004, one commentator, writing on *The Smoking Gun* website (a commercial, New York-based site specialising in obtaining and making available documents under the Freedom of Information Act) reviewed a series of law enforcement and government reports, grand jury testimony, and sealed court records and commented:

> If the harrowing and deeply disturbing allegations in these documents are true, Jackson is a textbook pedophile, a 46-year-old predator who plied children with wine, vodka, tequila, Jim Beam whiskey, and Bacardi rum. A man who gave boys nicknames like Doo Doo Head and Blowhole and then quizzed them about whether they masturbated and if 'white stuff' came out. A man who conducted drinking games with minors and surfed porn with them on a laptop in his Neverland Ranch bedroom, noting that if anyone asked what they were looking at, the kids should just say they were watching *The Simpsons*. A man who frequently talked sex with his little companions and explained that 'boys have to masturbate or they go crazy.' A man who told one pajama-clad boy that he wanted to show him how to 'jack off.' When the tipsy child declined the demonstration, Jackson announced, 'I'll do it for you,' and buried his hand in the boy's Hanes briefs, size small. And a man who emphasized to his little friends that these activities were 'their little secret' and should not be disclosed to anyone, even if a gun was at their head. (*The Smoking Gun*, 2005: online)

After much pre-trial media hype, the actual trial itself began 28 February 2005 and continued until the summer. On 13 June Jackson was cleared of all counts, the jury finding there was reasonable doubt about what had really happened. By August of that year, however, two of the jurors had publicly announced that they regretted the not guilty verdict and that they believed Michael Jackson to indeed be a paedophile who had molested children (*MSNBC*, 2005).

Between 2005 and his death in 2009, a slew of books attempted in various ways to explore (or cash in on) Jackson's trial. These books include Geraldine Hughes' *Redemption: The Truth Behind the Michael Jackson Child Molestation Allegation* (2004) on the original 1993 allegations; *FREAK! Inside the Twisted World of Michael Jackson*, by David Perel and Suzanne Ely, in 2005, as well as the possibly more balanced *Be Careful Who You Love: Inside the Michael Jackson Case*, by Diane Dimond, also in 2005. The following year, Lynton Guest's *The Trials of Michael Jackson* was published and, in 2007, *The Michael Jackson Conspiracy* by Aphrodite Jones, the comprehensive *Jacko, His Rise and Fall: The Social and Sexual History of Michael Jackson*, by Darwin Porter, and the cultural critique *On Michael Jackson* by Margo Jefferson. Meanwhile, other books such as the 2007 *Michael Jackson: For the Record* by Chris Cadman and Craig Halstead, and the 2009 *In the Studio with Michael Jackson* by Bruce Swedien continued to focus on 'the man and his music' rather than his trials. Since his death there will no doubt be many more books on the market, adding to the eulogies accorded him at his funeral.

What is interesting is that, of all the many books on the market dealing with Michael Jackson, there are only two which seem to have taken the perspective of the alleged victim rather than Jackson himself. The first, *Michael Jackson was my Lover: The Secret Diary of Jordie Chandler*, was authored by Victor Gutierrez in 1997, while *All That Glitters: The Crime and The Cover-up*, was written by Raymond Chandler, a lawyer and the uncle of Jordan Chandler, and published in 2004. As with Polanski, Jackson's status as a major artist and celebrity overshadows the experiences and emotions of the children at the heart of the court cases, and these books go some small way towards helping us to shift our gaze back to the child, rather than seeing the adult as the main victim deserving our sympathy.

2. Madeleine McCann

The case of Michael Jackson reminds us of the complex responses shown by society to alleged paedophile crimes. There is no straightforward and unambiguous condemnation of wrongdoing, as one might expect. Instead there is confusion, denial, resistance to the very idea that a man known and loved by millions of fans might be capable of anything more than naive foolishness. It is instead much easier to believe that Jackson himself was the hapless victim, the dupe of money-grubbing hangers-on and conniving lawyers. In the case of the disappearance of Madeleine McCann, also, we see reactions that perhaps we would not have expected, including a quite surprising level of confusion, denial, resistance and contested attempts to allocate blame. In both these stories, we – the public – would like there to be clarity, with obvious villains and innocent victims, but there is not. The discourses proposing such straightforward narratives are not maintained: they shift and alter at each step.

When I first began to write this book, in May 2007, there was one story dominating the headlines. This was the unfolding case of a little girl, Madeleine McCann, from Leicestershire, England, who was abducted from a holiday resort in Praia da Luz, Portugal, where her family were staying. At the time of her mysterious disappearance, on the night of Thursday 3 May, she was just nine days away from her fourth birthday.

Photographs of the little girl and her stunned and distraught parents covered the British and Portuguese media. There was huge and continuing interest in the case, not only in Britain and Portugal but also across Europe and in English-speaking countries such as Australia, where parallels were drawn with the case of Azaria Chamberlain, the baby who disappeared in the outback and was believed murdered by her mother until her clothes were found in a dingo's lair. Within days of Madeleine's disappearance, newspapers were reporting that the prime suspect was 'a paedophile' (*Telegraph*, 2007) or that she had been abducted 'to order' by an international paedophile ring (*Times*, 2007). The case of Madeleine (or 'Maddy'/ 'Maddie', as British tabloid newspapers dubbed her) garnered huge public sympathy and support from every quarter of British society. International footballers including Cristiano Ronaldo, John Terry and David Beckham made impassioned pleas for help. Madeleine's parents met with Pope Benedict XVI, who blessed a picture of the little girl and promised to pray for her safe return. Churches throughout the world offered prayers. In Britain, MPs in the House of Commons wore yellow ribbons as a mark of concern for Madeleine, as did the England cricket team for its Lords' Test match against the West Indies. In July 2007, the singer Bryan Adams dedicated his concert on Malta to Madeleine, advertisements asking for help in finding Madeleine were aired in cinemas before the showing of the popular film *Shrek III*, and author J. K. Rowling arranged for posters of Madeleine to be made available to booksellers all over the world at the time of the launch of the final Harry Potter book, *Harry Potter and the Deathly Hallows*.

Offers of help poured in and a fund of up to £2.6 million was pledged for rewards leading to Madeleine's safe return. An official website was quickly established to publicize the search, and within a short time of the disappearance many unofficial web-pages had also appeared to show support and sympathy for the McCann family, for example on social networking sites including Facebook and MySpace. Madeleine's disappearance even made an impact in the virtual world, with the website Second Life containing virtual posters advertising the search for Maddie. At least three books have been published so far on Madeleine's disappearance. There has also been a British documentary and a planned Hollywood movie on the case. Meanwhile, child kidnapping storylines in popular British soap operas, *EastEnders* and *Coronation Street*, due to be shown in May 2007, were cancelled and the release of a Hollywood movie, *Gone Baby Gone*, directed by Ben Affleck and centring on the abduction of a 4-year-old girl, scheduled for release in December 2007, was delayed to April 2008.

What is it about this story which so gripped the public imagination? For all of us who are parents, it is our worst nightmare: finding an empty space where our child should be. Madeleine represents innocence and brings out in us our protectiveness. But the story of Madeleine provokes darker questions about society and about human nature too. Who took her? Was she murdered by her own parents? Was she kidnapped to order by a criminal adoption agency? Was she, as newspapers suggested, taken by an international paedophile ring?

Madeleine has still not been found and no firm clues have yet been discovered. Some observers have noted that the idea of a paedophile ring based within Portugal is not far-fetched: a serious scandal came to light in 2002 when a number of high-profile members of Portugal's social and political elite were arrested on charges of child sexual abuse spanning decades and conducted in collusion with staff in Casa Pia, the country's oldest and most-respected state-run orphanage (Mitchell, 2003). After alleged victims came forward to speak out about the abuse, the former Secretary of State for Families, Teresa Costa Macedo, revealed that she had known about the abuse at Casa Pia since 1982, when she first sent a dossier of evidence to the police. She received death threats and the police closed the case in 1993, destroying all the evidence (Mitchell, 2003). Mrs Costa Macedo also revealed that the then-President, General Antonio Ramalho Eanes, was told by child victims of the abuse in 1980 but did not act (Mitchell, 2003; Tremlett, 2004). Portugal is a struggling economy within the European Union and this may make it more vulnerable to police corruption and to exploitation of its children. One report commented:

> Portugal has increasingly been under the scrutiny of anti-paedophile groups who have denounced its lax laws and uninterested courts for creating a paedophiles' paradise in Europe. Belgian and Dutch paedophile groups are reported to have operated in Portugal, with foreigners travelling to the island of Madeira to seek out young children. Investigators from the Swiss-based Innocence in Danger group, which claims children regularly disappear from the poorer streets of Portuguese towns and cities, say they too have been harassed and threatened. (Tremlett, 2002: online)

Years later, after Madeleine's disappearance and with the Casa Pia court case, begun in 2004, still grinding on (not until September 2010 did the case end, with seven defendants receiving convictions), another newspaper article drew similarities between the Madeleine McCann case, the Casa Pia scandal and the crimes of Marc Dutroux in Belgium during the mid 1990s, for which he was tried and eventually sentenced in 2004:

> Pedro Namora, a former Casa Pia orphan who witnessed 11 rapes on fellow orphans, during which they were tied to their beds, sympathizes with the McCanns. He believes elements in the force have conspired to suppress both scandals, fearing damage to the country's reputation. 'Portugal is a paedophiles' paradise', said Mr Namora, now a lawyer campaigning on behalf of the Casa Pia victims. 'If all the names come out, this will be an earthquake in Portugal. There is a massive, sophisticated network at play here – stretching from the government to the judiciary and the police. The network is enormous and extremely powerful. There are magistrates, ambassadors, police, politicians – all have procured children from Casa Pia. It is extremely difficult to break this down. These people cover for each other, because if one is arrested, they all are arrested. They don't want anyone to know.'
> … [Mr Namora] believes the case, which he brought to light in 2003, will underscore Portugal's growing attraction for paedophiles, which has seen six children disappear in recent years. One reason for this attraction is that the law was quietly relaxed last year, ahead of the forthcoming trial, meaning that repeat offences against the same child would merit only a single charge – and a lesser sentence.

...Amid allegations that paedophile networks have become endemic in Portugal – the European police force Interpol has named the country as one of the worst offenders in Europe – there are fears that the Casa Pia scandal will come to eclipse Belgium's notorious Marc Dutroux case, in which the arrest of a notorious paedophile and child murderer revealed a sordid picture of judicial and political corruption. (Malone & Allen, 2007: online)

The sexual attacks, taking place over a period of at least twenty years against many of the most vulnerable children at Casa Pia, some of them blind and many of them deaf and unable to speak about their ordeals (Popham, 2003), shocked the Portuguese people, just as other countries before and since have been shocked by revelations of systematic sexual abuse of children and its cover-up by those in authority. The allegations of corruption and indifference by those who ought to care pose a challenge to the very principles by which a country is run:

Underlining the challenge the system faces, Marcello Nuno Rebelo de Sousa, a law professor and social commentator, said: 'It is not just solving the Casa Pia case, it's believing in democracy. It is believing we belong to Europe, not just because we are in the European Union, but because we have a democratic system where justice works. Portuguese society looked in the mirror and said, "we are ugly".' (Popham, 2003: online)

These two narratives – Michael Jackson and Madeleine McCann – are two parts of the jigsaw puzzle building a contemporary picture of 'the paedophile'. Jackson, Polanski and other celebrities show us that, while unknown paedophiles typically excite hatred, those who are known to the public are more likely to receive a sympathetic and lenient reception even in cases where rape has clearly taken place. There are counterexamples, such as that of the British comic actor Chris Langham, who was convicted and imprisoned in 2007 for downloading child pornography and who encountered a veritable storm of public hostility and rage, but in general what the experience of well-known figures involved in aspects of sexual behaviour with children shows is that the public, when confronted with a famous face, cannot believe that such a person could truly be a paedophile or sex offender, no matter what the evidence. Such denial and avoidance of reality is a psychological process for dealing with emotional discomfort and has as its corollary the projection of hostility away from 'us' (well-liked figures such as

Polanski or Jackson) and onto the Other, the scapegoat figure of the 'evil paedophile'. These processes of denial and projection will be explored in more depth throughout this book as part of the study of conflicting attitudes to paedophiles in society.

While (some) paedophiles have arguably become overblown figures of extravagant hatred and loathing in the public imagination, scapegoats representing all that is evil and frightening about modern society, the suffering of Madeleine McCann and the many children of the Casa Pia orphanage, among many other silent victims, remind us of the sombre reality underlying public disquiet. Child sexual abuse and the disappearance of little children such as Madeleine McCann tell us uncomfortable truths about society, and about civilization in the twenty-first century.

The story of Madeleine McCann, since she disappeared in 2007, has crystallized for many people some of the most deep-seated fears in contemporary society: fears of risk, danger, loss, uncertainty, insecurity and lack of control. Madeleine McCann, the real, small, flesh-and-blood child, has become a cipher, standing in for all the horrors inflicted on children around the world. Harm to children arouses visceral responses of protectiveness. In acts against children we see both the evil and the compassion which lie at the heart of the human condition. For many people, the story of Madeleine McCann sums up the mysterious dread and horror which have become associated with the word 'paedophile'. This leads us to the third person to be introduced in this chapter, Kevin Brown, because Kevin is proud to be known as a paedophile. For Kevin, the connotations of the term 'paedophile' are not negative, they are positive and he has risked his life campaigning for the human and civil rights of paedophiles.

3. Kevin Brown

Kevin's story starts on 23 February 2005 when he phoned up a popular radio show in the United States and described himself, live on air, as a paedophile and a member of NAMBLA, the North American Man Boy Love Association. The radio show was hosted by Rick Roberts, a well-known conservative whose programme is known as 'The court of public opinion'. The programme airs on KFMB San Diego in California, but is accessible around the United States. At the time there was a continuing controversy about the posting of the names and details of convicted child sexual offenders on websites which could be accessed by members of the public, leading to possible harassment and attacks by vigilantes. For example, there had recently been a case in which a man, Lawrence

Trant, had attempted to murder two convicted sex offenders living near him, after he identified their addresses from the internet (MacQuarrie, 2004). It was within this context that Roberts announced a $1000 'bounty' for anyone with information on paedophiles and particularly members of NAMBLA.

Kevin, a husband and father in his thirties living in the United States, who describes himself as a paedophile or 'minor-attracted adult', decided to take up the offer of the bounty and phoned up during the programme to claim his $1000 and also make the point that he was proud to be a member of NAMBLA. This unusual step was prompted by Kevin's desire for honesty – a desire which later led him to contact and communicate with me over a period of four years during my research into this subject. Kevin had decided he would use the $1000 to fund a play he was writing, called *Adam's End*, which dealt with the situation of 'a decent man who was liked in his community and that community's reaction to him when they discovered his pedosexuality'. However, as Kevin was soon to discover, 'My art has become my life. I will never explore that topic on stage' (*Inquisition21*, undated: online).

Feeling that he needed to 'make a stand' on behalf of fellow-paedophiles, Kevin phoned the radio station without the knowledge of his wife. He was not given the $1000. Instead, the consequences of that phone-call were to shatter his family. As one commentator wrote, 'knowing that Roberts was engaged in the raising of a lynch mob, Kevin Brown phoned him live on radio, announcing his own status as a potential quarry' (*Inquistion21*, undated: online). He found himself having a hostile (if predictable) conversation live on air with Rick Roberts, in which Kevin explained how he 'took the risk of telling people [he was a paedophile] and lost friends over doing that, but it was fair, I think you would agree that if you had an acquaintance or a close friend that was a pedophile and you had children you would want to know that fact about them.' Roberts replied, 'Well, first of all I wouldn't have a friend that's a pedophile. Second of all if I could verify he was a pedophile, I would make sure that the nearest law enforcement agency knew about him...' to which Kevin could only respond, 'Well, and that's exactly what happened' (transcript of radio conversation from Brown, personal communication, 2006).

That might have been the end of this episode on the radio but, during the conversation, Kevin's little child could be heard in the background. Roberts got Kevin to clarify that he was a father and so, from a small-scale local difficulty, it now became highly publicized that Kevin, an 'out' paedophile, had a small child living at home with him. Within days, child protection services had taken the child into care. Subsequently, his wife divorced him and he became embroiled in a lawsuit which cost him his job, his home and his financial security. Why did Kevin do it?

Kevin had put his reputation, his friendships, his economic security, his family and even his physical wellbeing and his life on the line. Subsequent to this 'outing', Kevin was physically attacked on a number of occasions. He told me he was prepared to die and believed he would die as a result of his actions. What drove him to such an extreme measure appears to have been a deeply held conviction that one should be honest in one's dealings and that one should campaign for what one believes in. In Kevin's case, this included the civil rights of 'minor-attracted adults'.

I got to know Kevin during my research into the experiences of 'minor-attracted adults' and, over several years, Kevin wrote me numerous and lengthy emails and we also had a few telephone conversations. In his correspondence with me, he explained that he had realized that he was incapable of concealing his sexual orientation from others because doing so would require maintaining a façade, allowing people to assume his normative heterosexuality. He felt that this would be dishonest to those he cares about the most. In the interests of honesty, therefore, he decided to selectively tell people when appropriate. For example, if he and his wife socialized with a couple who had children 'and the circumstance was likely that I would be around their children unsupervised', he 'did not wish them to find out by other means at some point and carry suspicion about my activities; I have in the past, repeatedly, had people tell me that they felt it was more suspicious to find out by rumour than by me.' (Brown, personal communication, 2006). He therefore told them that he was sexually attracted to children.

The result of this personal policy, he discovered, was that 'most people will react well, and some will not, and will gossip widely'. Thus, through selective self-disclosure and his self-initiated 'outing' on live radio, Kevin Brown gained a high profile as a known paedophile. For Kevin, 'a moral life led me to the conflict that I am in currently, and it was unavoidable'. (Brown, personal communication, 2006). Having been put in a situation where he was known as a paedophile, and having had his own child removed from him, Kevin responded by initiating a civil law suit. This law suit was regarded by Kevin as a 'class action' on behalf of all self-defined 'minor-attracted adults' to defend their legal and civil rights to privacy and family life. At the same time, he also saw the law suit as defending the physical safety of NAMBLA members.

Kevin explained to me in his emails that a deep value he hoped to pass on to his own child was to 'stand up for what is right'. He wanted his child to be 'the one to stand up for the mentally handicapped, the obese, the ostracized in school'. He felt that 'minor-attracted adults', as a class, were a persecuted minority denied their legitimate legal, civil and human rights. He spoke about a 'very small group in our community [of "minor-attracted adults"] that is organized and aware of our enemy's actions and intents'. These enemies, as he saw it, had two goals. One was to pursue 'civil commitment statutes' throughout the United States, thereby depriving any known 'minor-attracted adults' of their liberty. The other was to act as a lynch-mob, 'engaging in violent acts against us and setting a precedent for local prosecutors to not pursue criminal charges for their actions.'

While standing up for what is right is always laudable, Kevin's young child may, of course, not wish to adopt quite such a kamikaze attitude as his father but has been pushed regardless into the fray. What perhaps strikes one most, however, is Kevin's use of the word 'enemies'. We are in very different territory here from that of Michael Jackson or Madeleine McCann. Jackson apparently had some vague notion that it was acceptable to take young boys into his bed, whether sexually or platonically (Niven, 2009), but he certainly never offered any political analysis or defence of his behaviour, and little Madeleine appears to have been swept up in some tragic encounter with unquestionable evil for which there can be no defence. But here Kevin is positing two opposed camps: the good guys (paedophiles or 'minor-attracted adults') on one side; the bad guys (legislators, campaigners and local vigilantes) on the other. Kevin, as a political activist, presents a view of paedophiles as a sexual minority campaigning for rights, in many ways equivalent to the Gay Pride campaigns of the 1970s in which lesbians and gay men won legal and civil rights comparable to the rights of mainstream heterosexuals. In this political campaign, others such as NAMBLA have gone further and argued, not overtly for the rights of adults to have sex with children, but rather for the rights of children to have sex with adults. Kevin is not here campaigning on a sexual libertarian platform but a civil rights one, insisting that a clear distinction be made between the status of paedophile (an involuntary sexual orientation which does not of itself lead to any crime) and the status of sex offender (which requires that the person must have acted on their desires and actually committed a sexual offence against a child). Kevin is not directly arguing for the rights of convicted sex offenders (although he is arguing for their protection from vigilantes). Fundamentally, Kevin is proposing that paedophiles can lead law-abiding lives in the community, being open about their orientation and working out appropriate child-safety plans with those around them so that children are not put at risk.

By having his child taken into care simply because it became known that he was a paedophile, Kevin's concern was that if the ruling against him set a legal precedent, then in future any adult who admitted that they were sexually attracted to children, no matter how law-abiding their lifestyle might be, would be at risk of losing their children to foster-care. He estimated this would initially affect 'one to two hundred men a year' in his state and then would go on to affect paedophiles all over the whole United States. As things turned out, Kevin did not lose custody of his child and his family survived the incident more or less intact. However, the 'goals' of his 'enemies' remained: civil commitment processes are now in place in the United States so that convicted child sex offenders, once they have served their term in prison, may not be released but committed indefinitely, possibly for the rest of their lives, within secure mental health hospitals. Meanwhile, outside in the community, vigilante activism against known paedophiles (whether offenders or not) remains a source of fear and threat. Does this matter? Is there any legitimate case that can be made for the civil rights of paedophiles?

The three very different case-studies presented here show some of the huge range of ways in which contemporary society currently thinks about adult sexual attraction to children and sexual abuse of children. To begin with, the case-studies chosen show the depth of our confusion over this topic. In each case, there is a disjuncture between the narratives presented and what may actually have happened. Michael Jackson may have been a paedophile – someone sexually attracted to children – or he may not. He may have been an innocent and misunderstood victim of other people's prejudices and cupidity, who genuinely behaved in no more than a child-like manner, like Peter Pan in his Neverland. Jackson was never convicted of any sexual crime against children. The narratives around him explore paedophilia, while at the heart of the narrative, the truth about Jackson's own sexuality may never be known.

Similarly, the narratives around Madeleine McCann's disappearance revolve around the concept of paedophilia and sadistic, predatory abduction for sexual abuse but there is still no clarity over what actually happened to her. We do not know if she is alive or dead. We do not know who took her, or why. Links have been made with known sexual abuse offences such as the Casa Pia scandal but these are speculative. In our need to make sense of the mystery, narratives of paedophilia stand ready to fill the gaps in our knowledge, much as narratives of child-stealing by gypsies, Jews, witches, fairies or aliens might provide explanations at other times or places. The narratives provide the comfort of a cosmology; they suggest we can know what is going on and can make sense of it. In the absence of incontrovertible knowledge, they are as scientific as we can get. And then these narratives are disrupted again by individuals like Kevin, who struggle to show us a radically different and challenging version of what it might mean to be a 'paedophile'. In this case, the disjuncture may be that society perceives a crime where there is not one. In Michael Jackson's case, crimes were alleged which the court decided were false; in Madeleine McCann's case, a crime has clearly taken place but the details of what crime (abduction? murder?), who committed it and why, remain unknown. In Kevin Brown's case, while the presence of a paedophile within the narrative is abundantly clear, the presence of a crime is less clear. Nevertheless, a crime was presumed either to have already taken place or inevitably to be about to take place, which was the reason for removing his child to a place of safety. As Rick Roberts said, when Kevin protested his innocence on radio and claimed he would never harm a child, 'Tick tock, baby, it's only a matter of time'.

Thus these case-studies begin to allow us to explore some of our confusion over this subject, our difficulty in accepting that someone we like might be abusing children, and our willingness to apportion blame or indeed to turn a blind eye in order not to face horrific realities. Finally, they show the moral and legal awkwardness we get into when trying to respond appropriately to protect children – and when attempting to discriminate between those who sexually offend against children and those who merely have a sexual attraction to children and may never act on that attraction. All these responses and more will be explored further in the following chapters. We will return to Roman Polanski and Michael Jackson in particular, as they enable us to explore our confusion over how we *think* we respond to 'paedophiles' in society and how we actually do respond. The abuse suffered by the children of the Casa Pia orphanage (and possibly also by Madeleine McCann since her disappearance) remind us again why understanding paedophiles is of such urgency and gravity. The book attempts to hold in tension our need as a society for empathic understanding of adults sexually attracted to children with the need never to underestimate the harm caused by adult sexual contact with children; it is only when both needs are met that children can be fully protected. It is therefore important to allow space for 'the voice of the paedophile' and this is where Kevin Brown and his peers are significant. I have published my findings from primary research in a separate book (Goode, 2009) and it is there that you will find 'the voice of the paedophile' most clearly articulated. This book builds on that research and provides a deeper understanding of the cultural context within which paedophiles and the rest of us live in society.

4. The scope and structure of this book

The function of this chapter has been to provide a discussion of some well-known examples which people often discuss when the subject of 'paedophiles' comes up. As this chapter indicates, we know that paedophiles exist in society; we just don't know how to respond to them.

The argument throughout the following chapters of this book is that we must understand them in new ways and respond to them in new ways. Previous books covering the topic of paedophiles can be broadly divided into two contrasting types: apologist texts which argue – to a greater or lesser degree – for tolerance of paedophiles while downplaying the harm they have caused to children; and more mainstream texts which focus on the 'demonization' of paedophiles and attempt to critique this demonization while firmly acknowledging the harm of child sexual abuse. In these texts, paedophiles (those adults who are primarily or exclusively sexually attracted to children) are typically discussed as being psychiatrically ill or criminal and are presented in relation to a model of the paedophile as 'the Other' or as 'monsters', as people very much outside the norms of society (Salter, 2003; Pritchard, 2004; Schultz, 2005; Thomas, 2005; Corby, 2006, Ward *et al.*, 2006) or conversely as misunderstood victims, even as rebels or heroes, again outside normal society but occupying in some senses a positive counter-cultural role (Wilson & Cox, 1983; Brongersma, 1986; Sandfort, 1987; Feierman, 1990; Li *et al.*, 1993).

Even where the phenomenon of adults sexually abusing children is located more obviously and directly within an everyday social context of home and family (for example, see Driver & Droisen, 1989; Cox, Kershaw & Trotter, 2000; Itzin, 2000) this does not always contribute positively to our understanding of paedophiles, as such adults are typically theorized not as 'paedophiles' *per se* but as opportunists who sexually assault children because they can. The characterization of child sexual abuse as explicable through an analysis of male sexual violence reflects the reality that there has been a pressing need to contest powerful and damaging myths about sexual abuse (for example, that 'little girls are seductive' or that adult sexual contact with children is not harmful). It also reflects the fact that there has rightly been a reluctance to endorse distinctions between forms of sexual assault – between 'incest', intra-familial assault, and assault by strangers, and between sexual abuse of children and of women – and rather to emphasize the underpinning coherent logic of male sexual violence running through all these varied manifestations. However, such theorizations fail to address certain key aspects of what it means to be 'a paedophile' and thus still leave significant gaps in our understanding.

Crucially, previous work has not adequately addressed the distinction between sexual attraction and sexual behaviour. There is almost nothing written on men who are sexually attracted to children but choose not to act on this attraction; simply attempting to locate such men within a continuum of male violence does not do justice to their experiences. More generally, portraying paedophiles as (contested) 'monsters' or as (contested) 'sexual radicals' means that they are seldom located within their everyday context as individuals who are quite ordinary and undistinguished other than by their sexuality.

It is the role of sociologists to locate individual everyday experience within its social context. The phenomenon of 'the paedophile' has been studied extensively and written about by clinicians, psychiatrists, psychologists, sexologists, legislators and criminal lawyers but considerably less by sociologists. In fact, sociologists have traditionally seemed to remain a little shy of it, as indeed of sex in general. Professor Ken Plummer, the doyen of the sociological study of sexuality in Britain, recently commented that sexuality 'is still largely isolated from the [sociological] mainstream because most people who do any other aspect of sociology, don't bother about us, they leave us to get on in our own little ghetto.' (Taylor, 2008: 7). This theoretical isolation is even more applicable in the case of paedophilia, despite extensive concern over the prevalence and impact of child sexual abuse, its portrayal by the media (Silverman & Wilson, 2002; Kitzinger, 2004; Critcher, 2003) and, more recently, critiques which re-visit and re-interpret 'sexual abuse' narratives (Reavey & Warner, 2003; Woodiwiss, 2009). Thus, while some areas within sociology such as media studies, gender studies, queer studies and childhood studies have all made valuable contributions to this field, 'the paedophile' as a problematic remains under-theorized. This book directly addresses this gap in our knowledge, primarily by stressing throughout the book that paedophiles are very much an integral part of society and cannot be understood without that context. Three overlapping but distinct concepts are recognized within this work: the concept of *the paedophile* as this individual is socially constituted through those everyday occurrences which go to make up their life-experiences and self-identity; the concept of *sexual attraction* which is experienced by adults towards children; and the concept of *sexual contact* which is committed by adults against children. All these concepts are distinct from any notion of *children's sexuality*, and this point is brought out in Chapters 4 and 5. Holding these three concepts separate helps to provide an original analysis of paedophiles and thereby opens up new theoretical possibilities and new ways of responding to the challenge which paedophiles present to society, allowing the final chapter and the Epilogue to explore the connections to, and implications for, human sexuality more generally.

Chapter 2 begins the process of locating paedophiles within society through an exploration of the importance of the internet, putting forward the case that the internet has both been shaped by paedophiles and has itself profoundly shaped the experience of being a paedophile in contemporary society. As well as a brief overview of functions of the internet generally, this chapter also provides a case-study based on Wikipedia and enables the reader to delve into the online world of pro- and anti-paedophile sites, exploring the way in which paedophiles use the internet to put forward 'pro-paedophile' arguments.

Chapter 3 moves on to a discussion of popular culture, looking first at examples from the media and then examining how concepts taken from the disciplines of history, anthropology and biology have become incorporated into popular discourse in an effort to shape and make sense of adult sexual attraction to children and adult sexual contact with children. This chapter concludes by arguing that what we have currently is a ragbag of disconnected concepts around paedophilia, and to suggest that we can begin to understand this better through an analysis of two main but conflicting discourses on 'sexual liberation' and 'child protection'. This leads on to Chapter 4 and a study of what was without doubt the most important work on human sexuality in the twentieth century and is still unsurpassed in its influence, particularly on academic, professional and lay notions of 'child sexuality'. The two Kinsey Reports (*Sexual Behavior in the Human Male* and *Sexual Behavior in the Human Female*), although little-read today, nevertheless underpin sexological concepts of children's sexuality and responses to adult sexual contact with children. This continuing impact of Kinsey's work is then explored in Chapter 5, which provides examples of work following on from Kinsey and thus brings into focus the body of academic and professional literature which presents a positive view of adult sexual contact with children.

Chapter 6 widens the perspective of the book by turning to explore connections between paedophilia and normative adult male sexuality. As noted earlier, a central thesis of this book is that paedophiles are not 'outside' culture or society but rather that they are part of our everyday human existence. That being so, sexual attraction to children is part of human sexuality. This theme is developed by looking first at how children are experienced and presented as 'sexy' in everyday contemporary culture and then by going back to the ancient past and the rise of the major world religions at the end of the Bronze Age in order to understand how ideology shaped civilizations to denigrate the material world, bodies, women and sex. We have got ourselves into a pickle sexually, with a heritage of normative adult male sexuality which has been historically and culturally shaped to be hostile, abusive and non-empathic.

The book concludes with an Epilogue which presents an optimistic view forward, arguing that both knowledge (popular discourse) and sexual response are socioculturally constructed and thus can – and do – change over time. The book proposes that we can distinguish between two fundamental concepts often buried beneath the one word 'paedophilia': adult sexual attraction to children and adult sexual contact with children. As the distinction between these two concepts is drawn, we may come to recognize and accept that adult sexual attraction to children may simply be a part of the continuum of adult (male) sexuality. The book also proposes that a more sustained and sophisticated analysis of the discourses on 'sexual liberation' and 'child protection' will identify ways in which these two currently conflicting discourses need no longer be opposed to each other but can be integrated to provide a richer, more nuanced and imaginative response to the complexities and challenges of human sexuality, strengthening the protection and care of children while enabling a more honest and mature acceptance of paedophiles in society.

2
Encountering Paedophiles on the Internet

Introduction

In Chapter 1 we saw how society attempts to make sense of situations where adults are (or seem to be) sexually involved with or attracted to children, and examples were given to show how popular culture has made us all aware, as a society, of what a 'paedophile' is, even though this cultural representation of a 'paedophile' may differ from reality. In this chapter we dive into the farther reaches of the internet, to explore what's out there and how it has affected all our lives. The aim is to understand the role of the internet in enabling paedophiles to contact one another and to influence wider society through online postings.

The importance of the internet cannot be overstated. It has opened up extraordinary new social, political and economic possibilities. When the American scientist Joseph Licklider first dreamed of a 'Galactic Network' at MIT in the early 1960s, he could have had no idea of where his original musings would take us. First the internet (the ability of remote computers to connect to each other) and then, developed from that, the world-wide web (the ability to search for and retrieve documents and files over the internet) have had a significant impact on almost all groups of people, but perhaps most on those who were previously isolated. Thus it could be argued that the one social change that has most dramatically affected the phenomenon of paedophilia in this generation is the internet. The internet has made possible anonymous communication across any distance, suddenly enabling – for the first time ever – people who want to keep their identities and actions secret to communicate easily and safely with other like-minded people.

It is easy to forget sometimes what a very recent innovation the internet is. It has become a key part of so many people's lives in a remarkably short space of time. Of the global population of almost seven billion people, the most recent (2011) estimates from the Internet World Stats website suggest that around two billion now have access to the internet. Over 77 per cent of the population of North America are online, as are over 60 per cent of the population of Australia and Oceania, and well over half (58 per cent) of Europe (Internet World Stats 2011).

As we all know, in the twenty-first century the geeks have indeed inherited the earth, and for those of us who are not geeks this is sometimes a bit confusing. Nevertheless, to understand the impact of this intersection of the human and the technical, and the huge changes it has brought about, it is useful to become familiar with at least some of the key technologies. If you are already entirely familiar with IRC, newsgroups and P2P file-sharing (maybe you even played on MUDs back in the old days), you'll probably want to skip the next section. If the last sentence made no sense to you at all, you'll almost *certainly* want to skip the next section – but please don't! At least we no longer have to learn hypertext mark-up language (HTML) before making websites! This is a very basic introduction to how we got from a few researchers playing about writing code for machines the size of the average living-room, to the current phenomenon of the average Western adult (and child) logging on every day and 'chatting' (often intimately) with people they've never met who live perhaps thousands of miles away – or just around the corner.

The internet began as the ARPANET (the network of the Advanced Research Projects Agency, a US military organization) and by 1971 it had 23 hosts (separate computers hundreds of miles apart, connected by code transmitted over telephone cables). Its first international connections (to England and Norway) were established in 1973 and in 1976 Queen Elizabeth II became the first head of state to send an email message – but who did she send it to? We are not told.

By 1977 the ARPANET had over 100 host-computers connected to it, by 1982 it was over 200, by 1983 (when the internet as we know it today replaced ARPANET) it was over 500, by 1984 it was 1000, by 1986 over 5000, by 1987 over 10,000, and by 1989, eighteen years from its start, the number of internet hosts reached 100,000. By this point, the internet was still a closed system, only available to those in government or academic settings, but now the big telecommunications companies began to take an interest and to run commercial internet service provider (ISP) access for the general public. Once commercial access was available, the internet exploded.

The world-wide web was established at the research centre Cern in Switzerland, with the first web-page going live in December 1990 (its address was http://nxoc01.cern.ch/hypertext/WWW/TheProject. html). By 1991 there were 600,000 hosts and ten web-pages. The following year, 1992, there were one million internet hosts and fifty exciting web-pages to browse! The next year it's two million hosts, the year after that three million, the year after that four million. When America Online and Compuserve got in on the act, in 1995, access more than doubled and by 1996, the number of hosts was up to nine million and the next year 16 million – the same year that the millionth internet domain name was registered. By the year 2000, 304 million people were online and the ten-millionth domain name had been registered (Anderberg, 2007). The internet and the world-wide web had become a global phenomenon and transformed our lives in under thirty years.

Although it isn't necessary to know all the tiny details of the history of how we got from there to here, having a broad overview does help our understanding of what exactly has changed, and what the impact has been on people's daily lives. Tracing the history of the internet from its beginnings in the 1960s to now will help us gain a clearer sense of which technologies have been most relevant in changing child pornography, for example, from something that was almost non-existent to something that is now ubiquitous, or in changing the experience of many paedophiles from one of utter isolation to one in which they can share their experiences with hundreds or thousands of other people. There are a great many books written now on web studies, cyberspace, online communities, 'cybersociety' and the like. Some of the books, particularly the earlier ones, concentrated on fears over 'the rise of the computer state' and increased surveillance (Burnham, 1983; Campbell & Connor, 1986). More recent works have tended to celebrate the wonderful opportunities the internet provides for new forms of media and new forms of community. There has been less emphasis on the hidden aspects of the internet, the 'darknet', where private deals take place and illegal activities can flourish.

If it is indeed true, as Spiderman discovered, that 'with great power comes great responsibility', then it's probably also true that with great anonymity comes great irresponsibility. If we do not know who someone is, we cannot hold them accountable for their behaviour, or for the negative consequences that may arise from the expression of their beliefs. There are few, if any, sanctions which can be successfully deployed against anonymous individuals who may hold a number of user-names and identities and perhaps operate from a number of different accounts, servers and computers. An understanding of how the internet has increased our capacity to interact anonymously also helps us to understand some of the threats as well as the benefits of the internet.

This chapter is divided into four sections, each dealing with a specific aspect of the online experience. Section 1 looks at playing in cyberspace and explores online communication; Section 2 examines file-sharing and the 'darknet'; Section 3 uses the example of an article on 'child grooming' on Wikipedia to illustrate how self-defined paedophiles disseminate their own 'point of view'; and Section 4 provides information on 'pro-paedophile' and 'anti-paedophile' websites.

1. Playing and chatting

Let's start with the fun stuff, playing with MUD – no, not that lovely squelchy brown stuff you enjoyed as a toddler, splashing about in your welly-boots, but something else that was equally fun for a lot of people. MUDs were interactive multiple-user adventure games which often drew on the hugely popular 1970s fantasy gaming world of Dungeons and Dragons, and they started almost as soon as internet connections could be made across the Atlantic, from England to the United States.

From the beginning, MUDs were non-commercial and were placed by their developers in the public domain, meaning that anyone was free to join and to develop further versions. MUDs, like Dungeons and Dragons (D&D), involved developing enormously intricate and complex fantasy worlds inhabited by warriors, shamans, princes and powerful wizards, having magical adventures that could last for weeks or even months at a time. Both D&D and MUDs gave participants a chance to develop a powerful shared alternative reality, one in which physically weak people had the chance to play at being conquering heroes and indomitable warriors, and shy individuals could take on the mannerisms of imperious regal lords or seductive lovers. Fantasy-games like these began to allow people to develop online persona quite different from their real-life personalities and identities, and interact with other people, in real-time, using these imagined personas. Unlike lonely fantasies in one's bedroom, these multi-user games are social and public, enabling other people to 'meet' and to interact with the invented persona, but unlike role-playing 'in real life' (off the computer screen), such personas need have no relationship at all to the actual physical body of the participant (Turkle, 1997). Out of the MUD came forth, eventually, complex multi-media fantasy-worlds such as *Second Life*, where individuals can take on new personalities, or avatars, and publicly explore parts of their inner lives which they might never have even known about otherwise.

As well as playing, a favourite human activity is talking, and discussion boards, in the form of bulletin board systems (BBS), came in at the very start of the internet, until they were largely overtaken by more sophisticated methods of cyber-talking such as email, newsgroups and, more recently, chat-rooms, blogs and tweets. BBSs began as a kind of virtual equivalent of the typical cork-board that any organization has up in the corridor or in the staff-room – a place to stick up photocopies of messages, post-it notes, invitations, circulars, pictures of your new baby or a car for sale, and general information for everyone to browse. They were often free, run as a hobby by the 'sysop' (system operator) and, because they ran over telephone-lines, they were restricted to fairly small geographical areas, so that people tended to know one another. However, as internet service providers (ISPs) set up cables and, later, broadband to connect more and more computers, more people were able to join and BBSs really took off. Pretty soon, people were able to use BBSs to access email and Usenet. Thus, for many people, their first taste of internet access came originally through their account on a discussion board. Today there may be millions of BBSs (now more typically known as discussion boards, online or community forums or message boards).

Unlike the friendly informality of most boards, some BBSs, known as 'elite boards' or 'WaReZ boards' had a different style. They were membership-only and were used exclusively for distributing illegal copies of software. The largest of these operated like an exclusive club, with members joining by invitation only. In the 1990s, bulletin boards became probably the most common way to share child pornography. These 'pedo boards' relied on individuals posting links to temporary websites where child pornography would be available (over a matter of hours or days) to download for free. In return, other posters were also expected to share their own 'collections' of child pornography. The subculture of 'pedo boards' is well-discussed in *Beyond Tolerance: Child Pornography Online* (Jenkins, 2003), where it is claimed that bulletin boards 'effectively serve as communal centers for the whole traffic in child porn' (p. 64). Law enforcement, or monitoring by the administrators, seems to have had very little impact on these boards. More effective has been hacking activism by anti-paedophile vigilantes who are sometimes able to post up information on the pornography users' actual identities, to deter them.

A safer way to communicate securely is through newsgroups, which are 'virtual' bulletin boards, not attached to any part of the worldwide web and thus not accessed directly through web-pages. Unlike bulletin boards, there is no registration process. Newsgroups started in 1979, long before the internet or the world-wide web, and are run on separate systems to the rest of the internet. Most people access newsgroups through their ISP or email provider, such as Outlook Express, or through an interface such as Google Groups. The earliest form was Usenet, which still exists and hosts around 100,000 newsgroups where individuals can post comments and share files on topics of interest. Early on, the newsgroups were divided into eight major categories (such as those for science or recreation) plus an additional category 'alt.*' for 'alternative' topics. It is sometimes suggested that 'alt.*' in fact stands for 'anarchists, lunatics and terrorists', as this category is where most fringe and sometimes illegal activity is found. Newsgroups identified as 'binaries' include sharing of photographs. Child pornography was said to be available in various 'alt.binaries' groups, with individuals putting online series of photo sessions (usually 100–150 pictures plus thumbnails) culled from pay-to-view sites back in the early 2000s (online comment from Beckett, 2009). Even avoiding alt.binaries sites, it is not difficult to find what appear to be advertisements for child pornography.

Example of a newsgroup post

---

alt.anime.shoujo

Description: Japanese animation targeted to young girls, and its origins.

20 Oct 2007, 05:03

Hi there. Looking to trade pics and mpegs of young lolitas and beastiality porn. Have hundreds of them to trade. Even have pics of nude little boys. If you are interested in trading please email me at Excaliber2 ... @webtv.net

(available at http://groups.google.co.uk/group/alt.anime.shoujo/topics?lnk=gschg, accessed 15 February 2008)

For many people interested in more mainstream topics, newsgroups may be less exciting than the more recent technologies like internet relay chat (IRC). IRC allows text-based conversation in real time and thus started the whole modern 'chat movement'. First developed by a student in Finland in 1988, IRC took off in 1991 when news on Iraq's invasion of Kuwait could be found only through an IRC link, after radio and television broadcasts were cut off. From IRC has emerged instant messaging and chat-rooms (which may also offer web-cam to supplement the on-screen text). Chat-rooms are provided by major organizations such as AOL. Such forms of communication tend to be fairly free and easy, often gossipy and flirtatious. They provide the opportunity for chatting more discreetly in 'private rooms', and are only lightly moderated, but do not offer a particularly high level of security. Alongside chat, there are now the burgeoning social networking sites (SNS) such as Facebook, MySpace, Bebo and so forth, which offer further advantages over the basic chat technology.

However, for those who wish to pursue hidden or illegal activities, newsgroups continue to provide a much more secure means of communication. While some newsgroups are moderated by administrators (and thus offer some check to illicit activity), it is easy to find ones which are not. Alongside the security of sophisticated pseudonymous servers ('nyms') to prevent anyone being able to track the websites visited, it is also possible to use secure email accounts which use encryption and 'anonymous remailing'. An anonymous remailer is a server computer which receives messages with embedded instructions on where to send them next, and which forwards them without revealing where they originally came from. Commercial companies providing these services can be easily found on the internet, for example at the following sites (accessed 15 February 2008), http://www.sendfakemail.net, www.ultimate-anonymity.com, or www.mixminion.net. Anonymous remailers may be used for postings when giving very personal and potentially stigmatizing information, such as for example on the support group alt.support.depression, and can also be used simply as a political statement on the right to privacy and opposition to surveillance (Donath, 1999).

2. File-sharing

As well as communicating, it is clear that another major function of cyberspace is to facilitate sharing, and in particular the sharing of files, whether those are software, photographs, audio or music files or film. File-sharing as a huge internet phenomenon began with Napster which, like IRC, was the brainchild of a student, Shawn Fanning. In 1999, Fanning designed a piece of software to combine the instant-messaging system of IRC, the file-sharing functions of Microsoft Windows and Unix, and the search capacities of a number of search engines, to seek out and download music files. The Napster software was free to download – and suddenly, peer-to-peer file-sharing meant that anyone could access any music, regardless of copyright. Within a year, Napster was prosecuted and re-launched as a fee-paying service, after the music business objected to all this free music-sharing (Brosnan *et al.*, 2002).

But after Napster came more sophisticated systems such as Gnutella. This avoided a centralized system (where enquiries were made centrally and anyone who had the file could then pass it on), to a de-centralized process in which all the information in the system is stored, not centrally, but in the ordinary users' individual PCs (known as 'nodes'). Thus the information is effectively scattered throughout the system, so that files can be searched and accessed without the need for a central store or for any human intervention in the searching process. This is therefore an anonymous system: because it makes use of members' personal computer hard-drives to store and transmit files, it becomes almost impossible to know who has sent or who has received any particular file.

The next step on from Gnutella is Freenet. Freenet is a file-sharing system set up by its originator, Ian Clarke, in order to counter online censorship. It uses encryption so that files are resistant to 'traffic sniffing' (finding out what is being sent). Anyone can publish information easily, without having to buy a domain-name as they would when posting files on a website. Thus, although file-sharing originally began as activity among friends or acquaintances, files can now easily be shared among total strangers anywhere in the world. As with bulletin boards or newsgroups, where posters are directed to temporary websites to download files, anonymous file-sharing may also take place outside the main system, via Freenet freesites or internet-based websites. These are likely to be restricted access, allowing small communities to share files privately. Parts of the internet such as these, which are not accessible to the general public and are not searchable by search engines, are known as the 'darknet' or the dark web. While much of the darknet contains innocuous material such as Facebook profiles, which are not available to search engines, it is also in the darknet that the dissemination of child sexual abuse images can take place. Ian Clarke does not appear concerned about this aspect of Freenet. As he reported in his blog, after being interviewed by a journalist:

> I told him what I tell everyone, which is that like most people I wish CP [child pornography] didn't exist, but there are many ways to get it other than Freenet, and I don't think people should be denied the freedom to communicate just because a small minority might use it for something we don't agree with. (Clarke, 2009: online)

Unlike 'most people', however, Clarke has carefully set up and maintains a site where child pornography is known to be distributed (Leurs,

2005). Child pornography is also, of course, not only 'something we don't agree with' but is a very serious crime. This does not faze Clarke. Referring to an article in the British newspaper, *The Guardian* (Beckett, 2009) which had suggested that the police are able to 'get round' the 'anonymity things', Clarke responded that:

> either they are mistaken, lying, or they know something about Freenet and Tor [another encrypted site] that neither I, nor anyone I've ever met or heard from, has discovered. This is extremely unlikely, I know many of the best security people in the world, and none of them work for the British police. (Clarke, 2009: online)

This brief overview of the online world demonstrates the multiple ways in which the internet, over a space of three decades, has radically changed people's recreation, communication and ability to share information. Crucially, it has facilitated the sexualization and exploitation of children. As Jenkins suggests, it was only the development of bulletin boards and newsgroups in the 1980s that revived the market for child pornography. Online file-sharing developed from the first 'pedo boards' in the early 1980s which, by the 1990s, were almost certainly the most important route for distributing such images (Jenkins, 2003). This continues with the most recent versions of Freenet and other parts of the 'darknet', which not only enable 'the largest online child pornography-oriented videotheque' (quoted in Leurs, 2005: 32) but also, as Jenkins (2003) and Leurs (2005) found, provide a forum for 'child lovers' to share views and justifications for their actions.

As well as secure and anonymous file-sharing, the internet also provides anonymity through pseudonymous servers ('nyms') and secure email accounts which use encryption and 'remailing'. All these provide the technological basis for a world in which, for the first time, those who find children sexually attractive can exchange illegal images in almost complete security while also discussing their sexual desires with others. Sexualized images of children have also expanded away from direct photography and film into other forms. The online paedophile presence has profoundly shaped the content and form of the internet and, in turn, the internet has shaped the experiences and self-perceptions of paedophiles. The following section explores this further, examining how the 'online paedophile community' has used the internet to present 'pro-paedophile' arguments.

3. Wikipedia: a platform for paedophiles?

As Chapter 1 demonstrated, there is a high level of cultural confusion over the subject of paedophilia and, from a psychoanalytical perspective, it can be argued that one way in which this confusion is dealt with, and to some extent resolved, is through the psychological strategies of denial, avoidance, projection and scapegoating. We see this manifested, for example, through denial of the prevalence of paedophiles in society and concomitant surprise when the internet is used to facilitate the exchange of child pornography. Contrary to such denial, I argue that paedophile desire is deeply integrated within our social and cultural systems; thus we should in fact *expect* to see the internet used in this way, and we need to confront and address that reality. This section provides another example of paedophile visibility on the internet, through the way in which self-identified paedophiles have edited particular entries on the online encyclopaedia Wikipedia.

Given the increasing significance of the internet as a direct, immediate and immensely popular source of information, Wikipedia plays a pivotal role in constructing and disseminating a shared understanding of paedophilia and issues related to it. Typing the word 'paedophilia' into Google or other search engines regularly brings up the Wikipedia encyclopaedia site at approximately the third entry. Google results are presented in order of the number of hits a site receives, and therefore a site which is consistently displayed in the top few results retrieved by Google (which is the most popular search-engine on the internet) demonstrates that Wikipedia is one of the most popular sites on the internet for people exploring this term, and therefore the entries provided by Wikipedia on paedophilia and related topics are likely to be highly influential. Both the spellings 'paedophilia' and 'pedophilia' produce this result, as do the alternative terms 'paedophile' and 'pedophile'. The Wikipedia entry also provides the searcher with links to related websites and to related terms within the Wikipedia site. Because the content of Wikipedia is not fixed but is 'open source', the links, related terms, entries and encyclopaedia articles change all the time, dependent on editing.

The significance of Wikipedia as a 'first port of call' for information on paedophilia has not gone unnoticed by the online paedophile community – nor, indeed, by the online anti-paedophile community, which has posted quotations from pro-paedophile activists, for example on the 'Wikipedia Campaign' page at the anti-paedophile activist Wikisposure.com website. In these quotations, one pro-paedophile activist, BLueRibbon, explained that the reason for spending so much time at Wikipedia is because the Wikipedia article on paedophilia is the top result for that term on Google, thus clearly making it an important platform for pro-paedophile activity.

Another poster, Student, comments on the topic of whether one should declare oneself as a paedophile on the editors' 'user pages'. Student, like BLueRibbon, explains that the most important function Wikipedia serves for the pro-paedophile community is directly through the paedophilia articles. What matters most, Student suggests, is that firstly they present a positive view of paedophilia and secondly that they have external links directly to the pro-paedophile support and activist community. Compared to editing the paedophilia articles, 'outing' oneself on the user pages is a much less important issue. Student stresses how important it is that any paedophiles who are 'newly daring' to search online terms related to paedophilia or look them up directly in Wikipedia, in an effort to understand themselves better, are able to get the information Student regards as unbiased and are presented with links to the various pro-paedophile support forums or sites which Student endorses. This applies also to the non-paedophile community, Student suggests, as Wikipedia can provide a widely recognized channel of authoritative information, thereby influencing the mainstream. Student concludes his exhortations to other paedophiles who might wish to be involved in editing Wikipedia by emphasizing that, if need be, one should 'lie and hide' rather than be prevented from editing.

There are numerous articles within the Wikipedia site, constantly changing, which could be explored in relation to the topic of paedophilia. One in particular provides a very clear example of how online knowledge is negotiated and how highly influential views can be presented. The example I have chosen to explore this process is the article on 'child grooming'. This article is significant because it is a clear example of a highly contested term, which does not even exist as an entry in other encyclopedias or dictionaries. This section explores how this article was edited, challenged and changed over a 14-month time-span from its initial inclusion in March 2005, and finishes with a review of what happened to this article, and other articles on the topic of 'paedophilia' up to the end of 2008.

Wikipedia is a free-to-access online encyclopaedia, described in its strap-line as 'the free encyclopaedia that anyone can edit'. A wiki is a type of website that allows users to add, remove, or otherwise edit content with few constraints. It is used for collaborative writing and for producing user-maintained databases for searching information. The word 'wiki' means 'quick' or 'fast' in Hawaiian and was coined by Ward Cunningham, the computer programmer who created the first wiki in 1994 and installed it on the web in 1995. This provided the software which subsequently resulted in the design of the Wikipedia encyclopaedia set up by Jimmy (Jimbo) Wales and Larry Sanger in 2001.

Wikipedia began as an English-language website which is also now becoming available in a wide range of other languages. The English language version, by 2011, had over three-and-a-half million articles. Having only been set up in 2001, it was already attracting daily hits running into the millions from 2004 onwards and, in 2010, attracted some 684 million visitors, with the number of people editing English-language articles rising from only 26 in 2001 to around 39,000 in 2011. (All statistics and quotations in this section are taken from various pages within Wikipedia itself, for example http://en.wikipedia.org/wiki/Wikipedia:About.) The exponential growth of Wikipedia has been credited to its 'democratic, all-encompassing nature'. Wikipedia has been 'designed to cater to all groups and is dedicated to providing balanced opinions and articles with the sole purpose of informing.' The explicit philosophy of wikis, as described on the Wikipedia pages, is to make it 'easy to correct mistakes rather than making it dificult to make them'. Wikipedia has set up a number of features to correct mistakes and allow editing of text. This is mainly done through the capacity to track editorial changes, for example through 'Recent Changes' pages, giving a revision history and a 'diff' feature. The diff feature works by highlighting the changes between two revisions, thus making it possible to quickly restore previous revisions. Wikipedia acknowledge that the open philosophy of allowing any content to be edited by any user makes any wiki vulnerable to what they term 'vandalism' (or bias). This approach – of making damage easy to undo rather than preventing damage in the first instance – is a form of 'soft security' and is consonant with the general Wikipedia philosophy of 'assume good faith'. The result, when compiling an online encyclopedia accessed by many millions of people as an authoritative source of knowledge, is to produce entries which are an amalgam of more or less convergent views on a topic.

For many encyclopedia entries, the agreed 'truth' on a topic may be regarded as relatively straightforward and non-controversial. For other subjects, the composition of an entry by multiple authors and editors clearly becomes a much more political and contested process, and Wikipedia have a list of over a hundred issues which are particularly controversial, ranging from abortion to zoophilia. For any article within Wikipedia, the capacity to track editorial changes means that to a large extent the negotiations and deliberations as each article is constructed and re-constructed become a transparent process. Unlike encyclopedias published in hard-copy, the process is visible to anyone who cares to go through and review chronologically the often extensive editorial changes (both minor and major) which have been made since the entry was first posted. Although at times it can be convoluted to follow the narrative of who made which changes, and wading through the many tiny editorial revisions of punctuation and grammar can also be tedious, the overall result is a fascinating document on the process of constructing a definition of a contested concept.

As part of the editing process, as well as a record of which edits were made, contributors frequently also leave comments on a discussion page, known as a 'talk page'. Thus the comments left as part of the background discussion to the 'child grooming' article can be found at http://en.wikipedia.org/wiki/Talk:Child_grooming. The discussion covered in this section took place between 13 April 2005 and 8 March 2006 and during this year seven topics on child grooming were covered, from a brief query on the UK Sexual Offences Act, and a short comment on the clarity and structure of the article, to longer debates on NPOV (the Wikipedia principle of always maintaining a 'neutral point of view'), paedophilia, moral character, pornography, and 'AfD' (an acronym for 'Article for Deletion', where someone complained 'This article is a bunch of fluff that either is or should just be covered elsewhere. I am contemplating nominating it for deletion.' Rather than being deleted, however, the article continued to be negotiated over and develop.

The original article on 'child grooming' was first posted on Wikipedia by a user named Patrick at 11.57 on 26 March 2005. The definition given (with hyperlinks underlined) is:

> Grooming a child is befriending a child, often in the negative context of preparing for the child to accept inappropriate behavior from the other person; in addition to acts which by themselves are legal, this may include showing pornography to the child, perhaps even child pornography, to give the child the impression that the depicted acts are normal. One form of grooming is 'internet grooming', e.g. through online chat. In 2003 MSN Chat was restricted to better protect children from inappropriate communication online.

The definition then goes to add, in a separate paragraph: 'The proposed Protection of Children and Prevention of Sexual Offences (Scotland) Bill would make it an offence for an adult to meet a child with the intention of later sexual abuse of that child', and Patrick later added a link to an academic paper by the University of Central Lancaster Cyberspace Research Unit.

The terms highlighted in the article were linked to web-pages on 'showing pornography to a child' (which links to a 'stub' on 'disseminating pornography to a minor' and is listed under 'pornography' and 'law'); 'child pornography' (which is an extensive entry, listing legislation in a number of countries); 'online chat' (which is quite a technical entry, with references to obscure early internet use of technology such as MUD. It also included a link to 'sexual abuse' (which includes a short entry on spousal abuse and a somewhat longer entry on child abuse). This entry therefore already gives a sense of the particular interests of the people who decide which definitions should be added to Wikipedia, what each definition should contain, and what each definition should link to.

In the 14-month period from 26 March 2005 to 20 May 2006, there were 117 revisions of the definition of 'child grooming' with over forty users contributing to the revisions (these details can be accessed via http://en.wikipedia.org/w/index.php?title=Child_grooming&action= history). Many of the revisions are marked as 'm' for minor, and are often the same user re-visiting the entry to tidy up the entry or add more detail. For example, Patrick makes fifteen revisions to his original entry, which remains uncontested until 20 May 2005, almost two months later. However, a substantial revision is then posted by a user named LuxOfTKGL, which is alleged online to be the username of a British man, Darren Cresswell (see http://wikisposure.com/Lux). LuxOfTKGL defined himself (http://en.wikipedia.org/wiki/User:LuxOfTKGL) as a girl-orientated paedophile. Prior to a prison sentence, he was active on 'girl lover' websites including the (now defunct) TKGL website. After Lux's revision, the definition of 'child grooming' now reads (underlining to show hyperlinks has been removed from all following definitions):

> Grooming a child is befriending a child, building a strong trusting bond.
>
> The term is often used in the negative context of lowering the inhibitions of the child to sexual behavior with the other person; It must be stated however that the relationship between Grooming and the adult act of seduction for a legitimate relationship is very similar – such Grooming in and of itself is not necessarily harmful, it all depends on the intentions and purposes behind the grooming.

It could be said parents groom their children to love them, and there are many models in which building a strong trusting bond with a child is beneficial, and indeed necessary. Therefore, Grooming a child used as a term on its own should at least make the reader ask for what purpose before a judgment on whether it is acceptable or not. In addition to acts which by themselves are legal, sexual grooming may include showing pornography to the child, perhaps even child pornography. The type of pornography may be such as to arouse the child, and/or an example of what the other person desires, to give the child the impression that the depicted acts are normal.

One form of grooming is 'internet grooming' or 'online grooming', i.e. nurturing an internet friendship, e.g. through online chat, possibly resulting later in real life contact. Again, the term is often used in the negative context mentioned above, but there are also many situations online where positive relationships have been forged and built out of such situations. In 2003 MSN Chat was restricted to better protect children from inappropriate communication online.

Legal information was also provided on the UK Sexual Offences Act. This definition remained uncontested on Wikipedia until the neutrality of the article was disputed a month later on 24 June 2005. This was flagged up by a sign showing a hand held up palm forward on a red background, in an international 'stop' sign, and the comment 'The neutrality of this article is disputed. Please see the discussion on the talk page.' The definition was also placed under a category shown as NPOV, relating to the contested neutrality of the point of view (POV) of the editor of the definition. Various links were added and removed, for example on 'cybersex', but the main text of the definition remained, and on 1 September 2005 the NPOV category was removed (meaning that the neutrality of the article was no longer disputed) even though the text remained the same.

On 8 September a user named Jdcooper then went further and added an additional paragraph to the definition, which was still regarded by Wikipedia as neutral:

Some critics have commented on the dangers of seeing the child's age as the sole criteria [sic] for their vulnerability and role in the relationship. There have been numerous cases of a minor effectively seducing a reluctant older person, a situation for which the law makes no allowance, assuming instead that everyone under the age of consent is vulnerable, immature, and always devoid of responsibility. Critics have described this view as naive and erroneous, though this same argument rages throughout the discussion of any activity for which there is a age [sic] of individual sovereignty.

On 14 September the NPOV category was reinstated, and the paragraph on minors seducing reluctant older persons was removed. The NPOV category remained, as various minor revisions were made and the definition of 'child grooming' was intermittently linked, and un-linked, to categories such as 'friendship', 'pedophilia' and 'child sexual abuse'. Not until 12 October was the NPOV category again removed, but the definition still remained substantially the same as before:

> Grooming a child is befriending a child by building a strong, trusting bond, though the term is most often used negatively to refer to an act of lowering a perceivedly inhibitory attitude of a child regarding sexual behavior with an adult.
>
> Grooming in and of itself is not necessarily harmful, it all depends on the intentions and purposes behind the grooming. In addition to acts which by themselves are legal, sexual grooming may include acts such as showing pornography to the child, perhaps even child pornography. The pornography may be used to arouse the child, or as an example of what the other person desires, to give the child the impression that the depicted acts are normal or common.
>
> One form of grooming is 'Internet grooming' or 'online grooming', that is, nurturing an Internet friendship, usually by means of online chat, which may later result in 'real life' contact. Again, the term is often used in the negative context mentioned above, but there are also many situations online where positive relationships have been forged and built out of such communications. In 2003 MSN Chat was restricted to better protect children from what they called 'inappropriate communication'.

The information on the UK Sexual Offences Act also remained in place, as did the links to both the categories 'child sexual abuse' and 'friendship'. On 1 November the befriending element of the 'child grooming' definition was strengthened, and the whole entry was substantially enlarged to incorporate material on sexual grooming and online sexual grooming as well as information on the UK Sexual Offences Act. This expanded definition was provided by a user named Rookiee Revolyob (which is alleged online to be the username of an American,

Damien Cole, see http://wikisposure.com/Rookiee), who describes himself (http://en.wikipedia.org/wiki/User:Rookiee) as a 'pedosexual and
boylover' (his username 'Revolyob' is 'boylover' backwards) and an
activist in the boylover and girllover communities. At this point the
basic definition of 'child grooming' in Wikipedia, which still had no
NPOV category at this point, was:

> Child grooming is the practice of instilling foundation of moral
> character within a child. It is often accomplished by forming an inter-
> personal relationship between an adult and a child, building a strong,
> trusting bond, thereby setting the stage for mentorship.
> The term has been held in both negative and positive light,
> depending on the user's context. It has recently grown a primarily
> negative connotation, most often when referring to adults who abuse
> their position of authority and trust to mold the child's views as their
> own. In this context, it is often compared to brainwashing. In this
> usage of the term, instilling values which society considers positive is
> not commonly viewed as 'grooming'; only values negatively held by
> society and/or for personal gain.

However, this definition lasted less than one day before being replaced
by the earlier style of definition which had lasted broadly unchanged
since first being posted by Patrick in March. Again, categories under
which to classify 'child grooming' continued to shift, and 'interpersonal
relationships' was added as a category on 3 November.

The NPOV category was added for the third time on 3 November and
a further category, Accuracy Disputes, was also added for the first time,
but these were both removed again by 9 November, and the definition
had been adjusted again to remove some of the more positive connotations of grooming. At this point a term, 'chickenhawk', was introduced
into the definition, posted on 9 November, removed on 13 November,
and reinstated again the same day. Various entries were made by different people, including a user named 'Psychedelicfrog' who stated on
his user-page (http://en.wikipedia.org/wiki/User:Psychedelicfrog) that
'Psychedelicfrog is a male boylover and advocate for NPOV in boylove-
related articles. His goal is not to spread pro-pedophile propoganda [sic],
but to ensure that the topic is represented in a fair and accurate way.'

On 30 November, eight months after the original definition had first
been posted, a substantial revision was made by a user named Rainbird,
re-presenting the original definition as a 'neologism' and providing a
new definition of 'child grooming' as 'common usage' which read:

The phrase 'Child grooming' has seen many varied kinds of usages over the course of the past several decades. In the 1970s and 1980s, grooming a child on the one hand, meant quite literally – keeping an eye out for a child's hygeine [sic] issues. On the other hand it meant preparing him for his future. Children were groomed to become artists, or doctors, or manual laborers. Parents had a vision for their child's future – and they made sure to find that child mentors, and give him or her experiences which would lead him on that pathway in life ... [ellipsis in original]

The rest of the entry remained broadly the same. This definition was not disputed, and a new web-link, to Perverted-Justice.com (a volunteer anti-paedophile computer watch-dog agency), was added in December. Given the positive connotations of 'grooming' given in this definition, it could be suggested that the Perverted-Justice web-link may have been added to alert chat-room users to the fact that some are watched by anti-paedophile volunteers. No other, more mainstream, child protection sites were linked.

On 22 December, the definition reverted to the earlier style:

Child grooming is a somewhat euphamistic [sic] term for the development of a relationship with a child by an adult for the purpose of engaging in sexual activities with the child. The 'groomer' is sometimes refered [sic] to as a 'chickenhawk'.

In addition to acts which by themselves are legal, sexual grooming may include acts such as showing pornography to the child, perhaps even child pornography. The pornography may be used to arouse the child, as an example of what the adult desires or to give the child the impression that the depicted acts are normal or common.

One form of grooming is 'Internet grooming' or 'online grooming', that is, nurturing an Internet friendship, usually by means of online chat, which may later result in 'real life' contact. In 2003 MSN Chat was restricted to better protect children from what they called "inappropriate communication". Yahoo! and the New York State attorney general's office agreed in October 2005 that Yahoo! will remove and bar user-created chat rooms with names that promoted sex between minors and adults.

Between December 2005 and May 2006, the definition became increasingly longer and with more legal content, but there appears to have been less online discussion of the issues and the NPOV and

Accuracy Disputes categories do not appear to have been used. Contributors to the definition at this point included Clayboy (http://en.wikipedia.org/wiki/User:Clayboy) who had this to say on his user-page:

> A proud member of the underground cabal of pedophiles who edit wikipedia (UCPWEW) (yes, I am being sarcastic, to be painfully clear) I am not here to manipulate content to skew it until it fits my perverted, wrong and harmful view of the world, nor am I here to meet boys. I am here because I believe strongly in the neutral point of view policy and I want to watchdog the articles pertaining to the boylove community or pedophilia at large. In my view, this is badly needed because most people who edit these articles are motivated by strong feelings and often blind hate, and not calm, proven facts and neutral wording such as they should be. [The term 'underground cabal' was given a web-link to an article by Perverted-Justice.com.]

By the end of May 2006, the definition of 'child grooming' was given as:

> This article is about the act of grooming a child for sex. For grooming to improve appearance or hygiene, see Personal grooming.
>
> Child grooming, in the context of this article, refers to actions deliberately undertaken with the aim of befriending a child, in order to lower a child's sexual inhibitions or establish an intimate friendship in preparation to the eventual introduction of sexual activities with the child. The phrase 'child grooming' can also mean preparing a child for a future activity or role outside of a sexual context. This can include educating the child, ensuring the child knows how to behave in a social setting as well as other benign activities essential for normal child development. This definition is outside of the context of this article. The act of grooming a child sexually may include activities that are legal in and of themselves, as well as acts which are illegal in some jurisdictions, such as showing pornography to the child by which the groomer may seek to arouse the child sexually, arouse his/her sexual curiosity, or to persuade the child that sexual activity is normal between adults and children. Sexual grooming of children also occurs on the Internet. The adult's goals may include online sexual activity – in chat rooms, for example – or meeting the child in person.

This definition was followed by expanded legal information, now covering Australia, Canada, the UK and the US.

In December 2009, when I last visited the 'Child Grooming' article, it remained active and had expanded considerably, but now resembled much more what one might expect from such a topic. Grooming to improve appearance or hygiene has been removed to a different article and there is no mention of mentoring or of children seducing adults Instead, there is a clear overview of sexual grooming behaviours, a paragraph on internet grooming, notes on criminal codes in various English-language countries, and references and external links to sites including child protection sites. The focus of the article has thus moved clearly and unambiguously to a child protection perspective (although there is also a link to a lengthy article on 'pederasty').

As noted earlier, alongside the edits being made to the article, there was also a fairly lively discussion going on behind the scenes on the 'talk page'. For example, regarding 'NPOV' (the policy of always holding a 'neutral point of view') the question of what the article should cover was mainly debated by two editors, LuxOfTKGL and Lepeu1999. LuxOfTKGL started the discussion by commenting:

> The article seemed severely biased to one side of the situation. The term 'child grooming' is not descriptive of the act that has taken place later, nor the intentions of the 'groomer'. Therefore, I felt it proper to add in the counter balance to this to state reasonably that other forms of 'grooming' are socially acceptable, and indeed beneficial.

To which Lepeu1999 responded:

> I disagree with the above. Your rational [sic] appears to be nothing more than an attempt to be disingenuous with respect to the entire concept. Given your public profile, I question whether or not you have an agenda here.

As the argument continued, another contributor suggested:

> Yes, I'm afraid that I, too, must take issue with this article. I feel that its tone, perspective, and very definitions are biased, or at very least misleading. Grooming is not synonymous with befriending, otherwise it would simply be called befriending. . . . It is my suggestion that this article be rewritten with a more accurate and neutral perspective.

The discussion continued, with increasingly personal comments being levelled as edits were made and removed. When someone remarked that child grooming is a felony, Rookiee snapped back, 'Which felony is 'child grooming' specifically?... there is no statute in the US that I'm aware of that says 'grooming' is illegal. That's a UK term, to be sure of. And thank God, the UK doesn't reign over the US anymore.'

Rookiee also took exception to the phrase 'the predatory tactic used by pedophiles', retorting, 'I contest that. I'm a pedophile, and I've never done that to anyone. That statement is biased and ignorant. It should read "For the predatory tactic used by child abusers" at the very least.' When another editor argued, 'Not everyone who sexually abuses a child is a pedophile. But child grooming is a much more involved, premeditated effort than simply molesting a kid. It means actively cultivating a relationship for the ultimate purpose of sex. Who but a pedophile would do so?, Rookiee's response was 'Aaaannnd you would know this, how?;) The way you're making it sound, either you've done it, or you've had it done to you.'

Throughout the year under study, what is perhaps most interesting is the information which is absent from the article and also which never gets mentioned in the discussion. For example, only one reference is made on the discussion page to another online dictionary, the *Free Dictionary*, where the two main definitions of 'grooming' are 'activity leading to skilled behavior' and 'the activity of getting dressed, putting on clothes'. No other primary sources external to Wikipedia appear to be examined, although other online encyclopaedia and dictionary entries, had they been searched, would have yielded similar results to the *Free Dictionary*. Wikipedia was the only online encyclopaedia at this point which contained an article on 'child grooming'.

Again, it is interesting that nowhere in the extended definitions and discussions related to this encyclopaedia entry is there any information given on the development of this term as a specific practice, or references to its first use in the media. For example, the Wikipedia entry could usefully have made reference to the *Tackling Sexual Grooming Conference*, held in London on 29 September 2003, where the keynote speech given by Will Gardner of Childnet International made the point that 'The new offence of 'Grooming'... was born from a Home Office Task Force on Internet Safety' (Childnet: Gardner, 2003). Another useful reference on the difficulties surrounding the derivation and meaning of the term was provided a few months later when the British Psychological Society made the following statement on its website to promote research findings presented on 23 March 2004:

Over the last few years the concept of sexual grooming is one which has come into common parlance and from May 2004 it was included as an offence under the Sexual Offences Act.

Yet two psychologists have presented research suggesting that sexual grooming is still something which both scientists and policy makers have yet to accurately define.... As the researchers tried to plot the development and acceptance of the term they found a surprising lack of empirical or theoretical research into the area. This, the researchers maintain, has meant that the range of behaviours referred to as sexual grooming is still not well defined.... High profile cases in 2004, such as the US Marine who contacted a young girl over the internet before abducting her, have made 'sexual grooming' a widely used term, particularly in relation to the activities of strangers over the internet. The researchers believe this has implications for parents, carers and teachers who may misunderstand the range of behaviours attached to 'sexual grooming' and for the effectiveness of future legislation, which may be reduced if the public are unable to identify the threat properly. (British Psychological Society, 2004: online)

References such as this would have contextualized the Wikipedia entry on 'child grooming' more clearly. Such unacknowledged omissions in the article and discussions demonstrate the implicit bias, and 'point of view', of the contributors at this time, who appear throughout most of the fourteen months under study to have been more interested in checking out what the legal status of certain activities might be, than in discussing effective mechanisms to protect children.

This 'point of view' among some Wikipedia editors did not go entirely unnoticed at the time.

4. 'Pro-paedophiles' and 'anti-paedophiles' online

In response to 'pro-paedophile' advocacy and activity such as the Wikipedia editing, there has been a rise in explicitly 'anti-paedophile' activity online. The first challenge to Wikipedia's neutrality, or the 'Wikipedophilia' debate, began on 12 December 2005 with a posting claiming that Wikipedia was a 'Gathering for Internet Predators'. This was originally posted by a group called Parents for the Online Safety of Children (POSC) and appeared on the Perverted Justice site, among others. It was this posting which originally claimed, as Clayboy ironically noted, that there was an 'underground cabal' of paedophiles on Wikipedia trying to make it a distribution centre for pro-paedophile propaganda. The posting by POSC attempted to 'out' a number of editors, including four self-defined paedophiles. Claiming that Wikipedia allowed paedophiles to edit pages and view the IP addresses of children freely, POSC recommended that parents and schools should block children's access to Wikipedia. Wikipedia responded rapidly to these claims with comments from an administrator named Linuxbeak (Alex Schenck), who pointed out various errors in the posting. Linuxbeak concurred that Wikipedia did indeed allow paedophile editors to edit paedophilia-related articles, but stressed the encyclopaedia's stance as neutral and unbiased and stated that neither would Wikipedia tolerate an anti-paedophile position to be adopted. The rebuttal concluded that it was not the job of Wikipedia to tell its users what is right or wrong, but only to avoid illegality. In a lengthy letter posted on the Wikipedia website, Linuxbeak robustly defended Wikipedia's integrity:

> To whoever I am talking to, please understand why I am so angry. I'm not against your cause; in fact, I'm totally for it. Pedophiles need to be kept in check and away from children. However, you have falsely insinuated that one of our administrators is pro-pedophile and in fact supported by this supposed pedophile underground. You couldn't be any further from the truth! (*Wikipedia*, 2005: online)

The argument continued and in June 2007 the founder of Perverted Justice, Xavier von Erck (also known as Phillip John Eide: posted on *Evilvigilante*, 2007) set up the Wikisposure website to investigate paedophile activists posting on Wikipedia and other sites. Since then, various changes have taken place at Wikipedia. For example, Rookiee's user-page was taken down and he was blocked on 21 September 2006 for using his page for advocacy; the user-page of LuxofTKGL seems to have been un-used since 26 September 2006; Clayboy's user-page was taken down on 7 March 2007 for 'activity detrimental to the activity of Wikipedia'; and an arbitration case was filed against the fourth named editor, Zanthalon, on 15 March 2007. These actions have removed four of the most outspoken pro-paedophile activists who were editing Wikipedia. In addition, anti-paedophile activists have edited new articles for Wikipedia, on 'anti-paedophile activism' and other topics, to counter the pro-paedophile articles still extant. However, Xavier von Erck (as username XavierVE), the founder of Perverted Justice, in a curious twist, was himself then blocked, apparently for too many contentious edits: his user-page was blocked as from 4 March

2008. (Parenthetically, Xavier also apparently behaved contentiously in another area: with regard to my own research, he claimed in 2010 to have submitted 'over a dozen' fake questionnaire responses in an attempt to 'poison the well' of my *Minor-Attracted Adults Daily Lives* research data in 2006–08. Another individual, Stitches77 – who may possibly be Xavier in another guise – made a similar allegation in 2009. However, when asked formally to provide evidence for this assertion or to point to examples of false data used by me, Xavier declined and has at no point offered any proof. Knowing Xavier's propensity to publicize his achievements if he does manage to fool someone, this suggests strongly that no such data were submitted and none were used.)

While the presence of self-defined paedophiles on Wikipedia fluctuates, elsewhere online there are more stable sites which allow individuals to debate topics openly and share their feelings. As noted earlier, paedophile activists such as BlueRibbon are very aware that Wikipedia provides 'the top result' for the term 'paedophilia' on Google, 'making it an important platform'. Any English-speaker wishing to learn about paedophilia (or related terms such as pederasty) is able to click through from a search engine to Wikipedia and then, through the external links (depending on the currents edits on Wikipedia), on to 'boy-lover' or 'girl-lover' sites which are legal and easily accessible. Thus, in two or three clicks, interested individuals are usually able to find themselves on websites where 'pro-paedophile' arguments are put forward.

As the phenomenon of 'pro-paedophile' websites has grown, so have the number of 'anti-paedophile' or 'vigilante' sites which track and challenge anyone advocating 'paedophile rights' or seeking sex with minors contacted online. The most successful of these sites is Perverted Justice, the strapline of which runs, 'Welcome to the most aggressive and innovative anti-pedophile organisation online'. Their stated aim is 'exposing, profiling, fighting and aiding to arrest and convict pedophiles and predators across the entire world'. Since 2003, they have been carefully monitoring and investigating the most outspoken paedophile online activists. At the same time, they also have volunteers who pose as children (aged between 12 and 15 years old) in chat-rooms. The volunteers do not initiate any sexual chat but wait for adults soliciting for sex. If an adult suggests a meeting, they provide an address to meet at and also collect telephone and other details from the adult (invariably a man). In this way, at least 544 men have been successfully prosecuted for sex offences against minors. Some of these men have arrived (for what they believed to be a meeting with a young child alone at a house) carrying items including guns, knives, rope, handcuffs and a gag.

It is clear, therefore, that there are a number of both 'pro-paedophile' and 'anti-paedophile' sites now existing on the internet. While the aim of the 'anti-paedophile' activity is to shut down sites advocating tolerance of paedophilia, identify and harass paedophile activists and prevent the online grooming and subsequent sexual abuse of children, it is less obvious, at times, what the aim of the 'pro-paedophile' community may be. The Canadian sociologist, Pierre Tremblay, has researched and theorized the role of online communities in the lives of paedophiles and he comments:

> Because law enforcement agencies pursue practical goals (arresting individuals) web sites have mainly been understood as providing new instrumental opportunities for paedophiles or hebephiles to reach juveniles and commit (or attempt to commit) offences. However, the most significant and long-term implication of this new mass medium of communication is that it allows individual paedophiles to participate in the development of an authentic subculture and 'community' and to perceive themselves belonging to 'a social movement'. The obvious implication is that a stable forum for in-group intimate, albeit virtual, contacts between individuals normally trapped by an unshareable secret will have lasting effects on their commitment and ultimately on the incidence of age of consent offences. (Tremblay, 2002: 32)

(The term 'hebephiles', which Tremblay uses, refers to those who are sexually attracted to minors who have reached adolescence but who are still below the age of consent. Some people regard this as a subset of the more general category of paedophiles.) Tremblay is here suggesting that online communities are likely to work as deviance amplifiers, by encouraging participants to become 'embedded in a deviant quasi-community or social movement' in which the influence of the peer-group will support the development of 'deviant careers' (Tremblay, 2002: ii). The online paedophile community, in this view, will act to encourage paedophiles to 'violate basic social norms'. This may not be entirely straightforward, however. Tremblay concludes:

> ...a sociological investigation of the current web-driven paedophilia subculture should increase our understanding of paedophiles and could provide a useful strategy for overcoming the inherent self-selection sampling biases shaping conventional clinical and correctional research. It could assess the extent to which this socialization

process (individual deviants becoming embedded in a collective set of exchanges) affects not only their motivation to act out but also their ways of acting out and even their motivation to cease or reduce the frequency and the seriousness of their violations. To the extent that age of consent offenders interact among themselves, they may learn from each other new 'tricks' or discover new 'opportunities' (an 'enhancing effect'). But, at the same time, they may also define for themselves a new set of norms about the 'appropriate' rules of courtship and about the appropriate settings for engaging in erotic interaction with juveniles ('a structuring effect'). Moreover, individuals engaging in age of consent offences may also realize that they are pursuing an altogether 'impossible dream'. As they persevere, they are likely to be disappointed by the juveniles that they have interacted with (the theme of 'betrayal' and the associated theme of the 'unreliability' of juveniles were recurrent topics in our interviews). They may also be disappointed by the callousness or insensitivity of other paedophiles they happen to exchange with (another recurrent theme). As they attempt to actualize their attraction, the personal costs they impose on themselves and on their personal entourage (including the juveniles themselves), may trigger a self-reflection process that will commit them into abstinence. (Tremblay, 2002: 33)

Here, therefore, Tremblay is raising the possibility that the online paedophile community, while it may enhance the potential for behaving sexually with children, may also, on the other hand, have the capacity to reduce that potential by encouraging alternative social norms and self-reflection. My research supports that assertion and suggests that there are indeed cases where the 'pro-paedophile' sites can help individuals to maintain a law-abiding lifestyle (Goode, 2009), even if only through letting off steam, by having a forum to share otherwise-hidden knowledge about oneself. As one research respondent explained:

An interactive message forum like [named site] provides the means for a community to develop, for GLers [girl-lovers] to interact with each other, question each other, discuss ideas, form bonds, provide mutual support. Also, of course, there are the related sites in other languages: [another site] for French-speaking GLers, and a number of BL [boy-lover] forums in other languages too. ('William', 2007, research data)

Another respondent commented, 'We have our own language, our own customs, our own websites. That's a community.' ('Gus', 2007, research data). While we may be fairly sanguine about adults coming across and joining such communities, and being able to take what they find with a pinch of salt, it seems that 'pro-paedophile' sites also attract people with less life experience who are therefore more open to taking on board an uncritical acceptance of such advocacy:

> These websites have helped me to understand my attractions to a greater extent, and to understand my place as a MAA [minor-attracted adult] in modern society. ('Ed' (aged 17), 2007, research data)

> I am 15 years old. After coming across this site through a random google search, I found myself entranced and quickly read through your entire story on the main page. I moved on to Essays after, then Testimonies, and finally the mailbag. I have to say that this is one of the most enlightening sites I have ever found on the internet. It transforms the dark, taboo world of Pedophilia into something wonderful and sweet – not to be ashamed of. I actually think I am proud to be the way I am, thanks to this site and the views expressed on it. I don't feel so alone anymore. . . . I know, now, there are more like me out there. I know that there are people, girls like me, willing to listen to this and not call me a pervert or whatever else close-minded insults others may throw at me. I know who I am – a boylover. I am not ashamed. ('Ginni', undated: online)

Belonging to a marginalized community may certainly encourage behaviour which is 'deviant' from the mainstream. Research on internet newsgroups for marginalized and stigmatized sexual groups suggests that concealing a stigmatized identity paradoxically brings it continually to mind (McKenna & Bargh, 1998), thus making that aspect of the self even more central to one's self-identity. Consequently, the centrality of this self-identity makes self-disclosure to trusted and empathic others even more pressing, in order to feel a sense of worth and acceptance. Newsgroups and other sites where people can 'post' and 'chat' validate such identities and, by doing so, they can make it more likely that they will 'encourage real-life behavior consistent with these identities' (McKenna & Bargh, 1998: 693). This may mean engaging in criminal behaviour: more benignly, it may simply mean that individuals, supported by the online community, are able to 'come out' to family and friends in real life and disclose what had previously been too embarrassing and taboo to speak about.

At the same time, the online community may also set up norms which channel and set a context for desires. These norms may be implicit and enforced through informal group approbation or disapprobation – whether posts on certain topics are picked up and discussed or ignored. The norms may also be more explicit. For example, on the (now-defunct) Human Face of Pedophilia website (one of the most influential 'pro-paedophile' websites until its demise in 2007), there were posted a *Manifesto* (dated 2005) and *Living with Pedophliia: A Practical Guide*, copyrighted to Lindsay Ashford, 2004. These set out expectations for behaviour, such as 'channel your sexuality, avoid child pornography, stay within the law' as well as arguments for a 'civil liberties' approach to paedophiles.

There are a number of sites online which hold an explicitly 'non-contact' position and where it seems to be the case that no illegal material is displayed or exchanged (or the site would rapidly be closed down). On these sites posters will, for example, chat about children they know or have seen and post wistful descriptions of 'girl moments' or 'boy moments', often describing a transient glimpse of an attractive child during everyday life in a way which links to longing and fantasy but not, it would seem, to actual sexual contact. On the 'girl-lover' sites particularly there is a strong sense of idolizing little girls: one of the most popular 'girl-lover' sites on the internet was headed 'A celebration of the splendor of little girls' as discussed in (Goode, 2008b). In psychoanalytic terms, this is another example of splitting and projection. One could describe this as the 'Madonna/whore' dichotomy taken to the extreme, where everything that is felt to be precious, pure, spiritual, beautiful, chaste and good is invested in the idealized image of the 'little girl', fetishizing a certain form of femininity – playful, nurturing, undemanding and protective of the adult male. In talking about 'girl moments', it is noticeable how each tiny gesture becomes imbued with intense meaning: she touched my fingers for a moment, she sat next to me, she brushed against me, I caught a glimpse of her, she smiled at me. One man wrote to me about his feelings for a little girl he knew:

[When I was very unhappy] this little girl would perceive exactly when I felt most 'low' and would come and give me a little hug, or hold my hand – and make me feel so much better. ... On one occasion, she was going to be away ... so she decided to lend me [a cuddly toy], so that I could still sort of 'keep in touch with her' through him! I kept [the toy] in my pocket the whole time, and whenever I needed to, I could hold him and feel close to her!

[Several years later, she occasionally emailed.] She ended the first mail she sent me with a *very* sweet 'PS', which made me almost die on the spot. I have it printed out here in a drawer by my bed, and it's a rare day when I don't read that particular mail before I go to sleep. The thing which frustrated me the most was definitely not a physical frustration, though yes, there was that. But that is fairly easy to 'deal with'. The ache inside me that drove me mad was the simple fact that I could never tell her those three words: 'I love you.' ('William', 2007, research data)

Another man described to me how, maybe forty years ago:

A girl of about four or five years old skated up to me and took my hand and claimed me as her partner for the dance, and we skated hand-in-hand for about ten minutes. At the end of the dance, I wanted to swing her up in my arms and kiss her and hug her and hold her, and go away from the crowd and do whatever else we wanted to do together. I didn't have a clear idea what I wanted to do. Of course I also wanted to skate with her some more. But I didn't get to do anything. ('Eustace', 2007, research data)

One ten-minute event, forty years ago, endlessly ruminated on: this gives a flavour of many of the 'girl moments'. Similarly, an individual sexually attracted to pubescent boys explained to me about his sexual fantasies:

[Sexual fantasies about boys were] the backdrop to a phenomenal and completely overwhelming feeling of failure and the deepest misery, hurt, isolation and fear that undermined the very value of my life itself... [When the boy] becomes the next Roy Keane then everyone else will say that my life and existence added to all that is positive and people would love me for it and I would be truly happy and have a purpose in this life.... The qualities I admired in boys, I now feel I've rediscovered within myself. I've come to the realisation that the transition to adulthood was not to leave them behind. They were merely buried under so much fear, confusion and pain. I feel I've now won back my sense of wonder, curiosity, questioning, optimism about the future, kindness, compassion, playfulness and wanting to do plain old good! ('John', 2008, personal communication)

What John appears to demonstrate here, as with the 'girl-lovers' celebrating 'the spendor of little girls', is the splitting of human experience into everything which is positive being located in the child and everything which is negative (failure, misery, hurt, isolation, fear, confusion, pain) in the adult. Only when John, through years of reflection, was able to re-integrate positive aspects back into himself was he able to let go of obsessional 'boy-love'.

Before he reached that point, John described the relationship between his own interior fantasies and what he found in the online 'boy-love' community:

> [The fantasies became] the basis of the creation of the garden of Eden I call 'Boy World.' A normal heterosexual's fantasy would last all of 5 minutes and end in an orgasm. My fantasy about boys was starting to last 2 full hours if not more. . . .
>
> Boy World was a sandy beach with blue skies and sunshine. It was filled with fun, laughter and games. . . . I'd give boys personalities, he'd be into Liverpool and so would I and we'd talk away about football. Sometimes another boy would be into Manchester United and we'd have a little banter going back and forth. Sometimes he was into computer games and we'd debate which is better – the super Nintendo or the Sega Megadrive – and which games were better. We'd become friends and he'd slowly, through our conversations and fun activities, feel comfortable enough with me to start to ask me about sex and if I had ever 'done it' with a girl. I'd always find a way to turn the conversation to the point where I'd end up giving him a back massage or foot massage. There was no rush to do anything in Boy World. It would skip forward in time and the boy would be asking for another massage and I'd cheekily suggest with a smile that there was another place on the human body that's very nice to massage as well and I'd wait until a grin crossed his face as he realized what I was getting at.
>
> There were so many scenarios played out, in so many places with so many conversations. Had I in later life ever gone down the 'groomer' path then this is where I would have been trained for it.
>
> . . . If you want to see what Boy World looks like then just go to the 'boy love' community. It's the online representation of Boy World. At its core is an archive of boy pictures. On the beach, in water parks, everywhere. All smiling and having fun with blue skies and sunshine. Around these pictures are the ideologies, beliefs and thoughts that structure this world. ('John', 2008, personal communication)

While activists such as Perverted Justice and commentators such as Eichenwald (2006) have seen 'pro-paedophile' websites only as promoting sexual contact with children and therefore as unremittingly negative, my research has suggested that they are also able to function as supporting a view which 'makes sense' of paedophiles as not predatory or evil, but as ordinary human beings with an involuntary sexual attraction which can be controlled, just as any other desire can be controlled. For example, one respondent wrote about where he found support as a 'non-contact' paedophile:

> Internet support boards are currently the only place I feel comfortable talking about it.... Wikipedia helped me discover that there were people who believed that attraction to children was not evil, and that the predatory paedophiles in popular culture were not necessarily accurate depictions. [Now-defunct website] taught me a lot about who these people are... [the online paedophile community] is the sole outlet for any thoughts I have relating to this part of myself. ('Kristof', 2007, research data)

One respondent ('Louis') summed it up, when he discovered the online 'pro-paedophile' community: 'It was such a relief just to discover that I was not alone in loving boys but having no desire to do anything socially / sexually harmful to them.' Thus, the online community may help to relieve loneliness and frustration, build a sense of trust and support and, at best, provide a positive self-identity which can buttress against law-breaking. Perhaps the most intriguing suggestion comes from John:

> The only good thing about the boy love community I can think of is that it can act as a sand trap to slow some people down. If a [predatory paedophile] finds his way on to the boy love community, he will suddenly find a lot of different opinions and points of view that I think will have the effect of slowing that person down quite considerably.... In the end it could be that the boy love community's existence has saved as many children as it is responsible for abusing. Not all good but then not all bad either, just a generally ineffective psychology that has a lot of confusion and therefore unable to deal with reality. In saying this I am not defending the boy love community, it's just if I were society I would not be so quick to judge! ('John', 2008, personal communication)

These quotations help to undermine the view of the online 'pro-paedophile' community as a homogenous group sharing identical views, and can begin to highlight, and contribute to, dissenting voices within the paedophile community which argue for a genuinely ethical and law-abiding stance to children and sexuality. (More details on the international English-language online 'pro-paedophile' community are provided in Goode, 2009.)

5. Conclusion

This chapter has sought to demonstrate not only that paedophiles have been involved from the start in shaping the internet, but also that the internet is radically re-shaping the paedophile experience. Over the last few years, paedophiles have become more vocal in society, as the internet provides hitherto-unobtainable opportunities for paedophiles to contact one another and for the anonymous dissemination of information to potentially millions of users.

The analysis of the construction of the 'child grooming' Wikipedia article over a 14-month time-span highlighted how 'sexual activity between an adult and child' either is or is not 'normal and/or acceptable', as one editor expressed it. This debate hinged not on illegality but on normativity or (potential) social acceptability, as a series of self-defined paedophile editors worked to build an implicit case that adult–child sexual activity falls within a continuum of normal human behaviour. This article provides us with an encapsulated moment of cultural knowledge-construction – a set of freeze-framed images – as one concept, 'child grooming', enters popular knowledge and negotiates its place within the cultural discourse. What is 'grooming'? Is it like 'friendship'? Like 'abuse'? Like 'mentoring'? Like 'parenting'? Like 'seduction'? Like being a 'chickenhawk'? Like 'brainwashing'? Linking the new concept to pre-existing concepts, whether positive or negative, allows 'grooming' to fit within existing models and become part of a cultural resource of 'common knowledge'.

Similarly, how we understand the discourses presented in online 'pro-paedophile' communities helps us to shape and make sense of social and cultural understandings of 'the paedophile' and adult sexual attraction to children. The following chapter continues this exploration of the cultural construction of knowledge, and the topic will be revisited in other chapters also, as the book seeks to demonstrate, not only that paedophiles exist as an integral part of society, but also that 'pro-paedophile' attitudes and beliefs lie deep at the heart of culture.

3
Popular Culture 'Making Sense' of Paedophilia

Introduction

Chapter 1 introduced the idea that, although paedophiles irrefutably exist within society, there is a great sense of confusion and bewilderment over how to respond to them – and what to do about child sexual abuse. There is a startling mismatch between the rhetoric – which is generally loudly hostile – and the reality, which tends to be far more muted. The examples of Michael Jackson and Roman Polanski in particular have demonstrated how, even where the circumstantial evidence seems highly convincing or indeed (in the case of Polanski) the perpetrator admits guilt, those around the alleged or actual abuser continue to support and excuse his behaviour. The Hollywood actress Whoopi Goldberg, for example, famously exonerated Polanski's crime by characterizing it as not 'rape-rape'. In an interview she stated:

> I know it wasn't rape-rape...All I'm trying to get you to understand, is when we're talking about what someone did, and what they were charged with, we have to say what it actually was not what we think it was...Initially he was charged with rape, and then he pled guilty to having sex with a minor, okay....What we were talking about was what he did, and that's what I wanted to clear up, and that's all I wanted to clear up. 'Cause I don't like it when we're passionate about something and we don't have all the facts...We're a different kind of society. We see things differently. The world sees 13 year olds and 14 year olds in the rest of Europe...not everybody agrees with the way we see things...(quoted in Markay, 2009: online)

Her remarks were contrasted with the evidence given at the trial by the 13-year-old, who explained how, after the 43-year-old had repeatedly refilled her champagne glass and given her part of a powerful sleeping pill, he told her to take off her clothes and invited her into the jacuzzi:

> He goes, 'Come down here' [next to him] and I said, 'No. No, I got to get out.' And he goes, 'No, come down here.' And then I said that I had asthma and that I couldn't – I had to get out because of the warm air and the cold air or something like that. And he went 'Just come down for a second.' So I finally went down... And he was like holding me up because it [the water] is almost over my head....Then he started to move [his hands] around and I just got out....I said that I wanted to go home because I needed to take my medicine. He said, 'Yeah, I'll take you home soon.'...I said, 'No, I have to go home now.' He told me to go in the other room and lie down....I was afraid.... He reached over and he kissed me. And I was telling him, 'No,' you know, 'Keep away' But I was kind of afraid of him because there was no-one else there....Then he went down and he started performing cuddliness...he placed his mouth on my vagina....I was ready to cry. I was kind of – I was going, 'No. Come on. Stop it.' But I was afraid....He was – sometimes he was saying stuff. But I was just blocking him out, you know....I was kind of dizzy, you know, like things were kind of blurry sometimes. I was having trouble with my coordination like walking and stuff....I wasn't fighting really because I, you know, there was no one else there and I had no place to go....He placed his penis in my vagina....He didn't answer me when I said, 'No.'...Then he lifted my legs up farther and he went in through my anus.... [I didn't resist] because I was afraid of him. [Someone came to the door.] And I got up and put on my underwear and started walking towards the door....He sat me back down again. Then he started to have intercourse with me again....I thought that I could just leave then and go home and say something, you know, because he was the only way I had to get home....I was sitting in the car [waiting for Polanski to drive her home] and I was crying.... (Extracts from transcript of 1977 court interview posted online, *The Smoking Gun*, 2003)

As he left her at her house, Polanski's parting words to the girl were, 'Don't tell your mother about this and don't tell your boyfriend either. This is our secret.' (Cohen, 2009).

This phenomenon of misinterpreting and trivializing child sexual abuse – and insisting that it 'wasn't rape-rape' – is not confined only to high-status celebrities. It is also seen in 'everyday' cases where the families of the victim and the perpetrator and those around them (such as the employer, school, church congregation or other institutions) are keen to hush up scandal and smooth over disturbing information. As Chapter 1 has also shown, using the example of the Casa Pia orphanage case in Portugal, there is often great social and cultural reluctance to face the reality of the abuse of children.

The discussion on the confusion and reluctance to get to grips with the reality of child abuse and the presence of paedophiles in society continued in Chapter 2 where it would appear, in some quarters at least, that there is a naive acceptance of the 'darknet' as protecting democracy rather than criminality. The internet has been linked to a massive rise in the distribution of child pornography, but crucially it also provides a platform for paedophiles to contact one another and to present 'pro-paedophile' arguments, either anonymously or under the cover of pseudonyms. Thus, as Chapter 2 discussed, paedophiles are active both in shaping the internet and in being shaped by it as, for the first time, they are able to talk online with others and share previously undisclosed experiences. However, paedophiles are in no sense hermetically sealed off from the rest of society. They, like any other individuals, live within society and the processes which influence them online also influence wider society. Because of the capacity of the internet to act as a secure, anonymous and powerful source of global information, one could argue that the 'paedophile voice' has, for the first time, found an amplifier through which to influence popular culture. However, this is not to suggest that the 'paedophile voice' is homogeneous, nor that it is uncontested, nor indeed that it was silent before. While the internet permits and amplifies, through access to many millions of users, the messages which individual paedophiles such as BLueRibbon or LuxOfTKGL can send out, it is the contention of this book that such a perspective is and has always been an integral part of human culture, alongside other forms of adult sexuality.

Before we proceed any further, it might be helpful to pause and get a clearer sense of what 'paedophilia' is and how many paedophiles there may be. A commonsense working definition of a paedophile (which is used throughout this book) was provided at the start of Chapter 1. A standard definition, widely accepted in clinical circles, describes paedophilia as involving recurrent, intense sexually arousing fantasies and sexual urges lasting for six months or more and involving a prepubescent child or children, and which are acted on or which cause marked distress or interpersonal difficulty (American Psychiatric Association, 2000). However, this leaves out any discussion of those adults who may find themselves aroused to children but only occasionally and not exclusively; this may include 'situational offenders' who become sexually aroused and orgasm while having sexual contact with a child or while using child pornography but who adamantly deny they are 'paedophiles' (for example, see Bell, 2003). It also leaves out those adults who sexually fantasize about children more or less recurrently but who have no intention of acting on such attractions and who manage any distress without 'interpersonal difficulty'. Thus, while this clinical definition attempts to differentiate between the two concepts of 'paedophiles' and 'non-paedophiles', there remain experiences of adult sexual contact with children, and sexual attraction to children, which are not adequately covered.

Very few studies have been conducted to date which explore how common sexual arousal to children may be in the general adult population, despite the significance of this topic in combating sexual abuse of children. An overview by Green (2002) cited a number of studies (Briere & Runtz, 1989; Fedora *et al.*, 1992; Freund & Costell, 1970; Freund & Watson, 1991; Hall *et al.*, 1995; Quinsey *et al.*, 1975) and there are also a small number of others. These studies have examined the responses of 'normal' men in the general adult male population (and one of the studies also included women). These are all relatively small-scale. They rely on three basic methods: direct self-report (what the research subjects themselves said about their sexual arousal to children); more general questionnaire responses (which included measurements such as 'sexual impulsivity' and self-esteem); and physical responses (measuring arousal when images were shown or tapes narrating a sexual story were played).

Such studies seem to suggest that somewhere between 12 per cent and 32 per cent of community or college samples of adult men report sexual attraction to children (Becker-Blease, Friend & Freyd, 2006; Briere & Runtz, 1989; Haywood, Grossman & Cavanaugh, 1990; Smiljanich & Briere, 1996) or show penile responses to paedophilic stimuli (Barbaree & Marshall, 1989; Fedora *et al.*, 1992; Frenzel & Lang, 1989; Freund & Watson, 1991; Hall *et al.*, 1995). For example, in a voluntary paid sample of 60 men (with an average age of around 30) recruited from hospital staff and the community, 17 per cent showed a penile response that was paedophilic (Fedora *et al.*, 1992). However, these figures can only be taken as indicative rather than any exact estimate: Freund and Watson

(1991), studying sexual arousal in a community sample of male volunteers, found that 19 per cent of the 'normal' sample were misclassified as having an erotic preference for minors – but also that a comparable number of the known paedophile sample were misdiagnosed as *not* having an erotic preference for minors.

An interesting example is the study by Hall *et al.* (1995), in which a sample of 80 volunteers was recruited from the general population. To explore their responses, the researchers showed the volunteers images and also used audio-tapes with sexual narratives. The images and tapes referred to adult women and to girls under the age of 12 years. Sexual arousal was measured using self-report and physical measurements of penile arousal. In this presumably 'normal' community sample of male volunteers, aged around late thirties, 26 of the 80 volunteers (32.5 per cent) showed sexual arousal to slides of prepubescent children that equalled or exceeded their arousal to the adult slides, and 21 volunteers (26.25 per cent) exhibited sexual arousal to taped stories of sexual behaviour with children which equalled or exceeded their arousal to the adult tapes. For eight of the subjects (10 per cent) the most arousing slide was one of the child slides. As well as the physical response measurements, 16 (20 per cent) of the volunteers self-reported paedophilic interest and three in this community sample of 80 men 'admitted to engaging in pedophilic behavior' (Hall *et al.*, 1995: 686).

The authors conclude:

> The slides and audiotape data combined suggest that most normal men are not sexually aroused by nude female children per se, but that some men who report no pedophilic activity are sexually aroused when a female child is depicted as enjoying sexual activity with an adult male. Consenting heterosexual activity, independent of the maturity of the partner, is sexually arousing to some men.... a major implication of this study is that sexual arousal to pedophilic stimuli does not necessarily correspond with pedophilic behavior.... Thus, arousal to pedophilic stimuli may motivate some, but not all, sexually aggressive acts against children, and a sizeable minority of men who do not report engaging in pedophilic behavior exhibit sexual arousal to pedophilic stimuli. (Hall *et al.*, 1995: 692)

These clinical studies therefore show a more complicated picture than the clinical definition of paedophilia might suggest. In addition to these laboratory studies there have also, to date, been three surveys which used questionnaires to explore adult sexual arousal to children

(Becker-Blease, Friend & Freyd, 2006; Briere & Runtz, 1989; Smiljanich & Briere, 1996). Smiljanich & Briere (1996) seems to be the only study to date which has investigated women's experiences as well as men's. They undertook a questionnaire study of 279 undergraduates which included 99 men and 180 women. This found 22 per cent of the male sample (and 3 per cent of the female sample) admitted 'some attraction to little children', with 14 per cent of the men using child pornography, 4 per cent masturbating to sexual fantasies involving children and 3 per cent admitting to the 'possibility of sex with a child if undetected' (figures for the female sample were respectively 4 per cent, 0 per cent and 0 per cent). The most recent study, Becker-Blease *et al.* (2006), used a self-completion questionnaire study of 531 undergraduate men. This study found only 7 per cent admitted sexual attraction to 'little children', but 18 per cent had sexual fantasies of children, with 8 per cent masturbating to those fantasies, and 4 per cent admitting that they would have sex with a child 'if no-one found out'.

Taken together, these studies therefore indicate that a sizeable minority of men, who do not describe themselves as paedophile, seem to be capable of being sexually aroused by young children, whether or not they act on that attraction. Until more research is done, using much larger samples, this is as much information as we have at present. Summarizing these findings suggests that, as a rough rule of thumb, in every group of a hundred men, at least one and possibly more are likely to be exclusively or primarily sexually attracted to children (in other words, paedophiles), and perhaps a quarter or more of adult males can be sexually aroused by images of children aged 13 or younger. Even though the figures are only indicative at this stage, this still seems a surprisingly high level of adult male sexual attraction to children. It is in this context that this chapter explores popular cultural responses to paedophiles and looks at how we 'make sense' of this phenomenon in contemporary society. This and the following chapters on scientific and academic texts lay the groundwork for theorizing a new understanding of paedophiles in society.

This chapter is divided into three sections. Section 1 looks at aspects of popular culture including the circulation of jokes and satirical humour about the topic of paedophiles and society's response, and films dealing with the topic of adult sexual attraction to children. Section 2 then looks at the specific concept of 'pederasty' and outlines some of the ways in which this term has been used to 'make sense' of or justify paedophilia or 'boy-love'. Section 3 then draws on wider themes in which notions of the sexuality of 'the Other' have been used to argue for the acceptability of adult sexual contact with children in Western society. This section includes contributions not only from anthropology but also from biology, as the sexual practices of a particular African ape, the bonobo, have recently entered popular culture as part of an argument for sexual tolerance and acceptance of adult sexual contact with children.

Together, these aspects of popular culture (including the incorporation of technical terms such as 'pederasty') help us begin to piece together some of the jigsaw puzzle of how contemporary Western society makes sense of events such as the court cases of Michael Jackson or Roman Polanski, or the political activism of Kevin Brown, the self-defined 'minor-attracted adult' introduced in Chapter 1.

1. Popular culture and 'the paedophile'

This chapter now turns to look in more detail at this relationship between 'the paedophile' and culture, especially popular culture in 'Anglosphere' countries (English-speaking nations which draw on a shared historical and literary culture). How is it possible to 'make sense' of paedophiles and the question of adult sexual attraction to children? As discussed in Chapter 1, and picked up again in Chapter 2, commonsense understandings of originally technical concepts such as 'paedophilia' or 'child grooming' are constructed through popular discourse by, for example, using celebrities as role-models and by linking the new, unfamiliar concept to other, pre-existing and more well-known concepts. In the case of 'child grooming', for example, the Wikipedia editors attempted variously to link this new concept either to 'child abuse' or to 'friendship', 'parental love' or 'mentoring'.

Popular discourse, and popular culture, emerge from a wide area of activity including news media, sports, music, films, animations, television drama such as soap-operas, literature (including fiction, poetry, popular science, biography and autobiography) and lifestyle features such as clothing and diet. Previously distinguished from the 'high culture' world of the subsidized arts (opera, ballet and classical music, for example), popular culture (or folk culture) was seen as of low(er) value. More recently, popular culture tends to be seen simply as the culture of everyday life; as the way in which social groups – through language, ritual and symbolism – construct and share a common consensus. Abstruse technical information (on climate change, for example, or disease) becomes mediated through popular discourse, with some aspects simplified and highlighted and others downplayed, distorted or misrepresented. Thus the complex science of climate change (itself a distillation of many fields of meteorology, oceanography, physics, computer modelling, environmental studies and so forth) becomes condensed into sound-bite slogans such as 'eco-friendly', 'global warming', 'carbon footprint' and indeed 'climate change' itself.

Discourse mediates emotion as well as information: for example, the public outpouring of grief in Britain at the death of Princess Diana not only allowed a ritual expression of sorrow and regret at the loss of one particular person but more broadly gave people an opportunity to feel a sense of social connection. Both her marriage and her death allowed rare – and brief – moments of powerful social cohesion, united initially in the emotions of joy and optimism and then of mourning. Humour also plays a key role in cultural discourse. The social function of humour is to divert or defuse psychological tension (emotions such as embarrassment, anxiety, fear and hate) and this can be done through slapstick, incongruity, teasing, ridicule and cynicism or through parody and satire – forms of humour which typically carry more overt political meanings.

In relation to paedophilia and the sexual abuse of children, all these elements come into play. Simplified stereotypes of the 'paedophile' are shared across society, changing over time. While Chapter 1 drew attention to the 'evil paedophile' and the 'nasty pervs' featured in contemporary tabloid newspapers over the period of the twentieth century, stereotypes of paedophiles have ranged from the clinically abnormal to the violent working-class sex offender, the pathetic, rather grubby old man, the louche and decadent member of the Establishment, the middle-aged European sex tourist, the faceless internet child pornographer, the fallen rock-star, and the cunning and evil member of a 'paedophile ring'. Similarly, culturally mediated emotional responses to paedophiles and to child sexual abuse have also varied widely from outrage to tolerance and indifference (Jenkins, 1992, 1998). This can be shown using the example of another public figure, this time the British musician Gary Glitter (the stage name of Paul Francis Gadd), who was convicted and imprisoned for possession of child pornography involving very small children and more recently convicted of the rape of two young girls. Despite considerable public anger and revulsion at his crimes, it is interesting that the official website of AOL Music contains a biography of Glitter which begins, 'Although the late '90s apparently saw the end of Gary Glitter's career, following his conviction for sexual offenses, there is no doubting that for a full 25 years before that tragic denouement, Glitter ranked among Britain's best-loved performers of all time', thus apparently suggesting that the sexual abuse of toddlers and small children which produced Glitter's 'denouement' was a tragedy only for *him*. The biography continues with a fulsome appreciation of Glitter's musical contribution and ends:

> Then came the news that Glitter was under investigation on child pornography charges and his world fell apart. Stores throughout the U.K. withdrew his records from the shelves, concerts were canceled; overnight, one of Britain's most adored icons became public enemy number one and even his staunchest allies now doubt whether Glitter will ever be able to pull one more comeback out of the bag. What cannot be erased, however, is the contribution he has made to the history of rock & roll – the creation of 'Rock and Roll' itself. (Thompson, undated: online)

This biography, by Dave Thompson of the *All Music Guide*, had not, as of January 2011, been updated to reflect Glitter's 2006 prison sentence for sexually abusing young girls in Vietnam. It is noticeable that, as well as the euphemistic use of the term 'tragic denouement' to describe Glitter's use of child pornography, Thompson also uses the emotive phrase 'his world fell apart' – again, the pain experienced by the *children* in producing the pornography (and, later, in being sexually abused by Glitter himself) is invisible in this biography. It is only Glitter who suffers in this account.

The case of Gary Glitter is also worthy of note in another regard. The issues of paedophiles and child sexual abuse clearly provoke psychological tension and emotional reactions such as anxiety, so it is not surprising that humour plays a part in sociocultural responses, and an interesting phenomenon spawned by the Glitter trial is the presence of 'Gary Glitter jokes' on the web. These, along with 'Maddie jokes', 'sick jokes', 'dead baby jokes' and so forth, rely for their effects on incongruity and shock, and are typically extremely bleak. At one point, Gary Glitter appeared to be facing the death penalty in Vietnam for his crimes. The sentence was due in December and there were a number of jokes about the tradition of 'hanging up Glitter at Christmas'. Such jokes, and variations on them, are likely to be applied to whoever becomes the latest well-known paedophile:

- What's worse than Gary Glitter babysitting your kids? Ian Huntley giving them a bath. [Huntley is well-known in the UK as a sexual abuser who murdered two children]

- What's the difference between Neil Armstrong and Gary Glitter? Neil Armstrong was the first man on the moon: Gary Glitter fucks children.
- The Police have raided Gary Glitter's house. They found class A drugs in the lounge, class B drugs in the kitchen and Class 5c in his bedroom.
- What's the difference between Gary Glitter and greyhounds? Greyhounds wait for the hares.
- What's the difference between Gary Glitter and acne? Acne waits till you're a teenager to come on your face.

Jokes relating to Michael Jackson, as well as including the more generic types, also relied for their comic impact on specific biographical facts about Jackson himself, which changed over time:

- Michael Jackson first wanted to look like Diana Ross, then a white person, now he wants to be a Roman Catholic priest.
- Michael decided to have a boy of his own because it's too expensive to rent them at $2 million a pop.
- Michael Jackson has been spotted dangling children from a balcony again. It makes a change because he usually tosses them off.

When we can laugh at horror, we are able, at least to some extent, to put it in perspective and thus contain it. As well as the circulation of online jokes, humour in popular culture (ranging from the heartbreaking to the tasteless and tacky to the genuinely witty) has also been expressed through television shows produced as a comic backlash to poke fun at and deflate what can sometimes be regarded as a self-righteous and overblown sense of horror. Although paedophilia is a highly sensitive subject, there are examples of risqué humour including an episode in the well-known cartoon series *South Park*, in 2000, called 'Cartman Joins NAMBLA'. Eric Cartman is the 8-year-old protagonist who decides his young friends are much too childish for him and advertises online for mature friends who like little boys. To his surprise, he is inundated with responses. Soon he is invited to attend a dinner as the 'poster-child' for NAMBLA, the North American Man Boy Love Association (an actual organization in real life, mentioned in Chapter 1). Confusion arises when the (presumably fictitious) North American Marlon Brando Look Alikes also meet in the same place. The episode ends with a paedophile making a heartfelt plea for tolerance, understanding and recognition as a sexual minority (similar to the kinds of arguments put forward by paedophile activists such as Kevin Brown and Lindsay Ashford, mentioned earlier). While the adults are deeply touched by his appeals, the blunt reply of the unimpressed 8-year-olds is simply, 'Dude, you have sex with children.'

An example from Britain comes from the award-winning spoof documentary series, *Brass Eye*, which poked satirical fun at the public and celebrities by setting up absurd situations which people nevertheless believed to be factual. The *Brass Eye* special on paedophilia, aired twice in July 2001 and coming less than a year after the murder of a little girl, Sarah Payne, and subsequent mass anti-paedophile riots, caused huge offence and the channel was forced to issue an apology. Despite this, the actual show itself is so patently silly that it is now surprising that anyone could find it realistic enough to be offensive. The spoof suggested, among other things, that internet paedophiles can project poison gas through a child's keyboard, using a new system known as HOECS (pronounced 'hoax'). It also included an item on a paedophile disguised as a school (yes, really), and a pair of 'Trust Me' trousers which inflate like a balloon. The producer, Chris Morris, even managed to include Syd Rapson, the Labour MP from the Paulsgrove estate in Portsmouth (which had witnessed the worst of the anti-paedophile rioting), commenting on these trousers: 'I think it's an absolute disgrace that somebody should use the internet to market these "trust me trousers" . It makes it very difficult to pin them with the offence because it covers the fact that they're stimulated in the groin area.'

Another British example is the figure of the 'Paedofinder General' in the cartoon series *Monkey Dust*, which ran from 2003 to 2005 and was an award-winning series shown first on the digital channel BBC3 and later, presumably due to high viewing-figures, shown on the more mainstream channel BBC2. The Paedofinder General is a terrifying hooded character based on Matthew Hopkins, the seventeenth-century 'Witchfinder General' immortalized in the eponymous 1968 film by Michael Reeves, starring Vincent Price. The Paedofinder General accosts any adults seen with children and accuses them of paedophilia. In one episode, for example, the accusation is on the grounds that the man is wearing swimming-trunks with the logo 'peedo' on them. The man protests that the logo is in fact 'Speedo' (a well-known brand) but this does not save him: he is summarily executed. A father playing on the beach with his children is accosted and accused of giving his child a '69' (a euphemism for simultaneous fellatio and cunnilingus). When he protests that it was in fact a '99' (a type of ice-cream), the Paedofinder-General is horrified at how much worse a '99' must be than a '69' and again, the man is immediately executed, by hanging, along with the children, who are also hanged on the basis that abused children grow up to be abusers. A family watching the public execution are delighted at the outcome and the little boy of the family comments happily that this is the best holiday he has had. These and similar episodes clearly draw for reference on events such as the anti-paedophile riots in Bristol and Portsmouth in 2000, and the infamous incident in which a paediatrician had her house daubed with the slogan 'paedo' (Allison, 2000).

These examples from satire and parody show that not only is the paedophile the target of humour but also those around him – perhaps especially those who allow their anxiety over child abuse to degenerate into unthinking 'moral panic' (Cohen, 2002). These are thus examples of the way in which humour can be used to subvert, deflate and thereby manage some of our deep-seated, realistic – and very painful – anxieties about harm to children.

Other forms of popular culture which have addressed the topic of paedophilia include Hollywood and independent films. Many films touch on the subject of adult sexual attraction to children or adult sexual abuse of children, a topic treated in for example Kincaid (1998), Green & Goode (2008) and Goode (2009). Obvious examples of this genre are of course *Lolita* (1962, directed by Stanley Kubrick, and 1997, directed by Adrian Lyne) and *Pretty Baby* (1978, directed by Louis Malle). A more recent example from mainstream Hollywood cinema is *The Woodsman* (2005), directed by Nicole Kassell and starring Kevin Bacon as the main character, a 45-year-old paedophile named Walter. In the film, Walter is opposed to and attacks another paedophile, a mysterious and evil character whom Walter calls Candy (from the Candyman who gives treats to children), who is clearly shown seducing young boys. Walter himself is presented as gentle and loving, perhaps almost a rescuer of children – like the Woodsman of the title who rescues Little Red Riding Hood from the Big Bad Wolf. Alongside the tormented Woodsman and the malignant Candyman, other Hollywood images of paedophiles could be said to include Jean Reno as Leon, the professional assassin with a heart of gold, flirting with 12-year-old Natalie Portman playing the role of orphaned Mathilda (*Leon / The Professional*, 1994, directed by Luc Besson). *Leon* contains a scene which appears almost entirely tangential and extraneous to the plot-line, in which little Mathilda dresses up in a series of costumes to represent famous people (Madonna, Marilyn Monroe, Charlie Chaplin and Gene Kelly) ostensibly to demonstrate to Leon how little he knows about ordinary life, but also gratuitously giving the viewer the opportunity to see a little girl in make-up and acting 'sexy'. This scene is reminiscent of a comment by a journalist who infiltrated a NAMBLA meeting to discover their 'secret eroticism' and found it was simply network television, the Disney channel and mainstream films: 'I had found NAMBLA's "porn", and it was Hollywood.' (quoted in Kincaid, 1998: 115). As Sinclair (1988) and others have pointed out, Hollywood has always done a line in 'nymphets', from Shirley Temple to the present day.

Like the later films *Lawn Dogs* (1997, directed by John Duigan) and *Man on Fire* (2004, directed by Tony Scott), the emotional energy in *Leon* comes from the sympathetic and low-key portrayal of the relationship between the man and the young girl. In these films, there is no sexual violence. This is in contrast to, for example, the controversial *Hounddog* (2007, directed by Deborah Kampmeier) which was banned from general release. *Hounddog*, like *Man on Fire*, stars the actress Dakota Fanning as a young child but in this movie she is raped. The director defended her portrayal of child rape, arguing 'I have a daughter; I am a daughter. I cherish and honor the souls of girls and women. If I did anything to harm Dakota or anything exploitative, that would be betraying the whole reason I made this film.' (Kampmeier, 2008). The 12-year-old Fanning also defended the scene, pointing out, 'I know my mom would take me to see it. You have to prepare your children for things that happen in the world. Everything isn't rosy.' (Fanning, 2007).

What is interesting in this selection of films is less the predictable sexualization and voyeurism (available in spades in films such as *Pretty Baby*) but rather the moments of affection and friendship between the grown man and the young child as they goof around together. Paradoxically perhaps, what films such as *Lawn Dogs* express is not that men find prepubescent girls sexually attractive (after all, as Fanning comments, everything isn't rosy) but that they can have comfortable non-sexual friendships with them. Warm friendships between men and (unrelated) children are seldom presented in modern popular culture, so the nuanced depictions in these films provide an unexpectedly sophisticated contribution (Green & Goode, 2008).

Models of adult–child friendship provide one way of 'making sense' of paedophilia, and these films have been cited by paedophiles as important in developing their own sense of self (Goode, 2009). However, for 'boy-lovers' rather than 'girl-lovers', there are fewer films in modern popular culture which portray such a relationship, although *Long Island Expressway* (2001, directed by Michael Cuesta) and *Mysterious Skin* (2004, directed by Greg Araki) are two fairly mainstream films dealing with adult male sexual desire for boys. This dearth in films is not matched in literature or online. For many, the most significant model of adult–child relationships is that of 'Greek Love' or 'pederasty' from the world of Ancient Greece, and this is discussed in the following section.

2. The concept of 'pederasty'

Pederasty, like paedophilia itself, has for most of its career been a technical term dealt with mainly in historical works. Largely ignored in mainstream culture for many centuries, this notion has more recently – and often enthusiastically – been taken up by theorists and campaigners within the gay rights movement and now references to 'Greek Love' frequently emerge in discussions on paedophilia, making pederasty part of contemporary popular discourse when discussing adult sexual attraction to children. A search of internet sites will show that the concept of pederasty features on a number of gay and pro-paedophile sites and, for example, is on the NAMBLA site and was also discussed in an online encyclopaedia of gay, lesbian, bisexual, transgender and queer culture available at GLBTQ.com (now defunct). Thus it is clear that, although its origin may lie in the rarefied domain of science (the realms of the clinician and the historian), the term 'pederasty' has, in the twenty-first century, entered popular culture through internet-mediated sexual politics and political activism. These two spheres of science and popular culture are not and never have been separate; recent academic books concerned with pederasty have found themselves vulnerable to fierce controversy – championed and castigated in equal measure. While *The Greeks And Greek Love: A Radical Reappraisal of Homosexuality In Ancient Greece*, by James Davidson (2008), *Images of Ancient Greek Pederasty* (Lear & Cantarella, 2008) and *Historical Pederastic Relationships* (Miller, Vandome & McBrewster, 2009), seem to have escaped difficulty, the book *Same-Sex Desire and Love in Greco-Roman Antiquity and in the Classical Tradition of the West* (Verstraete & Provencal) encountered a storm of criticism and was originally withdrawn from publication by Haworth, who then published it a year later, in 2006, after removing one essay. The offending essay, titled 'Pederasty: An integration of cross-cultural, cross-species, and empirical data', was later published separately in the *Journal of Homosexuality*.

These publications indicate an increasing level of interest in this concept. Pederasty was also implied in the discussion on 'child grooming' in Chapter 2, where the concept of 'grooming' was linked by some activists to the concept of 'mentoring' – a concept closely allied to pederasty and with a long pedigree in pedagogical models of older males educating young boys.

The term 'pederasty' comes from two Greek words, *paides* (boy) and *erasteio* (to love or long for) and therefore is used to relate only to situations in which adult men are sexually attracted to young boys, with the synonym 'boy-lover' also being used in place of 'pederast'. The equivalent situation in which adult men are sexually attracted to young girls appears not to have been recognized with any formal or informal term until the 1970s, when the expression 'girl-lover' was published in *Paedophilia: The Radical Case* (O'Carroll, 1980).

According to studies such as that by William Armstrong Percy III, author of *Pederasty and Pedagogy in Archaic Greece* (1996) and an enthusiastic commentator on this subject (personal conversation, March 2008), pederasty as a recognized social convention within the ancient world arose in Crete in the eighth century BC as a response to delayed marriage to stem population growth. Men were not expected to marry until their thirties and began developing relationships with young boys in order to deal with sexual frustration. This became an elaborate institutionalized practice which then, over a few generations, spread first to Sparta in the seventh century BC and thence to the other Greek city-states, including Athens. For these fiercely militaristic cultures, based on rigid elitism and segregation, a benefit of pederasty was that it could build strong emotional ties between soldiers who might previously have been lovers, and thus could promote loyalty and bonding within military cohorts. It was also seen as a way of transmitting virtues such as honour and civic-mindedness from older to younger men. Thus pederasty was regarded as a solution for military cohesion and for population control (alongside war and institutionalized infanticide) and as a specific form of pedagogy emphasizing athletic skill as well as intellectual and moral development. Later, as continual wars took their toll and as emigration shifted populations out of Greece into the wider empire of Alexander the Great from the fourth century BC onwards, the practice of pederasty gradually declined. It had arguably almost disappeared by the second century BC, although the persistence of myths with pederastic themes (such as that of the god Zeus and the young boy Ganymede) suggests that positive attitudes to the practice remained. It was not until the rise of Christianity from the second century AD onwards that sex outside marriage, and non-procreative sex generally, was discouraged.

Thus pederasty seems to have existed as a significant institution within ancient Greek culture for some five hundred years or so. It appeared as a theme in both literature and in art, particularly vase-paintings. A striking example is that of the Warren Cup, an embossed and engraved silver cup presently in the British Museum. The Warren Cup is a Roman artefact, made in the first century AD. It depicts two fairly explicit idealized scenes of an older bearded male having sexual contact with a younger, adolescent, beardless male. When it was bought for £1.8 million by the British Museum in 1999, it caused controversy due to the nature of these explicitly pederastic or homo-erotic images (Williams, 2006). The Warren Cup, although a later Roman example, has similarities with earlier Greek vase-paintings depicting pederastic relationships. A number of vase-paintings have been found, showing scenes of courtship, gift-offering, foreplay and sexual inter-course between men and youths. The vases also show scenes from mythology, such as Zeus with Ganymede, and they include painted inscriptions in praise of the beauty of boys (Lear & Cantarella, 2008). These vases portray idealized images of pederasty, conjuring a world of beautiful elite males sharing and displaying highly admired physi-cal and intellectual qualities. Perhaps they are the classical equivalent of the airbrushed pin-ups of today, where every body is perfect and every relationship is ideal.

Certainly pederasty seems to have been a pursuit only of the wealthy and land-owning classes: privileged men with the money to afford the armour and weapons to fight as a 'hoplite' (a citizen-soldier); the influ-ence to vote and control the fate of their city; and sufficient resources (obtained through warfare and slavery) to be able to send their sons to be educated. Only the leisured gentry would also have the time to pursue a pederastic relationship, viewing the naked boys practising their athlet-ics, courting a boy at his school and bestowing expensive gifts on him; and only a well-connected man would be likely to be acceptable to the boy's father. Thus 'Greek love' or pederasty, as a form of stylized and ritu-alized relationship with similarities to mediaeval European courtly love, seems to have been a relationship specifically tied to hierarchy, privilege and wealth, as well as to a militaristic and hyper-masculine culture in which women and girls were excluded from citizenship and confined to an extremely circumscribed domestic role. As with the traditions of courtly love, the relationship may well at times have been 'chaste' with no overt physical sexual contact but with a strong emphasis on faithfulness, loyalty and commitment.

Another parallel which we can associate with classical pederasty is of course the traditional British public school system. Based on wealth, privilege and hierarchy, the great English public schools (private schools founded over almost a five hundred-year period between 1179 and

1611 and including Westminster, Winchester, Eton, Shrewsbury, Rugby, Harrow and Charterhouse) were all based on an ideal of classical education and athletic prowess that would have been familiar to the young men of ancient Greece. As with the schools first founded in Crete and Sparta, British public schools prepared their pupils for adult roles in public and military service and provided an entry into the elite class. Discipline was traditionally harsh, with corporal punishment inflicted by senior pupils on younger pupils. Sexual initiation, too, was also likely to be performed by an older boy on a younger boy. And, just as appears to have been the case with classical pederasty, the institutionalized sexual abuse of young boys appears to have repeated itself over generations, with boys growing up, becoming fathers and electing to send their sons to the same schools, to undergo the same ritual humiliations, punishments and sexual experiences that they themselves had endured as youngsters.

However, it would be a mistake to draw any parallels too closely: each cultural context is unique. For example, although we may think of classical Greece as a 'democracy' and thus similar to forms of society we know today, in fact we would find many aspects unrecognizable and indeed morally repellent. The Greek democracy only recognized land-owning adult men as 'citizens' – the vast majority of the population, including adult women, slaves and 'barbarians' (anyone not a member of that city-state), were all excluded from any form of public life. Women were regarded primarily as a means to breed citizens and soldiers: only when a man reached his thirties would he marry, usually taking a teenage bride. Greek culture emphasized male beauty over female and male love over female. Alongside the decorous and idealized love between the *eromenos* (young male lover) and the *erastes* (older male lover), so beautifully painted on vases and praised in epic literature, lay the reality of the widespread rape of slaves, non-citizens and those captured during war.

The notion of pederasty has been taken up and used, not only implicitly in British public schools, but quite explicitly in some models of pedagogy, using terms such as 'pedagogic Eros', where the emphasis has been on men mentoring young male protégés, developing intimate sexual relationships with them as a way of benefitting their general education and development. This is discussed in, for example, *Boys on Their Contacts with Men* (Sandfort, 1987), *Male Intergenerational Intimacy: Historical, Socio-Psychological and Legal Perspectives* (Sandfort, Brongersma & Naerssen,1991) and *Pederasty and Pedagogy in Archaic Greece* (Percy, 1996). Sandfort's work is discussed in more detail in

Chapter 5, but we now turn to a further example of how concepts orig-inally derived from the work of scientists (in this case, anthropologists and biologists) are incorporated into popular discourse on sexuality.

3. Contributions from anthropology and biology

Turning from examples taken from classical Greece, two thousand years ago and more, what other sources of popular culture may individuals draw on when attempting to explain and 'make sense of' the phe-nomenon of contemporary adult sexual attraction to children or adult sexual contact with children? Judging by the material in scientific and popular books dealing with paedophilia (for examples of these, see Chapter 5) and by the 'chat' posted on internet forums, it seems that another significant body of evidence from which contemporary culture tends to draw when thinking about paedophiles is the example of 'other countries' and 'other cultures'. Clearly, this is a vast area, potentially encompassing literally every country and every culture other than the one within which any particular researcher or writer happens to cur-rently reside! Such an ethnocentric position traditionally tends to divide the world into two segments: the 'normal' one in which the writer lives; and the 'exotic' beyond, housing inscrutable others, primitives and sav-ages, with their quaint rituals and strange superstitions – much indeed as classical Greeks viewed all their neighbours as the 'barbarians', those aliens who did not speak Greek and thus only made meaningless 'bar bar' sounds whenever they opened their mouths.

For any culture, a part of the attraction of 'the Other' is its strangeness and often, mixed with that, its erotic allure – or repulsion – marked by its differences in sexual practice. We are often intrigued by how strangers look, how they speak, what they eat – and what they do in bed. As the anthropologist Mary Douglas has pointed out, if we want to criticize a group of people, it is typically their sexual behaviour that we will focus on to mark them out as 'other' than us (1966, 1992). From travellers' tales to contemporary anthropology and cultural studies, the sexual practices of 'the Other' continue to fascinate and titillate us, whether it is the lure of the sensual Orient, as for example popularized in Sir Richard Francis Burton's 1885 translation of the Arabic classic *A Thousand and One Nights* (also known as *The Arabian Nights*), or the guiltless frolicking of the 'noble savages' of Tahiti painted in a deliberately 'primitivist' style by Eugenè Henri-Paul Gauguin in the 1890s.

Key scientific works in this field include the writings of Margaret Mead and Bronislaw Malinowski, both of whom focused, as had Gauguin,

on the remote (from a European and North American perspective) cultures of the South Pacific. Mead's most important text was a study of
sexual practices among adolescent girls on one South Pacific island,
*Coming of Age in Samoa: A Psychological Study of Primitive Youth for Western
Civilisation*, (2001; first published in 1928) and followed by a study of
gender-differences in New Guinea, *Sex and Temperament in Three Primitive Societies* (2002 [1935]). Mead's fascination with the sexual life of
'primitive savages' in the South Pacific was echoed in the work of her
contemporary, Bronislaw Malinowski, who, like Mead, is regarded as a
founder of modern social anthropology. Malinowski's classic, *Sex and
Repression in Savage Society* (2001), was first published in 1927.

It would be difficult to over-estimate the impact of these texts on
the development of sexual attitudes within twentieth-century Western
society. As scientific explorations into the universal phenomenon of
human sexuality, these books laid the groundwork for theorizing sexual behaviour, feeding directly into the work of later sexologists such
as Alfred Kinsey. Both Mead and Malinowski wanted to test European,
specifically Freudian, theories of sexual development, for example the
concept of the Oedipus complex, in order to confirm whether or
not they had universal applicability. Both of them ended up painting
utopian portraits of 'savage' life which powerfully indicted their own
cultures' sexual hypocrisy and repression. Malinowski, in *Sex and Repression*, provides a vivid contrast between a miserable, guilt-ridden, shame-
faced upbringing typical of middle-class Europeans, and a charming,
sunny, relaxed, uninhibited and playful childhood in the Trobriand
Islands (now known as the Kiriwina Islands). For example, he described
children engaging freely in sexual contact from the age of 5 or 6 years
onwards into puberty:

> At an early age children are initiated by each other, or sometimes
> by a slightly older companion, into the practices of sex. Naturally,
> at this stage they are unable to carry out the act properly, but they
> content themselves with all sorts of games in which they are left
> quite at liberty by their elders, and thus they can satisfy their curiosity
> and their sensuality directly and without disguise. (Malinowski, 2001
> [1927]:44–5)

Any individual piece of evidence drawn from such a heterogeneous and
polyphonous evidence-base as 'other cultures' is usually likely to say far
more about the agenda of the writer than about any one culture's values.
This will be particularly true in such a vexed area as adult–child sexual

contact and children's sexuality, and when we look at contemporary discussions what is perhaps most remarkable is the breadth of evidence drawn upon, from a vast range of cultures over a vast span of time. This section can only point to those examples which tend to be most used in discussions on the English-language internet and which thus have most salience in contemporary 'pro-paedophile' debates. Again, we find a particular example from the South Pacific, this time from Papua New Guinea, which is repeatedly referred to. This time the anthropologist in question is Gilbert Herdt, who has written in a number of publications about his periods of fieldwork among the Sambia tribe from 1974 up to 1993. Professor Herdt is now the Director of the National Sexuality Resource Center, based at San Francisco State University. When conducting his fieldwork back in the 1970s, as a gay man with a commitment to integrity and transparency, Herdt found himself the first Westerner to be permitted to know about 'boy-inseminating rites' or the tribal culture of ritual fellatio of adolescent men by younger boys:

> My empathy for and closeness to these men facilitated their 'confession' to me. I was in turn deeply grateful to them, and felt the desire to 'confess' my own secrets too. These friends knew that I could be trusted to keep my word, and over the years I have been true to this promise. When Moondi asked me whether I knew of this practice [by 'this practice' Herdt appears to mean fellatio by a male] and had ever done it before, I could say yes; and my own revelation sealed a pact that has endured many years. (Herdt, 1999: 11)

Herdt further comments, 'My ability to apprehend and interpret Sambia sexuality depended upon acceptance of my own sexuality and the intuitive use of myself to understand how homoerotic relations were built into the Sambia design for life.' (p. 13). However much we might regret Herdt's inability to apprehend and interpret Sambia *female* sexuality (and thus half the population and culture he is studying), one still gains an impression of Herdt as generally self-aware and sensitive. Sadly, others who have made use of his research have been somewhat less sensitive. Herdt describes a specific cultural practice, which has now apparently died out since it was studied in the 1970s. In this initiation rite, young boys aged from around 7 onwards are taken from their families and initiated into a number of secret practices by the elders in the 'cult-house'. One of the ritual practices is to repeatedly fellate older adolescents from 15 onwards, swallowing the semen, until they themselves are considered old enough to be fellated in turn and subsequently to marry and start families. Herdt reports that the young boys involved in this practice were often reluctant but that it was considered essential to becoming a man. For the Sambia, boys needed to 'eat penises' and suck the semen or 'milk' of 'junior warriors' in order to grow strong and to, literally, ingest masculinity. Only in this way, it was believed, would they become masculine enough to grow up as full men capable of fathering children.

Similar rituals have been reported among the New Guinea tribes of Etoro and Kaluli (Bauserman, 1997). As Herdt has described it, 'boy-inseminating rites' are a specific cultural practice which take place in a society in which men engage in other similarly unusual ritual practices such as the use of nose-bleeds as a form of blood-letting in order to purge themselves of pollution after having sexual contact with women and in which, for example, kissing is 'completely unknown and absent' (Herdt,1999: 5). What makes this 'boy-insemination' practice relevant to modern Western society is the rhetorical use made of it by those who point to it as an example of cross-cultural 'inter-generational intimacy' and who use it as evidence to argue that, since such evidence of 'inter-generational intimacy' seems to be widespread in many cultures then it cannot be a bad thing. Other examples of adult–child sexual contact within cross-cultural contexts are given in works by Ford and Beach (1951) and in Bauserman (1997), with specific examples on Tahiti by Oliver (1974) and on Hawaii by Milton Diamond (1990).

As well as looking at examples from history and examples from other countries and other cultures, a third way of 'making sense' of human sexuality and particular forms such as adult sexual attraction to children is through the contribution of biology and its sub-disciplines such as ethology and primatology. Cross-species parallels with aspects of human behaviour have been studied 'in the field' (using observation of natural behaviour), using captured populations (such as animals in zoos, where behaviour can be manipulated) and clinically (using laboratory experimentation and dissection).

A leading author in this field was the American scientist, Professor Alfred Kinsey (discussed in the following chapter). Kinsey was a zoologist before he became perhaps the most famous and influential sexologist of the twentieth century. He himself did not experiment on animals (his field of research prior to human sexuality was the study of gall-wasps, which he collected and classified). Nor did Kinsey first initiate interest in this field, which was already very well-established when he began researching sexuality in the 1930s but Kinsey and his colleagues are nevertheless hugely important in popularizing this mode of study, drawing heavily and uncritically on published studies of laboratory work with rats, monkeys and other mammals to make points about human sexuality, including inter-generational sexual behaviour (Kinsey, Pomeroy & Martin,1948). In many ways, Kinsey's work – including this use of animal data to draw conclusions about human sexuality – has become firmly incorporated into modern ways of understanding sex and sexuality: it would be extremely difficult to find a single book on sex published in the last fifty years which does not make reference to Kinsey's work.

While many people today may be a little less sanguine about just how much we can really learn from dissections of monkeys' brains, or stimulus-response experiments on laboratory rats, the study of one animal in particular has sparked the popular imagination and re-ignited interest in what animals may be able to teach us about human sexuality. This is the bonobo ape (also known as the pygmy or 'Left Bank' chimpanzee), an ape which lives on the left bank of the Congo River in equatorial Africa. The bonobo was identified as a separate species only in 1926, from bones held in a museum, and has been studied in the wild only since the 1970s. Due to violent conflict in the area and inroads into the forests by mining companies, the bonobo is now feared to be on the verge of extinction, despite being recognized by the international scientific community as uniquely significant in its ability to teach us more about human evolution. The bonobo is now considered to be as close a relative to humans as chimpanzees.

Excitement about the bonobo began in 1995 with an article, 'Bonobo sex and society: the behaviour of a close relative challenges assumptions about male supremacy in human evolution', by Frans de Waal, published in the popular and prestigious science magazine, *Scientific American*. In his article, de Waal made the following points:

> At a juncture in history during which women are seeking equality with men, science arrives with a belated gift to the feminist movement...females play a central, perhaps even dominant, role in the social life of one of our nearest relatives. In the past few years many strands of knowledge have come together concerning a relatively unknown ape with an unorthodox repertoire of behavior: the bonobo....The species is best characterized as female-centered and egalitarian and as one that substitutes sex for aggression. Whereas in most other species sexual behavior is a fairly distinct category, in the bonobo it is part and parcel of social relations – and not just between males and females. Bonobos engage in sex in virtually every

partner combination (although such contact among close family members may be suppressed)..... Bonobos become sexually aroused remarkably easily, and they express this excitement in a variety of mounting positions and genital contacts... the frontal orientation of the bonobo vulva and clitoris strongly suggest that the female genitalia are adapted for this [face to face sexual] position.... Instead of a few days out of her cycle, the female bonobo is almost continuously sexually attractive and active.... The diversity of erotic contacts in bonobos includes sporadic oral sex, massage of another individual's genitals and intense tongue-kissing. Lest this leave the impression of a pathologically oversexed species, I must add, based on hundreds of hours of watching bonobos, that their sexual activity is rather casual and relaxed. It appears to be a completely natural part of their group life. Like people, bonobos engage in sex only occasionally, not continuously. Furthermore, with the average copulation lasting 13 seconds, sexual contact in bonobos is rather quick by human standards.... sexual behavior is indistinguishable from social behavior. Given its peacemaking and appeasement functions, it is not surprising that sex among bonobos occurs in so many different partner combinations, including between juveniles and adults. (de Waal, 1995: online)

The initial article was followed up by a book, *Bonobo: The Forgotten Ape* (1997). The message that bonobos are 'sexy apes' who can beat any humans in the 'sexual revolution' stakes is one that has found a receptive audience (the other key message of de Waal's paper, on the female-centric culture of the bonobos, fell on stonier ground). As a commentator on the *Primates' World* website remarked, in an article entitled 'Sex-crazed bonobos may be more like humans than thought', bonobos 'make the human sexual revolution of the sixties and seventies look tame.' (*Primates World*, 1998). They have gained the tags of the 'make love not war' primates and the 'Kama Sutra ape'. In the United States, they are used – to the disgust of the conservative movement – to bolster perceived left-wing or liberal views on evolution theory, on homosexuality within animals, and also to counter arguments on the naturalness of male supremacy and the biological inevitability of violence and war; for example, see the article 'Do you bonobo? Meet our make-love-not-war primates' (Wiker, 2001, online). Commentators, bloggers and other posters on the web have used the 'argument from bonobo' to make varied political points about male dominance and to discuss the 'naturalness' of homosexuality and the positive qualities of 'free sex'. For example, the following exchange took place on 11 July 2006 on a discussion board hosted by *USA Today* on gay marriage (spelling corrected and presentation adjusted, this web-page is now defunct):

> *Person A*: And you certainly don't see primates having same sex sexual relations with each other. Seems to me the animals act better than some humans do.
>
> *Person B*: Actually, the Bonobo monkey (a primate) is a well known example of exactly that: http://www.colszoo.org/animalareas/aforest/bonobo.html. The most telling part of the Bonobo article I cited is this:
>
> 'Sex is an important way to ensure group stability and ease tensions. Bonobos substitute sex for aggression, and sexual interactions occur more often among bonobos than among other primates. Reduced male aggression, strong bonds between males and females, and frequent sex (including male-to-male and female-to-female) characterize bonobo society.'
>
> Hmmm...I seem to see the same pattern in human society. Where sexuality is feared, repressed, and combated, violence reigns. Where sexuality is free, violence is greatly reduced. Compare the violent cultures of the Middle East (and the high murder rates of the Bible Belt) with the low violent crime rates of progressive Northern European countries – kinda supports the theory.

But sexuality is arguably not all we have inherited from our ape cousins. Humans are as closely related to chimpanzees as they are to bonobos and, along with sexuality, it seems our violence may also stem from our primate ancestry. In *Demonic Males: Apes and the Origin of Human Violence* (1996), a study of the 'deep origins' of human violence, Richard Wrangham and Dale Peterson argue that the strong connection between sex and male violence among many species is related to its reproductive advantage:

> Sexual selection, the evolutionary process that produces sex differences, has a lot to answer for. Without it, males wouldn't possess dangerous bodily weapons and a mindset that sanctions violence. But males who are better fighters can stop other males from mating, and they mate more successfully themselves. Better fighters tend to have more babies. That's the simple, stupid, selfish logic of sexual

selection. So, what about us? Is sexual selection ultimately the reason why men brawl in barrooms, form urban gangs, plot guerrilla attacks, and go to war? Has it indeed designed men to be especially aggressive? (Wrangham & Peterson, 1996: 173)

Aggressive sexual behaviours exist widely among animal species including mammals – but not across all primate species. Indeed, only among two species on Earth are these instinctive aggressive behaviours expanded into certain more complex forms including male-bonded intergroup hostility, lethal territorial raiding parties, deliberate killing of adults and infants, battering of adult females and forced copulation of females by males. These behaviours are not even typical among great apes. They are found *only* among chimpanzees and humans.

Chimpanzees and bonobos are the two closest living relatives of modern human beings. While chimpanzee (and human) males have social groups based on hierarchical political alliances, bonobo society is different. It is organized into stable, cohesive parties in which mother–son bonds and female–female bonds are particularly important. Any threat from an aggressive male is likely to be met by a concerted rebuff from a group of determined females and it is this female solidarity which appears to have fundamentally altered male behaviour among bonobos, diluting violence and making rape unknown. Among chimpanzees and humans, however, males have not changed: their aggression and sexual dominance remain untamed. These traits of violent physical and sexual attack – in which individual males, or groups of males, attack all those less dominant than they are – have been termed by Wrangham and Peterson as 'demonic'; instinctual, unthinking, hard-wired into us from our evolutionary past:

> Our ape ancestors have passed to us a legacy, defined by the power of natural selection and written in the molecular chemistry of DNA. For the most part it is a wonderful inheritance, but one small edge contains destructive elements; and now that we have the weapons of mass destruction, that edge promotes the potential of our own demise.... The problem is that males are demonic at unconscious and irrational levels. The motivation of a male chimpanzee who challenges another's rank is not that he foresees more matings or better food or a longer life. Those rewards explain why sexual selection have favored the desire for power, but the immediate reason he vies for status is simpler, deeper, and less subject to the vagaries of context. It is simply to dominate his peers. (Wrangham & Peterson, 1996: 199)

They conclude their study on 'demonic males' by highlighting the paradox at the heart of humanity, as we increasingly move towards the possibility of total annihilation:

> Ingenuity now serves the demon with new weapons, new tactics, new kinds of deception in the ever-escalating game of conflict.
>
> For us, the biggest danger is not that demonic males are the rule in our species. After all, other demonic male species are not endangered at their own hands. The real danger is that our species combines demonic males with a burning intelligence – and therefore a capacity for creation and destruction without precedent. That great human brain is nature's most frightening product.
>
> But it is simultaneously nature's best, more hopeful gift. If we are cursed with a demonic male temperament and a Machiavellian capacity to express it, we are also blessed with an intelligence that can, through the acquisition of wisdom, draw us away from the 5-million-year stain of our ape past. (Wrangham & Peterson, 1996: 257–8)

Primatology therefore seems to suggest that we can learn about sexuality, violence (and female solidarity) from our ape cousins. Sexual dominance and aggression will be explored later in the book, but we finish this discussion on bonobos with an example of the way this animal has been used to argue for the 'naturalness' of adults having sex with juveniles. This is from a blog and video podcast called *Child Love TV* by Norbert de Jonge, a Dutch paedophile activist. It includes the following comment, posted 13 May 2007 (the site on which it was posted, CLogo, was taken down in May 2008):

> [E]veryone should *accept* their pedophilic feelings, because, generally speaking: 1. pedosexual contacts are *healthy* for children, and when these contacts *can't* take place it is because, 2. a *third party*, like politicians or parents, abuses its power over the child in order to deny the child its sexual freedom.
>
> ... You realize how absurd it is to even have to explain the benefits of greater sexual freedom for children, when you see a child – when you see child pornography of consensual sexual contacts.... Sex can be an expression of love and is a pleasant liberation of tension. Touch and affection are the cure for the social diseases of violence and fundamentalism.... children have to indulge their sexuality to become peaceful. Did you know that animals who are known to do this, like dolphins and Bonobo monkeys, will patch

up quarrels by having sex? Our world leaders can learn a valuable lesson from them. (de Jonge, 2007: online, emphases in original, ellipses
added)

De Jonge, therefore, provides a clear example of a quotation linking 'pedosexual contacts' and 'sexual freedom' with the behaviour of
bonobo apes. Primatologists would of course be surprised (and those
I have spoken with are horrified) by such a misunderstanding of primate behaviour, and its misapplication to human behaviour, but what
is relevant here is not the accuracy or otherwise of the science but its
use by some groups as a legitimizing discourse. De Jonge, in his attempt
to normalize adult sexual contact with children, makes use of 'dolphins
and Bonobo monkeys' to argue that children should be free to express
themselves sexually (with adults).

This chapter has therefore looked at three main discourses which
are used – in academic and popular culture – to make sense of
paedophiles and adult sexual contact with children. All these discourses
(on pederasty or 'Greek love', on cross-cultural examples and cross-
species examples) have been used throughout the twentieth century
and now, in the twenty-first century, form part of contemporary 'intergenerational studies'. They are presented, for example, in *Paidika*,
an international journal on paedophilia; in the international *Journal of Homosexuality*, which frequently features articles on aspects of
paedophilia; in an edited collection, published in the United States,
on *Pedophilia: Biosocial Dimensions* (Feierman, 1990); and in an edited
collection, published in Britain, called *Dares to Speak: Historical and
Contemporary Perspectives on Boy-Love* (Geraci, 1997).

There is a sense among the 'pro-paedophile' community that its time
has come and that long-stifled voices will now be heard more clearly.
The edited collection *Dares to Speak* ends with the following assertion:

Surprisingly, there has been a plethora of publications that are positive, or at least scientifically neutral, on the subjects of childhood
sexuality and intergenerational sexual relationships. . . . That a virtual
reference library of more open material on intergenerational relationships should exist is of course not at all evident in the general
discussion today. . . . There has been a more varied response to childhood sexuality issues than that presented to us by the religious right,
the recovered memory movement, some feminists, or the child-abuse
industry. It can be safely said, without appearing to exaggerate, that
Intergenerational Studies has just begun, and that there are shades of

grey and white in the discussion that do not appear in the literature of abuse. (Crawford *et al.*, 1997: 255–6)

The reader will note that the authors of this quotation, in distinction to 'Intergenerational Studies', make reference in passing to the 'child-abuse industry'. These two terms ('intergenerational' and 'child abuse') could be said to summarize the nature of the confusion experienced by society, and perhaps begin to account for the 'jigsaw puzzle' or 'rag-bag' sense that is experienced when one attempts to piece together how contemporary society makes sense of paedophilia.

The three ways of understanding paedophilia which have been focused on in this chapter are all part of a discourse which sees paedophilia as being about 'intergenerational sexual relationships'. The notion of 'intergenerational sexual relationships' – to make sense – must itself be based on an understanding of 'childhood sexuality'. Whether it is practices from ancient Greece, from New Guinea or allegedly from bonobo behaviour, the common thread is that it is about 'juveniles' being (in some sense) sexually attracted to adults and choosing (more or less) to engage in sexual practices with them. This discourse is strongly at odds with what Crawford and colleagues, quoted above, call the 'the child-abuse industry'. It is worth concluding this chapter with a brief overview of these two main, but conflicting, discourses. Both discourses are primarily about adult sexuality while also commenting on children. Both have their academic roots in nineteenth-century Western thought (from anthropology, sexology and social policy in particular) but achieved their most significant popular impact in the 1970s with the rise of sexual and identity politics.

The first discourse relates to the liberatory potential of 'less orthodox' 'new sexual minorities' (Weeks, 1989) including bisexuals, sado-masochists, transvestites, transsexuals and paedophiles (Plummer, 1995). These sexual orientations have been seen as part of a broad continuum of alternative sexualities. Both paedophiles and children find themselves positioned within this discourse of 'alternative sexu-alities', alongside lesbians and gay men, the logic being that anything other than 'straight' is by definition dissident and radical. Thus Gayle Rubin (1992), in a celebrated essay on 'Thinking sex' written for a conference in 1982, lumped together as 'sexual radicals' just about any-one with any kind of possible 'alternative' sexual experience: prostitutes, fetishists, adults with incestuous desires... and children. This confla-tion of hugely varying sexual experiences – encompassing economics, paraphilias, crime and child development – have in common only their difference from normative heterosexuality

Rubin reminded her readers of the importance of this diversity, urging that '[w]e have learned to cherish different cultures as unique expressions of human inventiveness rather than as the inferior or disgusting habits of savages. We need a similarly anthropological understanding of different sexual cultures' (1992: 284). Writing sympathetically of NAMBLA, Rubin suggested that 'the community of men who love underaged youth' (she does not mention other forms of paedophilia) 'have been the victims of a savage and undeserved witch-hunt. A lot of people will be embarrassed by their collaboration with this persecution' (1992: 273). Thus, proponents of 'intergenerational intimacy' saw themselves as being at the forefront of a wholesale revision of normative and 'compulsory heterosexuality' (Rich, 1996), arguing for a relaxed and joyously liberated sexuality which could embrace everyone, including children. A generation later, this view remains profoundly influential even though at least one key thinker has now reconsidered its impact on children. In the early 1980s, Pat Califia wrote enthusiastically of the erotic possibilities of adult sexual contact with children. In 2000, he published a more sober analysis:

> I'm alarmed by the way people who want to justify imposing their sexual needs on young people have made use of my name and work.... these articles [published in 1980] were interpreted as giving permission, here and now, for things like father/daughter incest or adult American men traveling to southeast Asia to buy sex from prepubescent boys. Although that was never my intention, I hope this reexamination of the issues can serve as a way to make amends for harm that might have been caused inadvertently by my misguided idealism.... Sex radicals have often avoided or glazed over the damage done by child sexual abuse.... I was naive about the developmental issues that make sex between adults and prepubescent children unacceptable. (Califia, 2000: 57, 61, 62)

While Califia has reconsidered, other 'sexual radicals' continue to critique the 'child abuse industry' or 'CSA [child sexual abuse] industry' (Jones, 1991), arguing that it is no more than a late-modern 'victimological' discourse which acts to silence potentially positive accounts from boys (this 'victimological' critique is not extended to the experience of girls). More recently, but drawing on the same intellectual tradition, the author Judith Levine (2002) has put forward a case for a more relaxed approach to children's sexual contact with adults, without discussing questions of children's age.

During the time that 'sexual radicals' were developing their theories on 'intergenerational intimacy', the experience of consciousness-raising among another radical group made it possible, for the first time in history, to provide a very different critique of normative sexuality. Authors such as Rush (1980), Driver and Droisen (1989), Danica (1989) and Itzin (2000) have all repeatedly drawn attention to the abusive nature of adult sexual contact with children, drawing on reports of the direct lived experiences of adults as well as on statistical data to provide evidence of its long-term impacts. Among the very first of such texts, Louise Armstrong's *Kiss Daddy Goodnight: A Speakout on Incest*, published in 1978, broke a profound taboo by bringing into public view the hidden trauma of children's actual sexual experiences. These reports, breaking the silence of many generations, first came almost exclusively from women but, more recently, men have also begun speaking publicly about sexual contact with adults in their childhood: an example of this is the British documentary *Chosen* (dir. Woods, 2008) which received a BAFTA award for its sensitive portrayal.

As with the first perspective discussed, this second theoretical tradition also makes connections between adult sexual attraction to children and other forms of sexuality, but in this case it is likely to link the phenomenon of adult sexual attraction to children not to 'alternative sexualities' but, on the contrary, to mainstream male sexual behaviour, seeing a continuum of sexual violence (Kelly, 1987) which is expressed through sexual harassment, rape and the sexual abuse of children. Thus, this second discourse, which takes a child protection perspective, does not present paedophilia as a radical or dissident alternative but conversely as an integral part of normative adult male sexuality as expressed (and problematized) within patriarchal systems.

4. Conclusion

This chapter has attempted to provide an overview of some of the main ways in which contemporary society understands adults who are sexually attracted to children. Rather than any coherence, the ways in which society 'make sense' of this phenomenon may strike one almost as a disparate ragbag of disjointed ideas, with tabloid newspapers shrieking about 'evil paedos' and 'nasty pervs' (and finding themselves the butt of satire), while celebrities and their fans shrug off concerns over child abuse and mainstream Hollywood 'nymphets' act out fantasies which then, it appears, become the content of NAMBLA's porn. The nineteenth-century technical psychiatric term of 'paedophilia erotica' (and the considerably older 'pederasty') have emerged alive and kicking in the twenty-first century, drawing fresh energy from the capacity of the internet to disseminate ideas, shape global discourse and, as a by-product, provide an amplifier for the 'paedophile voice'. The field of 'intergenerational studies' draws on pederasty, cross-cultural and cross-species examples to put forward a view of both paedophiles and children as 'sexual radicals', while perspectives on child sexual abuse and child protection, one could argue, get rather lost and almost drowned in the cross-currents. Where paedophiles do feature in the academic literature, it is often simply to acknowledge that typically they are misrepresented and demonized (Kitzinger, 2004; Meyer, 2007). Individualized and apolitical notions of 'stranger danger' only serve to add to the confusion, merely adding to the confusion and throwing a smokescreen over the reality of child sexual abuse (Kelly,1996; Cowburn & Dominelli, 2001).

Given these conflicting academic analyses of paedophilia, which each critique normative masculine sexuality but from substantially different perspectives, it is perhaps less surprising to find such a level of confusion within contemporary mainstream society – and a response in everyday popular culture which ineffectually falls back on sardonic humour, satire, cynicism, indifference, furtive titillation or baffled hatred. Instead of being able to critique adult sexual attraction to children as a social phenomenon, explicable within its cultural and political context, when confronted by the reality of sexual offences against children popular culture tends to draw on asocial narratives of individualized moral deviance; the 'bad apple' approach. In this way, paedophiles find themselves explained in the popular press and in criminal justice cases neither as outside the mainstream (as 'sexual radicals', free-wheeling counter-cultural libertarians in the style of Allen Ginsberg or André Gide, for example), nor as within the mainstream (as normative hegemonic patriarchs) but typically as monsters, not inside or outside but simply *other than* society; individualized and pathologized perverts, people who have left behind their common humanity.

How did we get here? The next two chapters seek to answer that question by exploring some of the most influential work published on 'intergenerational sexuality' over the last half-century or so. As will be obvious by now, there is, as quoted above, a 'plethora of publications that are positive' on adult–child sexual contact, too many to cover in this one book, so only a small selection will be discussed. Readers wishing to find out more about the second perspective (that on the abusive nature of adult sexual contact with children) are encouraged to read the statistical, clinical and experiential data provided in a number of mainstream texts. The following chapters in this book focus on the perhaps less obvious but nevertheless hugely influential work which follows the logic of the first perspective, that there is 'a more varied response to childhood sexuality issues' and that adult sexual contact with children has 'shades of grey and white'. We begin with the most influential author of all, Professor Alfred Kinsey.

4

'Early Sexual Growth and Activity': The Influence of Kinsey

Introduction

Following on from the discussion on 'making sense' of paedophilia through historical, cross-cultural and cross-species examples, this chapter now turns to one specific body of data and analysis developed by the biologist Alfred Kinsey and his colleagues at Indiana University and set out in a key text published in 1948, *Sexual Behavior in the Human Male*. Since its first publication, Kinsey's work has been the focus of controversy and misinterpretation and it is therefore essential to return to this famous but little-read original source-material for analysis. The impact that this work has had on modern Western society has been profound, and the extraordinary fame of Kinsey's study on sexual behaviour has recently been revived in the popular imagination by the Hollywood biopic *Kinsey* (2004), written and directed by Bill Condon and starring Liam Neeson and Laura Linney. The unique data from Kinsey's survey of sexual behaviour – and the manner in which they were published and discussed both in Kinsey's original book and in Condon's film almost sixty years later – not only provide us with a lens through which to examine changes in attitude to the idea of adult–child sexual contact but also show us how such changes in attitude were effected.

Dr Alfred Charles Kinsey (1894–1956), Professor of Zoology at Indiana University, has been a household name since the publication of *Sexual Behavior in the Human Male*, which he published in conjunction with his two research associates, Wardell Pomeroy, a prison psychologist, and Clyde Martin, an undergraduate student taken on as the 'numbers man'. Without doubt this book remains a fascinating text. Within its tables and descriptions of findings a particular moment of understanding human sexuality is preserved like an insect caught in amber.

Radical and taboo-busting as Kinsey's work undoubtedly was, and scientifically neutral and objective as it claimed to be, it is suffused with the prejudices – both amusing and disturbing – of its three WASP (White Anglo-Saxon Protestant) male authors.

First published on 5 January 1948 by W. B. Saunders, a well-established medical publishing house, the book excited intense popular interest and was likened to the H-Bomb in impact. Despite the relatively expensive price of $6.50, to keep up with demand the publishers needed to reprint the book three times in the first month alone and a further four times during that year, with numerous reprintings being issued throughout the 1950s and 1960s. In total, the book has had at least thirteen re-issues, the most recent being on 1 June 1998 by Indiana University Press, to mark the book's fiftieth anniversary. During its heyday, the book sold 275,000 copies in the United States alone, with numerous translations abroad (Wallechinsky & Wallace, 1981). Kinsey received many accolades, even appearing on the cover of *Time* magazine when the second book, *Sexual Behavior in the Human Female*, was published in 1953. The media coverage was unprecedented for a book (Gathorne-Hardy, 1998) and has probably only been rivalled in modern times by J. K. Rowling's *Harry Potter* series. Over the decades, Kinsey's books, his sex survey, his research team, his Institute for Sex Research, and more recently the film about his life, have all been the subject of considerable controversy, adulation and anger.

Section 1 sets out some of the key points of the original text and identifies Kinsey's focus on 'sex offenders' as a central theme running through his work. Section 2 provides a brief biographical context within which to make sense of Kinsey's work and Section 3 homes in on what is without doubt the most significant part of Kinsey's work in relation to adult–child sexual contact, Chapter 5 of *Sexual Behavior in the Human Male*. Section 4 brings the work up to date by looking at the ways in which the data in that chapter have been critiqued and the portrayal of Kinsey's work in the film *Kinsey*, and by exploring how Kinsey's work has been incorporated into the body of contemporary academic literature dealing with adult–child sexual contact, with the enduring influence it has had on our thinking.

In order to demonstrate Kinsey's thesis clearly, I have drawn extensively on quotations from *Sexual Behavior in the Human Male* and, to a lesser extent, on *Sexual Behavior in the Human Female*. However, for copyright reasons, I have not been able to use as many direct quotations as I would have wished and so I have needed to paraphrase in places. The reader is encouraged to check all quotations and assertions of fact with the original work to confirm the veracity of my portrayal of Kinsey's views.

1. The Kinsey study and 'sex offending'

In order to analyse Kinsey's work, it is necessary to understand what he and his research team believed they were doing, and the language that they used to present their findings to the public. When *Sexual Behavior in the Human Male* was published, it was meant as the first tranche of findings from a huge project on human sexuality which, it was intended, would continue for another twenty years or so and encompass interview-data to be obtained from up to 100,000 individuals throughout the United States. At the time of publication, Kinsey and his team claimed already to have interviewed approximately 12,000 individuals and they viewed their work as providing an analysis of data from the most thorough, comprehensive and scientific study of human sexuality ever undertaken. Kinsey saw his work as primarily biological and taxonomic, building from his expertise in zoology and the meticulous entomological studies of gall-wasps which had been the focus of his academic work until middle-age.

The book opens by stating that it is 'a progress report from a case-study history on human sex behavior', a 'fact-finding survey in which an attempt is being made to discover what people do sexually' and what factors account for differences in sexual behaviour among individuals and among different groups within the population (*Sexual Behavior in the Human Male*, 1965: 3; please note that all quotations and page-numbering in this chapter are from the 1965 re-issue of the original 1948 text, but page-numbering is likely to be the same in all re-issues).

Sexual Behavior in the Human Male, and the subsequent *Female* volume, were credited as being authored by Alfred Kinsey and two of his research staff, Wardell Pomeroy and Clyde Martin (and, for the *Female* volume, Paul Gebhard as the fourth author). Both of these texts were in fact written solely by Kinsey himself (Gathorne-Hardy, 1998: 61) who habitually wrote using the first person plural, 'we'. Throughout the text, and particularly in the opening chapter, Kinsey was at some pains to represent his work as fully within the traditional and conventional positivist model of 'hard science', authored by a serious, disinterested group of dedicated scientists. Thus the first few pages are larded with scientific terminology and an emphasis on 'the desirability of obtaining data about sex which would represent an accumulation of scientific fact completely divorced from questions of moral value and social custom'.

Within just the first page alone, Kinsey manages to squeeze in reference to all of the following terms: 'progress report', 'case-studies', 'Research Council', 'fact-finding survey', 'data', 'accumulation of scientific fact', 'physicians', 'patients', 'objective data', 'psychiatrists', 'analysts', 'educated intelligence', 'education', 'social control of behavior', 'science', 'laboratory animals', 'physiologic activities', 'scientists', and 'scientific investigations in this field'. This is a careful scene-setting, leaving the reader in no doubt that, with that kind of opening, the rest of the book will be thoroughly scientific!

It is not until p.16 that Kinsey feels confident enough in having established the research team's scientific credentials that he begins to let his hair down and show some emotion, referring to his interviewees' 'satisfactions and heartaches' and his own 'sympathetic acceptance of people as they are'. As Paul Gebhard, one of the co-authors, was later to say, 'I felt that it was anthropology; we were just studying our own culture instead of some primitive culture. And I felt this was really important, pioneering work. We all felt that way.' (quoted in Brown, 2004, online).

A key part of this 'pioneering work' was the development of a new model of human sexuality and a new model of how such sexuality articulated with 'our own culture'. Thus Kinsey's model of sexuality drew on previous conceptual models taken mainly from biology, whilst developing new sociological implications. Kinsey saw himself as in contradistinction to the psychological or psychodynamic model of sexuality developed by Freud. He had no patience with psychology. The terminology of 'New Biology' and 'Scientific Sexological' concepts – humans as instinct-driven animals – saturates his work. There is no mention of 'men' or 'women', but only the 'human male' and the 'human female', with repeated reference to research on 'anthropoids' and on 'other mammalian species' – apes, monkeys and especially rats. Kinsey was, after all, a zoologist by training, and a determined Darwinist to boot, who delighted in seeing humans as simply another species of mammal, so it is not surprising that, for him, animal research was an important source of confirmation for his theories on 'sexual behaviour in the human animal', as he liked to term it. At the same time, Kinsey seems to have been influenced by the Freudian idea of the sex drive or libido constantly existing as a powerful force within bodies, demanding a 'sexual outlet' for its expression and release in orgasm.

Throughout Kinsey's book, we are not really exploring sex – we are certainly not being given information on developing sexual relationships or love-making. A central concept of the book is this notion of a 'sexual outlet' – almost as impersonal and mechanistic as plumbing: place the penis into an 'outlet' and orgasm results. Kinsey's model of sexuality is thus a straightforward one: the human male is a biological organism with an innate drive to achieve coitus and to orgasm. The amount and type of 'sexual outlet' is affected by biological factors; the main factor, according to Kinsey, being the age at which adolescence occurs. Measuring the onset of adolescence by signs such as physical growth, pubic hair, voice-change, and ability to ejaculate, Kinsey demonstrates from his data that if adolescence occurs early (around 10 or 11 years old), then the individual is more likely to have sex early and have more sex throughout life than a boy who reaches adolescence later (age 14 or 15). As he expresses it, the boys who reach adolescence earliest are the ones who most often have 'the highest rates of outlet' in later life (p. 213). (It may be relevant that in the film *Kinsey*, there is a scene where Kinsey is asked when he developed pubic hair and his voice broke: he reports that this occurred when he was about 11, although he is reported to have remained a virgin until his marriage at age 27.)

Throughout the book, there is built up a picture of male sexuality as focused on 'sexual outlet' and in which the earlier sexual activity starts, the better. Because of the centrality of the concept of 'sexual outlet', any notion of slowly developing sexual maturity is almost irrelevant. The idea of a human being passing incrementally through developmental stages, from baby to child to adolescent to adult, to arrive at full emotional, psychological and social maturity ready to participate in adult, sexually expressed relationships seems entirely foreign to Kinsey's model of sexuality. The plumbing metaphor works whatever the chronological age of the penis concerned, or the 'outlet' concerned.

Kinsey is keen to emphasize throughout the book that young males do (or should) start sexual activity as soon as they are capable of ejaculation or indeed 'would be capable of ejaculation if the proper opportunity were at hand' (p.189). (This oblique statement about 'the proper opportunity' is discussed further in Section 3.) On pubertal boys, Kinsey states that, after the initial experience of ejaculation, practically all boys become regular in their sexual activity, thus 'more than 99 per cent of the boys begin regular sexual lives immediately after the first ejaculation', whether this involves monthly, weekly or 'even daily ejaculation'. (pp. 191–2). As well as emphasizing that young males should start sexual activity as soon as they are capable of ejaculation, Kinsey finds that those who do start early have many advantages. Not only do they have much more frequent sex 'for a matter of at least 35 or 40 years', but they are 'more alert, energetic, vivacious, spontaneous, physically active' and generally outgoing (p. 325). This highly positive description appears to be derived from 'personality ratings' but it is not clear who – if anyone – administered these ratings or whether they were not simply anecdotal impressions of the interviewer. Late-adolescent boys were described using the terms 'slow', 'quiet', 'mild in manner' and so on. These listless, unforceful males do not appear to deserve much sex, and never get much sex, according to Kinsey.

As well as admiring the 'vivacious' young males who begin sexual activity early, the book also admires what it terms 'lower level males', in other words, working-class or blue-collar youths. Again, this comes out throughout the book. Kinsey distinguishes between 'upper level', that is, college-educated, and 'lower level' males. As with the 'early-adolescent' and 'late-adolescent' distinction, there is a similarly clear and value-laden distinction made between 'upper level' males, who don't get the sex, and 'lower level' males, who most certainly do. (Again, it may be relevant that Kinsey, and also his researcher Clyde Martin, had come originally from distinctly 'lower level' working-class roots, although they were of course also 'college-educated'). There is a tension in the book between the inability of 'upper level males' to 'achieve coitus' and the contrast this makes with 'lower level males' who are presented, enviably it seems, as 'natural', uninhibited, sexually free and sexually successful. Throughout the book the argument is that 'upper level males' fail to get what they want in socio-sexual relations' (p. 363) while 'the lower level male comes nearer having as much coitus as he wants' (ibid.) and indeed 'the lower level male is likely to have had intercourse with hundreds of girls' (p. 369).

As well as age and social level, the book analyses other factors which are seen as affecting 'sexual outlet'. These include marital status, religious background, and rural or urban background. Marital and religious factors are treated fairly uncontroversially, but Kinsey proposes that rural or urban background is particularly important because the majority of boys living on farms will have sex with animals – as will city boys who visit farms. It is rather startling to discover that *Sexual Behavior in the Human Male* contains an entire chapter, Chapter 22, on bestiality. This seems never to have attracted any particular interest or comment. Re-reading Kinsey's work now, however, one of the most striking characteristics of the book is the contrast between the way in which sex with animals and sex with women is presented. Thus, whenever 'petting' (that is, heterosexual love-making which does not involve penile penetration) is discussed, the language becomes noticeably stilted and medical: rather than any reference to a man caressing a woman's breast with his hands or mouth, one finds only 'manual manipulation of the female breast' and 'oral eroticism', and an almost complete absence of reference to affection or emotion. Unexpectedly, it is in the chapter on bestiality where we find the most explicit references in the entire book to affection, where Kinsey talks about 'many a farm boy' who fantasises about sexual contact with animals and 'may develop an affectional relation with the particular animal with which he has his contacts' and who may be 'quite upset emotionally' when 'situations force them to sever connections'. Kinsey also writes about 'male dogs' who 'may become considerably attached' to the boy who masturbates them and may 'completely forsake the females of their own species in preference for the sexual contacts that may be had with a human partner.' (pp. 676–7).

Consonant with the tenor of the whole book, the overall impression is formed that, since the function of sex is orgasm, an activity such as 'petting' (hugging, kissing or caressing) is largely a waste of time. 'Petting' is presented as something that is only done by 'high school and college levels' (p. 345) and provides few orgasms. The implicit advice is not to bother too much with 'petting' women: better for the 'human partner' to head straight for the affectionate (male) animals on the farm. Indeed, the anthropologist Margaret Mead commented acutely in a review, 'The book suggests no way of choosing between a woman and a sheep' (quoted in Gathorne-Hardy, 1998: 272).

The 'sources of sexual outlet' which are covered in separate chapters in the book encompass: masturbation, nocturnal emissions, heterosexual petting leading to orgasm, heterosexual coitus (whether pre-marital, marital, extra-marital or sex with prostitutes), homosexual outlet, and animal contacts. Alongside the emphasis on bestiality, there are other strange anomalies such as the recurring questions on 'urethral insertions', a very rare activity statistically but one enjoyed by Kinsey himself, apparently from early adolescence onwards (Jones, 1997). Similarly, specific survey questions in the Questionnaire on 'breast knots' in adolescent males and 'thickness of lips' (1965: 64) seem also to indicate interests peculiar to Kinsey, as it is not clear what their general scientific value might be to sexology.

Despite its much-vaunted scientific neutrality, therefore, the biases within the book are glaringly evident for those who take the time to read it. For example, throughout the book there is an obvious impatience with and intolerance of women, particularly those who withhold, demand payment for, or otherwise constrain male 'sexual outlets'. Women, as they appear in this book, have little sexual interest and no imagination or empathy. In fact, they are really rather irritating and get in the way of men having sex. Kinsey expresses annoyance that women, whether as mothers, as school teachers or as 'voting citizens' (he was

26 when women finally attained suffrage in the United States), are the main carers for boys and are the ones who 'control moral codes, schedules for sex education, campaigns for law enforcement, and programs for combating what is called juvenile delinquency'. He dismissively conjectures that it is 'obviously impossible for a majority of these women to understand the problem that the boy faces' in dealing with sexual arousal (p. 223).

It is extraordinary to find that, in an 800-page book on male sexuality, there is only one reference to rape (pp. 237–8) and this sole reference is not actually about the reality of rape but only about false allegations (in this case, false allegations of sexual abuse against children), which is a 'problem which deserves noting' (p. 237). As one author has astutely commented, remarking breezily that Kinsey thus put in 'a good word for child molesters':

> This represented the only instance in the Reports [on Male and Female Sexual Behavior] where adults appeared in the role of victims and children in that of oppressors...Throughout this discussion, it should be noted, Kinsey assigned the villainous role not to children as such but specifically to female children, just as in his examination of the sexual hardships endured by teenagers he assigned the role of repressor to mothers and female teachers. Inevitably one feels that his sympathies went out not so much to the young in general as to those among them who happened to be males. (Robinson, 1976: 92)

Thus, in what is purported to be a comprehensive and scientific compendium on sexual behaviour in the human male, the sexual behaviour of actual rape or sexual abuse – committed against adults or children – does not appear. It is only false allegations which 'deserve noting'. This silence on sexual assault, along with the tone of contempt for women's desires and experiences, is consonant with Kinsey's thesis on the importance of coitus and 'sexual outlet'. For him, 'sexual outlet' is central and he expresses only exasperation for any moral codes which reduce the amount of coitus available to males. Throughout his writings, his many public lectures and his campaigning activities over twenty-odd years, Kinsey's vision, shared by the members of his research team, is a powerful image of 'human males' craving and needing 'sources of sexual outlet' by which to relieve the biologically ordained pressure of their libidinal drives.

Kinsey, partly for reasons which will be explored in the next section, was driven by a great sense of sympathy for sexually active men and an equally strong sense of outrage and injustice at social systems which prevented, circumscribed or punished men whose sexual behaviour contravened norms or laws. His book, ostensibly an objective and dispassionate scientific study on all sexual behaviour in the human male, is in fact a sustained argument for the legal and social freedom for all males to achieve coitus without hindrance, via whatever 'outlet' is available. This argument leads logically to Kinsey's campaign, introduced in the *Male* volume and continued actively and unceasingly for the remainder of his life, for the reduction and even removal of 'sex offender' as a criminal category.

Even prior to beginning the study on which this book is based, Kinsey was already declaring in his lectures to students, 'there are only three kinds of sexual abnormalities: abstinence, celibacy, and delayed marriage. Think about this.' (quoted in Gathorne-Hardy, 1998: 124). Reading his words, we do indeed need to 'think about this'. Kinsey is stating baldly that, in his opinion, the only 'abnormal' sex is no sex. Kinsey does not qualify this contention in relation to consensual or non-consensual sexual acts. In Kinsey's world-view, the very concept of 'non-consensual sex' appears to be an oxymoron, since apparently there would never be a reason not to consent to sex: certainly in his written work there appears to be no mention of such a situation. For Kinsey, therefore, there are no forms of sexuality which are wrong. The only form of wrongdoings or crimes which can be committed in relation to sex are to abstain from or to prevent sex.

At the time when Kinsey was researching, in America just prior to and during the Second World War, society was shifting awkwardly between a general relaxation of sexual mores and an increasing hostility towards male homosexuality. The categories of sex offending for which a man might be imprisoned ranged from rape of an adult or sexual abuse of a child to 'victimless crimes' such as masturbation in public, consensual heterosexual oral or anal sex, or consensual sex between two adult men. Kinsey's sympathies were strongly with the 'sex offender', seemingly regardless of the offence committed. Since he regarded sex as an essential biological drive, all 'sources of sexual outlet' as equally morally neutral, and orgasm, however obtained, as an unproblematic and unalloyed good, his research provided a compelling argument against the concept of 'sex offending' and for all sexual behaviour to be socially tolerated and legally de-criminalized. This was no mere rhetoric. Kinsey's work inspired and underpinned substantial reforms of sex offender laws in both the United States and Britain from the 1950s to the present day. (More details on this are provided in Section 4.)

2. The man behind the book

Professor Kinsey, as the instigator and leader of the largest survey into human sexuality ever conducted and as the founder of the prestigious Institute for Sex Research at Indiana University, was a powerful personality, domineering and charismatic. He was also, as noted, the sole author of the two major texts resulting from the survey (as both *Sexual Behavior in the Human Male* and *Sexual Behavior in the Human Female*, although credited to several authors and written in the formal third person, were in fact written solely by Kinsey himself, Gathorne-Hardy, 1998). It is to Kinsey's biography therefore that we must turn in order to understand something of the provenance of his key ideas on human sexuality and on 'sex offenders'.

We all take our early childhood experiences into the rest of our lives and our work. The dramas, the fears and the comforts of childhood inform our emotional and intellectual lives and provide the ground for our particular ways of knowing, embedded in and inseparable from our socio-economic and cultural contexts and the accidents of our biographies. It is the task of biographers and theorists to tease out possible relationships between early experiences and later intellectual work. This embedded, situated knowledge, of course, affects both the subject (in this case, Kinsey) and those who choose to study the subject (as well as those who choose to study those who choose to study the subject, and so on *ad infinitum!*)

Kinsey has been studied by two biographers in particular. The first, James Jones, is an American who conducted his doctoral research at Indiana University and went on to publish his research as *Alfred C. Kinsey: A Public/Private Life* in 1997. The second major biographer is an English author, Jonathan Gathorne-Hardy, from an aristocratic family fallen on hard times (Gathorne-Hardy, 2004) who had been one of Benjamin Britten's young boy friends in the 1940s (Bridcut, 2006) and who has written on topics as diverse as English nannies and the public school system as well as on Kinsey. Gathorne-Hardy, like Jones, was given privileged access to files at Kinsey's Institute at Indiana University. His 1998 biography, *Alfred C. Kinsey: Sex the Measure of All Things* provided the basis for Condon's film *Kinsey* in 2004. Facts cited in this section are taken, unless otherwise referenced, from Gathorne-Hardy's work, and page numbers given in this section therefore refer to Gathorne-Hardy (1998).

Alfred Kinsey was born in Hoboken, New York, in 1894. His early life was dominated by chronic ill-health, the humiliations of chronic poverty, and by bullying both at home and at school. His health problems, including rickets, rheumatic fever and typhoid, were linked to poor diet and housing and, when not ill at home, he was isolated at school and socially. A school-acquaintance recalled many years later, 'He kept himself alone, stayed by himself...We thought he was a sissy guy, feminine-like, like a girl.' (p. 16). He had a stern Methodist upbringing from his intensely religious dictatorial father and he himself went on to bring up his own children unusually strictly, chastising them on occasion (p. 7). His hated childhood left him with an 'almost insane' emphasis on personal cleanliness and neatness (pp. 8 and 9). At age 10 the family moved fifteen miles out of town to a village, South Orange, and here, 'Even thirty years later Kinsey could remember the excitement, the great surge of relief he got from at last escaping out into the surrounding countryside – away from his bed, from illness, from home, from the bullying streets and cramped houses' (p. 12).

Socially awkward, self-absorbed, an obsessive collector, Kinsey is presented even by sympathetic biographers such as Jones and Gathorne-Hardy as someone who found it hard to empathize with others, someone perhaps with almost autistic difficulty in understanding how others might perceive the world. The impression that comes through most clearly, however, from anecdotes of his childhood is his overwhelming sense of 'furious hatred'. Kinsey had an abiding sense of rage against his upbringing, his father and especially religion. He seems to have been furious, throughout his life, about the effects of his upbringing. It is this powerful sense of frustrated fury, an engine of rage, which comes through clearly in his later work. When he shows empathy, it is with men denied opportunities to express themselves sexually. When he argues most eloquently, it is for the rights of such men to do what they please. Generations of men, reading Kinsey, have found echoes of their own frustration and their own desires.

As Kinsey grew older, more confident and more assured in his social standing, leaving behind his working-class background and settling into the comfortable lifestyle of a successful professor with an international reputation, aspects of his character began to be expressed more assertively. Kinsey was not shy about sex within his circle of colleagues and associates. He had a fascination with masturbating and watching masturbation, insisting to a photographer, 'I need 2,000 orgasms...All I want is the genitalia – close up....I have to see the semen coming out.' (p. 296). It is well-documented by Jones and Gathorne-Hardy that he had sex with a large number of men, among them most of the members of his research team which became 'a group of interacting open marriages' (p. 168), including Clyde Martin, Wardell Pomeroy and others, in which 'we all sucked one another' (p. 290). Kinsey had 'about nine other partners during his life' in addition to 'anonymous and casual "tea-room" [homosexual] sex' (p. 248). During Kinsey's lifetime, homosexual acts were criminal and the damage to his reputation, to his work and to his university and funding bodies had his activity been known would have been immense. Kinsey relied on people around him to remain silent.

Homosexual sex was not the only sexual interest which Kinsey had and which, had it been more widely known about, might have affected the public's uncritical acceptance of his work. Both his major biographers, Jones and Gathorne-Hardy, document masturbation practices which included inserting pencils and even toothbrushes into his penis through the urethral opening (p. 337). He also tied rope around his testicles and on one occasion suspended himself from the ceiling, possibly for a couple of hours, by this rope (pp. 206 and 414). He was also known to have circumcised himself as an adult (p. 414), and it seems clear that quite extreme pain comprised an integral part of his sexual life. Given such unusual and extreme practices, it would be surprising if Kinsey's own idiosyncratic sexual experiences did not colour his relationship to sexual behaviour in general. Kinsey himself hints that these practices are relevant in his professional work. For example, in *Sexual Behavior in the Human Male* (1965: 60), in a discussion on interviewing skills, he includes a paragraph on interviewing men who have 'greatly elaborated' their 'masturbatory techniques' and he comments favourably on the importance of the interviewer's 'background of knowledge' in this regard.

Other idiosyncratic details about Kinsey may also be relevant to the final shape of the study and the published results. He was apparently very proud of his penis, which was said to be 'unusually large' (Gathorne-Hardy, 1998: 60) and he had a habit of wearing few or no clothes, which some people found disconcerting (pp. 90, 105–6). With young male students he was especially relaxed. He had been a very enthusiastic member of the Boy Scouts since his adolescence and continued to enjoy camping trips all his life. Before his career switch into sexology, Kinsey was a zoologist studying the gall-wasp, a tiny flightless insect, and this research involved camping trips with students to collect samples. These camping trips continued later, when Kinsey took his young male research staff around the United States to interview respondents for the survey on sexual behaviour. Some young men on these trips were taken aback when Professor Kinsey appeared naked, engaged them in intimate conversations and offered to teach them masturbation techniques. One researcher, Vincent Nowlis, who had recently joined the team, left promptly when he realized he was expected not only to work for but to have sex with the Professor (p. 228). After that, Kinsey determined that he would only accept research members who were more open about sexual issues.

From the information provided by his biographers, we can see that Kinsey was not the conventional scientist of impeccable sexual probity whom the American public believed him to be. When he argued for tolerance of sexual difference, and a freeing-up of sex offender legislation, including that which criminalized male homosexual acts, he can be seen to be ahead of his time, a courageous advocate for sexual liberation and the unashamed enjoyment of sexual pleasure, and this is how many people today understand his work. Offering to masturbate the young men working under him could be interpreted as the gesture of a relaxed sexual libertarian eager to release his students from stuffy and repressive inhibitions. After all, such young men, although constrained by job and career considerations, could still choose to leave the project if they did not wish to participate sexually. There was a sense of sexual permissiveness and experimentation about the research team which many relished, although there was also a rigid and compulsive quality: the research team all had to fill in sex calendars, detailing each orgasm and its 'source' (p. 218). Kinsey was a controlling and dominating character and those around him regarded him as a powerful father-figure not to be thwarted. Nowlis described him as 'a guru surrounded by disciples' (p. 217) and there are many similar comments.

For Kinsey, as we have seen, sex was genuinely 'the measure of all things', the central organizing principle. For men, the need to orgasm was a biological demand that must be met. The idea of an orgasm which is unwanted is outside Kinsey's conceptual framework. Kinsey could, and in his writings and speeches frequently did, sympathize with those who did not have sex when they wanted it; we never hear from him any sympathy for those who might be exposed to sexual acts they did not want or which they were unable even to comprehend.

3. The data in Kinsey's Chapter 5: 'Early Sexual Growth and Activity'

Turning from Kinsey the man and back to an examination of his hugely influential publications, it is worth taking a moment to examine how the data on sexuality were collected. (All page-references in this section are to *Sexual Behavior in the Human Male*, 1965, unless otherwise noted.)

The question of data-collection is more complex than would at first appear. The authors (again, actually only Kinsey but drawing on support with statistics from Martin) outline their methodology in the context of a thorough overview of previous 'sex studies' (pp. 21–34), again in order to demonstrate how this study is a development of earlier scientific work. The book is a presentation of data 'secured through first-hand interviews' which are 'limited to persons resident in the United States' and include persons from ages 'three to ninety' (p. 5). It is stated on p. 6 that the present study is based on 'about 5300' white males, which is not the whole sample of 12,000 histories taken at that point, which presumably included women and Black men whose histories were intended to constitute later volumes. However, a casual reader might be misled on this point by the Dedication at the front of this volume to the 'twelve thousand persons who have contributed to these data'.

Information is given on pp. 13–16 on the different groups involved in contributing interviewees, from hospitals, universities, schools, psychiatric clinics, prisons and 'Travelers on Trains', but there is no way of telling from the information contained within this volume exactly how many sex histories were derived from which groups. Further, since the discussion on sources of data seems to cover all 12,000 case-studies and not simply the 5300 selected for this volume, it is not at all clear where the sample in this volume was drawn from or even whether this is the whole of the white males who had contributed to the study by that point or only a subset. Particular reference is made to penal and 'correctional institutions' where the inmate populations 'have voluntarily cooperated in splendid fashion' (p. 15). Although not mentioned in the book, Kinsey's colleague Pomeroy, through his contacts, was able to recruit a large number of prison inmates (particularly sex offenders) as interviewees. In one rare admission of who contributed, there is mention of 'several hundred male prostitutes who have contributed their histories' (p. 216) to the overall sample of 'about 5300' men. Since male prostitutes probably do not constitute anywhere near 5 per cent or more of the general male population, this is evidence of skewing the sample.

On p. 7 the question of normal sexual behaviour is raised, with the strong statement that no preconception of what is normal or abnormal has affected the choice of the histories or the selection of data recorded. Kinsey also states that the study does not distinguish between 'sexually well-adjusted persons' and those whom psychiatrists would regard as neurotic, psychotic or psychopathic. However, since sexual or mental health is not used as a variable in the research, it is impossible, from the data presented, to know whether the sample was representative of the wider population within the United States or, by apparently relying heavily on samples of prisoners including sex offenders, whether it skewed the findings towards the 'psychopathic' end of the spectrum. Kinsey's research team also took histories from individuals based at a State Training School for the Feeble-Minded, a Children's Home, and a Salvation Army Home for Children (p. 15). It is not clear what ages the interviewees were from these institutions and no further details are given in the book. However, Gathorne-Hardy tells of Kinsey collecting data from Washawaka Orphanage (1998: 169) and of collaborating with a graduate student, Glenn Ramsey, who, for reasons which are unclear, had independently decided to collect a large number of masturbation histories from boys at Woodruff Senior High School in Peoria, Illinois where Ramsey was teaching; he subsequently agreed to join Kinsey's team after being dismissed as a teacher (Gathorne-Hardy, 1998: 129, 136, 192–3).

Years later, in 1979, Paul Gebhard, a man at the heart of Kinsey's research team and the one who took over as Director of the Kinsey Institute after Kinsey's death, published a version of the original data which had been re-analysed (Gebhard, Johnson & Kinsey, 1979). In the first chapter of this volume, he attempted to explain some of the difficulties with the data. Even his explanations are fairly convoluted and opaque. He advises: 'we must warn readers that attempting comparisons between this volume and the first two 'Kinsey Reports' is complex and often frustrating' and goes on to say that *Sexual Behavior in the Human Male* is:

> one of the most difficult books to work with ever written. Some of the problem stems from the fact that in those days we lacked computers and our card sorters were slow. A relatively simple table could easily take a full day or two of sorting – assuming the machine was available. Consequently, some tabulations were made a year or more before others and since our interviewing continued, our Ns [sample-sizes] varied. (Gebhard *et al.*, 1979: 8–9)

In fact, Gebhard admits that the sample of 'older males' (which appears here to mean anyone aged over 45!) was 'often so small that no calculations should have been published' – he gives the examples of a table based on 14 cases and one table based on a mere three cases (1979: 9). As well as varying sample-sizes and difficulties working with the data, a more fundamental problem was that the data themselves were skewed, containing unrepresentatively high proportions of 'delinquents', prison-inmates, prostitutes and homosexuals. The Kinsey research team had deliberately 'sought out groups and organizations known to have a high proportion of homosexual members and interviewed large numbers of these' (1979: 5). Gebhard explains that this was done because the team intended later to publish these findings as part of a separate study on homosexuality, but this was never indicated in the 'Kinsey Reports', where the samples were presented as being representative of the general population.

In the 1979 volume, the original interview-data have been 'cleaned' by dividing them up into four groups: the 'Basic Sample', 'Delinquents' (including sex offenders), 'Homosexuals' and 'Special Groups' (including 'sources with known deviant sexual bias', 1979: 5). A sample of 'prepubescent children' is included under Special Groups. Thus, in the 1979 volume, only the Basic Sample appears to be meant to be representative of the general population while, in the original *Male* and *Female* volumes, data from all these four groups were presented as representative not only of the average American citizen but indeed as representative of the entire human population, 'the human animal', in general. Gebhard, however, stands by the findings from Kinsey's work and asserts:

> Despite the flaws of our earlier pioneering publications and the difficulties of comparing them with this volume, it is clear that the major findings of the earlier works [*Sexual Behavior in the Human Male* and *Sexual Behavior in the Human Female*] regarding age, gender, marital status, and socioeconomic class remain intact. Adding to and cleaning our samples has markedly increased their value, but has not as yet caused us to recant any important assertion. In using our new Ns [sample-sizes] in analyses, we anticipate we will discover relationships previously unknown to us and we will undoubtedly have to modify some prior statements, but we feel the important contributions of Dr. Kinsey will stand. (Gebhard *et al.*, 1979: 9)

This approach of continuing to stand by Kinsey's findings has continued to this day (see Section 4), despite what would seem to be the increasingly untenable nature of such a stance, particularly 'the major findings of the earlier works regarding age', as concern centres on the way in which children's experiences were included in the study and the ways in which information about such experiences was obtained. Gebhard states that, in *Sexual Behavior in the Human Male*, those interviewed included 536 prepubescent children, of whom he says 'Most of these were too young to have received our standard interview and were given a variant of it.' (1979: 6). Later he clarifies this sample as comprising 380 'prepubertal males' and 156 'prepubertal females' (1979: 45). Their experiences were discussed in both the *Male* and the *Female* volumes. The following discussion mainly addresses the data in the *Male* volume, where the subject was treated more fully.

Returning to the original work by Kinsey, the most important section of *Sexual Behavior in the Human Male* in terms of children's sexual development and adult–child sexual contact is presented immediately after the background and methodology of the research have been laid out in Part 1. The first chapter of Part 2 ('Factors Affecting Sexual Outlet') is Chapter 5, 'Early Sexual Growth and Activity'. This is therefore the first chapter which gives actual findings from Kinsey's survey. Given the nature of the material presented in this chapter, an important question to ask at the outset is how this chapter fits into the rest of the book. Is it an anomaly, an aberration which can safely be ignored or excised, leaving the value of the rest of the book unscathed? Or is it central to the argument of the entire book?

The evidence suggests that, for Kinsey and his team, this is not by any means an insignificant or anomalous part of the book, but is indeed central to the overall argument. This is shown in the way that data from this chapter are integrated into the themes of the book, with the findings repeatedly referred to throughout the other sections of the book (for example the comment 'The existence of multiple orgasm in the pre-adolescent male has been discussed in Chapter 5' is given on p. 215, in the chapter on 'Total Sexual Outlet'). As well as references in other chapters to statements in Chapter 5, attention is drawn to the chapter itself all the way through from the beginning to the end of the book. At the start of the book, in the introductory section, on p. 6, Kinsey explains 'We have only begun to accumulate data for the highly important chapter that involves infants and very young children'. On pp. 58–9 he provides a section on 'Interviewing young children', which refers to interviews with children from ages 12 down to 3. Although it is stated 'One of the parents has been present in all of our interviews with these younger children' (p. 58), and this assertion is repeated by a subsequent Director of the Kinsey Institute, John Bancroft, it is known that in fact this is quite untrue. Kinsey conducted all the interviews with children personally and at least a proportion of them were conducted with no other adult present (Gathorne-Hardy, 1998: 214–15). It is possible that children were also interviewed through schools and Children's Homes (as listed in the groups interviewed, pp. 14–15).

Kinsey and his team found the whole area of children's sexuality sufficiently important to state 'A later volume will cover this aspect of the study' (p. 59). Although this intended volume was never published, members of Kinsey's research team, notably Wardell Pomeroy, continued research in this area. Pomeroy later went on to write *Boys and Sex* (1968) and *Girls and Sex* (1971) (both books re-issued most recently in 1991), and *Your Child and Sex: A Guide for Parents* (1974). In a published interview, he stated his view that:

> Girls should learn to have an orgasm as part of their growing up. It isn't nearly as important whether she has intercourse when she is young, or pets when she is young. The real important ingredient is whether she has orgasm. The girls who have orgasm when they are young – as early as three or four – but anywhere along in pre-adolescence, are the ones who have the easiest time having an orgasm in marriage, or as an adult. It's a real learning experience. And it doesn't make much difference how she gets it. Those who masturbate have just as easy a time as those who have intercourse or pet.
>
> ...We compiled all the sex histories we got of women who as children had traumatic sexual experiences with adults: rape, cruel and unusual punishment, etc. We found that as adults, they were more responsive sexually than the rest of the population. (Quoted in Arnow, 1977: 5, 53)

This view has developed from the work Pomeroy undertook with the Kinsey research team and fits with the thesis presented in the previous section, that the earlier a boy enters adolescence and starts sexual activity, the better he will function. This thesis is made clear in numerous remarks throughout the book, for example in the statement that, when assessing age of onset of adolescence, one should pay attention to the time of first ejaculation 'or to evidence that the boy *would be capable of ejaculation if the proper opportunity were at hand*' (p. 189, emphasis added). Kinsey also comments that most people could be much more sexually active if they were as 'unrestrained' as those who 'openly and regularly' defy the law and social convention (p. 213).

He then develops his view that the 'primitive human animal' must prehistorically have engaged in 'unrestrained pre-adolescent sex play' – an activity which he believes also occurs in 'the other anthropoids', in 'some of the so-called primitive human societies' and 'among such of the children in our society as escape the restrictions of social conventions' (p. 222). In relation to escaping 'the restrictions of social conventions', Kinsey then adds a reference to Chapter 5.

Throughout the book, Kinsey is making a case that not only is early sexual experience good but that more children should be enabled to have this experience of 'unrestrained pre-adolescent sex play', without restrictive 'sex taboos', and that 'proper opportunity' should be 'at hand' to assist this to happen. As Pomeroy continued to insist, in 1977, the 'girls who have orgasm when they are young – as early as three or four' will be the ones who are 'more responsive sexually' later on. For Kinsey, Gebhard, Pomeroy and the rest of the research team, sex is 'the measure of all things' and overrides any other consideration. Given this view on pre-adolescent and prepubertal sexuality as benefitting from an 'escape' from 'the restrictions of social conventions', it is unsurprising that Chapter 5 is not presented as anomalous in any way. It is presented with no apology and no explanation and no special treatment is regarded as necessary in discussing data on erotic arousal and orgasm among 'younger boys', including babies.

Like all the chapters presenting data, this chapter contains charts and tables. The four tables which are most relevant are Tables 30 to 34. Table 30 (p.175) is titled *Pre-adolescent Eroticism and Orgasm* and gives samples of children from age 1 to age 15. The part of the table on 'Erotic Arousal' covers 471 children and gives data from age 4, 'based on memory of older subjects'. The part on 'Orgasm' covers 273 children from age 3 and again is 'based on memory of older subjects'. In other words, the data have been collected, as one would expect, by asking respondents to recall the first time they felt sexually aroused or first had an orgasm. However, a separate section gives data from age 1 and covers 214 children, using 'original data gathered by certain of our subjects' on 214 cases of which 'all but 14 were subsequently *observed* in orgasm' (p. 175, emphasis added).

Table 31 (p. 176) is titled *Ages of Pre-Adolescent Orgasm: Based on actual observation of 317 males*. This table includes one 2-month-old baby, two babies aged 3 months and so on. In total, this table includes data on 28 babies up to 1 year old, of whom it is claimed orgasm was observed for nine babies. There are, in addition, a further 49 children aged between 1 and 4 years old; 112 children aged between 5 and 9 years old; 115 children aged between 10 and 12 years old; and 13 children aged between 13 and 14. All the children in the table are aged under 15 years. Cumulative tabulations and percentages are carefully given to one decimal place. The corresponding text accompanying this table states that better data on 'pre-adolescent climax' has come from 'the histories of adult males who have had sexual contacts with younger boys' and who have interpreted the boys' experiences. Kinsey states:

> Unfortunately, not all of the subjects with such contacts in their histories were questioned on this point of pre-adolescent reactions; but 9 of our adult male subjects have observed such orgasm. Some of these adults are technically trained persons who have kept diaries or other records which have been put at our disposal. (*Sexual Behavior in the Human Male*, 1965: 177)

From these 'technically trained persons', Kinsey and his team obtained information on '317 pre-adolescents who were either observed in self masturbation, or who were observed in contacts with other boys or older adults' (*ibid.*). He characterizes these children as 'a somewhat select group of younger males...based on more or less uninhibited boys...many of whom had had sexual contacts with one or more adults' (*ibid.*) These boys were less 'inhibited' or 'restricted by parental controls' than typical children, and in this sample he claims, 'Orgasm has been observed in boys of every age from 5 months...Orgasm is in our records for a female babe of 4 months.' (*ibid.*)

To be clear, then, what Kinsey is here describing is not a situation where children or adults were asked to remember back to their first sexual experiences. Nor is it a situation where mothers or other carers are asked about when they noticed their child's first genital exploration or masturbation. The data in Table 31 are based on the observations of nine 'adult males who have had sexual contacts with younger boys'. Kinsey calls some of them 'technically trained persons' – this phrase has never been adequately explained by the Kinsey Institute but apparently means that they were taught to use a stopwatch. In order for this to happen, the Kinsey researchers did not have one-off interviews with these men; they corresponded with them and, when told that these men were having sexual contact with small children and babies, they supplied them with stopwatches. There is a name for such behaviour in civilized countries, but that name is not 'science'.

It is also important to note that, of these 317 children, there is little emphasis on boys who are beginning to reach an age at which they might choose voluntarily to masturbate in front of an adult man. Of this sample, only 13 children are aged over 13 years. *Seventy-seven of these children are not even 5 years old.* There is no data given on how many of these babies and young children were 'observed in self masturbation' and how many were 'observed in contacts with other boys or older adults' but it is stated that 'many' of this group of under-15-year-olds 'had had sexual contacts with *one or more* adults' (emphasis added). The only fact which is seen as 'unfortunate' here is that not all 'adult males who have had sexual contacts with younger boys' were asked enough questions about it.

The Kinsey research team was generally composed of married couples with young families: for example, the Kinseys themselves had daughters born in 1924 and 1925 and a son born in 1928. The first formal data-collection for the project started in 1938, although Kinsey had been interested in this area for years before this date, in fact from 1926, he told Gebhard (Gathorne-Hardy, 1998: 127), that is, when he himself had babies at home. It is known that Kinsey and his research team were heavily engaged in discreet multiple sexual relationships with one another and were used to keeping sexual secrets from the outside world (as documented extensively in biographies and other material). It is known that Kinsey, Pomeroy, Gebhard and Tripp – and possibly other members of the research team also – shared strong views on early sexual experience as being not only neutral but actively beneficial. It is known that they wished to gather research-data from every source available. Knowing all this, one reads the highly detailed description of the 'female babe of 4 months' and the other descriptions of orgasm in babies and young children, one looks again at the term 'technically trained persons', and questions are raised in one's mind to which there are as yet no answers available in the public realm. In this context, one also looks again at a comment on children masturbating, where Kinsey makes the point that children can be taught that, if known outside the family, such activity may cause 'social difficulties' but that it is possible to work out 'careful adjustments' in the home. Kinsey then makes the oblique comment that there are 'cases' of parents who have succeeded in accomplishing this 'delicate adjustment' between things which are acceptable in the home and 'things that other people outside the home "just don't understand"' (p. 506). If Kinsey is here referring to simply allowing young children the privacy to explore their own bodies from time to time, that would be both an understandable and a commendable position for a scientist and a parent to hold. However, given the data presented in Chapter 5 and elsewhere on situations in which Kinsey tells us of babies under a year old who have 'learned the advantage of specific manipulation, sometimes as a result of being so manipulated by older persons'; and where, for children, 'an older person provides the more specific sort of manipulation which is usual among adults' (1965: 501), it would be irresponsibly naive to assume, without further consideration, that this is what Kinsey is saying, and in this context the comment by Kinsey on children learning to keep quiet takes on a more sinister tone.

We should remember also that Kinsey found masturbation personally fascinating. He had himself filmed masturbating, wanted the photographers Clarence Tripp and William Dellenback to film two thousand sequences of men masturbating to orgasm, and was known to raise the topic of masturbation with his students in lectures and on camping trips, whether such a topic was welcomed or not. His biographers report also that masturbation had occupied his thinking very much as a boy. Kinsey writes feelingly of boys living in 'continual mental conflict' over masturbation and the damage such conflict causes psychologically (p. 514). One can understand a man, filled with 'furious rage' at his own repressed and inhibited sexual upbringing, reacting against it by an excessive lifelong obsession with masturbation, sex, penises, orgasms, 'sexual outlets' and everything which is 'taboo' and forbidden. One can also imagine such a man, in his zeal to undo what he considered harmful repression, impelled by an obsession with collecting statistical data and a compulsive need to watch sexual activity (Gathorne-Hardy, 1998: 206), deciding that it would be a good idea to give matters a helping hand, or to watch others doing so.

Considering the attitudes expressed so consistently by this group, one has to ask, in fact, why this group of men would *not* have sexually abused children, if they really believed the statements which they averred so frequently. To their minds, an adult sexually touching a young child would not have been regarded as sexually abusive and would, on the internal evidence from their publications, have been seen as a non-exploitative, mutually pleasurable and kind thing to do – teaching a child, even a baby, how to take greater pleasure in their own body. If they seriously believed, as they claimed, that early sexual experience led to sexual benefit in later life, what would have stopped them? If, rather, they believed that small children should be protected from adult sexual contact, that information is never conveyed in any form.

Gathorne-Hardy touches on this issue several times in his detailed and thorough biography. On p. 175 he claims that, 'to begin with [Kinsey] would tell men who had or wanted to have sex with children ... to stick to adults'. This claim is referenced (Chapter 9, reference note 31, p. 476) to a 'Frank Banta' (possibly a pseudonym for 'honest chat'?) from interviews conducted by the BBC in 1995: in other words, only to an obscure and possibly pseudonymous individual, not to any published source. It seems a very weak source for such an important assertion.

Again, Gathorne-Hardy asserts, 'It should go without saying, but should nevertheless perhaps be said, that Kinsey was fiercely against any use of force or compulsion in sex.' (1998: 223). Gathorne-Hardy is a careful biographer who meticulously references his assertions. It is noticeable that this assertion, however, is un-referenced and at no point anywhere in this whole biography does he quote any actual statement from Kinsey himself on force or compulsion. He repeats this view on pp. 376–7, stating: 'However obvious, I should perhaps stress again that Kinsey was implacably opposed to any sort of violence, coercion, or pressure of any sort in sexual matters.' This time, he adds a foot-note in support: a reference to the *Female* volume, pp. 17 –18 and 'still more specifically to lectures and conversation' attributed to Gebhard (Chapter 19, reference note 26, p. 489). Pages 17 and 18 of the *Female* volume contain no condemnation of force at all, rather a diatribe on 'Social Control of Sexual Behavior' which begins by stating:

> Most societies have recognized the necessity of protecting their mem-bers from those who impose sexual relationships on others by the use of force, and our own culture extends the same sort of restriction to those who use such intimidation as an adult may exercise over a child, or such undue influence as a social superior may exercise over an underling. In its encouragement of marriage society tries to provide a socially acceptable source of sexual outlet, and it considers that sexual activities which interfere with marriages and homes, and sexual activities which lead to the begetting of children outside of marriage, are socially undesirable. The social organization also tries to control persons who make nuisances of themselves, as the exhibi-tionist and voyeur may do, by departing from the generally approved custom. In addition our culture considers that social interests are involved when an individual departs from the Judeo-Christian sex codes by engaging in such sexual activities as masturbation, mouth-genital contacts, homosexual contacts, animal contacts, and other types of behavior which do not satisfy the procreative function of sex. (*Sexual Behavior in the Human Female*, 1953: 17)

Kinsey's argument in this section then continues by claiming that 'sex offenses' are common and 'sex offenders' are ordinary people. This hardly warrants the description of being 'fiercely against' or 'implacably opposed to any sort of violence'! This therefore seems to be the strongest statement Gathorne-Hardy was able to find in Kinsey's *oeuvre* on the harmfulness of coercion. The implication is that Gathorne-Hardy looked hard at all the published material, all the thousands of papers and letters Kinsey wrote, the lectures he gave, and the interviews and all he can find is an unpublished reference to a 'Frank Banta', this quotation from the *Female* volume, and unquoted, footnoted support from Gebhard. It seems clear therefore that Gathorne-Hardy was actually unable to find *any* published quotation from Kinsey or his research team to back up this view that Kinsey disapproved of force in sex.

And of course it is unlikely that, even if Kinsey did disapprove of 'force or compulsion', he would have regarded adult sexual contact with children or babies as in any way comprising 'force or compulsion' (see the comments by Tripp in the following section). In addition, to wish for protection against sexual contact for one's own children, while publicly recommending the opposite for children in general, would have been a strangely inconsistent position to adopt. Kinsey was a noted public lecturer as well as a writer; he had many opportunities throughout his long and influential career to make a public statement about the harmfulness of adult sexual contact with children. He did not. On the other hand, he made repeated explicit comments about the harmlessness and positive value of such behaviour.

One fact which we do know about the home-life of the Kinseys is that Mrs Kinsey, who was not a member of the research team but was closely involved throughout, spent a number of years (possibly as many as 12 years, from 1944 right up to 1956) meticulously typing out the voluminous diaries of one apparently 'technically trained person', known variously as Kenneth Braun or 'Mr Green'. Gathorne-Hardy says that in February 1956 she had 'finally finished typing Braun's Masterwork and her typescript was bound in board and cloth' (1998: 433). These diaries contained horrifically disturbing material on the sexual abuse of literally thousands of individuals, including the rape of small children. Typing away, day after day for more than a decade, perhaps this material eventually came to seem quite normal to Mrs Kinsey.

After detailed descriptions of orgasm 'in an infant or other young male', the text from Chapter 5 of *The Human Male* continues with a report on five cases of 'young pre-adolescents' on whom observations are said to have continued 'over periods of months or years, until the individuals were old enough to make it certain that true orgasm was involved'. Kinsey asserts that, for a minority of these children, they 'fail to reach climax even under prolonged and varied and repeated stimulation' – a failure which he attributes to 'psychologic blockage' rather than 'physiologic incapacity' (pp. 177–8). Again, this tells us very clearly that these are not casual observations of everyday life in which little Johnny plays with his 'willy' or his 'pee-pee' while Daddy benignly watches. Some children had a 'psychologic blockage', they didn't *want* someone using 'prolonged and varied and repeated stimulation' to try and make them orgasm just to prove a point.

In case of any lingering doubt about what exactly is being discussed, the chapter in *The Human Male* continues with Table 32, on p.178, titled *Speed of Pre-adolescent Orgasm*, which details 'Duration of stimulation before climax; observations timed with second hand or stop watch. Ages range from five months of age to adolescence.' In this table, there are 188 'cases' but we are not told how many children are of which ages, although we are told in the text that there 'are two-year olds who come to climax in less than 10 seconds, and there are two-year olds who may take 10 or 20 minutes, or more.' (pp. 178–9). The orgasms are carefully timed to two decimal places, with the mean time to climax, for example, put at 3.02 minutes. A person or persons unknown has timed 188 children from as young as 5 months with a stopwatch over periods ranging from up to ten seconds to over ten minutes.

A key text in *Sexual Behavior in the Human Male* is the comment given on Table 32, which remarks that this is an unusual group of children because, in the population as a whole, a much smaller percentage would 'experience orgasm at any early age' because few babies or children 'have the opportunity' or ' find themselves in circumstances that test their capacities' but, in Kinsey's view, 'half or more' of all babies and 'younger boys' in an 'uninhibited society' would be capable of orgasm 'by the time they were three or four years of age' (p. 178). This is presumably where Pomeroy, his research associate, also gained his view (Arnow, 1977: 5, 53) that girls should have orgasms 'when they are young – as early as three or four'. As Pomeroy complacently remarked, it 'doesn't make much difference' how she had this experience, whether as 'traumatic sexual experiences with adults: rape, cruel and unusual punishment, etc.'.

If any further evidence was required that we are not discussing children's own freely chosen genital exploration and masturbation here, this is it. These children are quite clearly and deliberately having their 'capacities' tested. The 'inhibition' referred to in this quotation is that inhibition which restrains us from sexually touching babies and toddlers. So what exactly is this 'capacity' which is being tested? It is sexual stimulation to 'orgasm', described graphically by Kinsey as including 'convulsive action, often with violent arm and leg movements, sometimes with weeping... There are observations of 16 males *of up to 11 months of age*, with such typical orgasm reached in 7 cases.' (p. 177, emphasis added).

Table 33 (p. 179) is titled *Multiple Orgasm in Pre-adolescent Males: Based on a small and select group of boys. Not typical of the experience, but suggestive of the capacities of pre-adolescent boys in general.* This table reports on 182 'cases' and again ages are not given. The focus of the table, and this part of the chapter, is a fascination with orgasm, trying to find out how quickly small children can be made to orgasm and how many orgasms they can be stimulated to have in any period of time. There is an obsessional detail shown here. The 'Mean No. of Orgasms' are given as 3.72, the median as 2.62, with a 'Mean Time Lapse' of 6.28 minutes and median time-lapse 2.25 minutes. Any sense of reality has been lost here. Babies, at least one as young as 5 months old (p. 179), toddlers and children are being recorded as having orgasms on a minute-by-minute basis, for thirty minutes or more, while some 'observer' timed the whole procedure with a stopwatch.

The final table in *Sexual Behavior in the Human Male* which is focused solely on pre-adolescent sexual experience is Table 34, titled *Examples of Multiple Orgasm in Pre-adolescent Males: Some instances of higher frequencies.* This table shows children aged from 5 months up to 14 years old. Although there are data given on 24 children, it is not clear if, for example, the two 11-month-old babies are the same baby. If the repeated age indicates the same child, then the sample-size would be a minimum of 13 children involved. This table therefore gives data on somewhere between 13 and 24 babies and children. The time-periods given for 'multiple orgasm' range from 70 seconds to 24 hours. The text comments, 'The maximum observed was 26 climaces in 24 hours, and the report indicates that still more might have been possible in the same period of time.' (p. 180).

Kinsey and his colleagues are pleased with their data. Kinsey quotes previous researchers as wishing for information on 'specific sexual experience in infancy and early childhood' and boasts that his work has now addressed this and complied with the 'scientifically fair demand for records from trained observers' (p. 181). By the time of the publication of *Sexual Behavior in the Human Female*, in 1953, Kinsey and his colleagues had continued collecting data, and continued to espouse the same views. On p. 15 of the *Female* volume, Kinsey states that, in addition to studying adults, 'we have engaged in a more detailed study of younger children and particularly of children between two and five years of age'. He goes on:

Because early training may be so significant, most parents would like to have information on the most effective methods of introducing the child to the realities of sex. Most parents would like to know more about the significance of pre-adolescent sex play, about the sexual activities in which children actually engage, about the possibilities of their children becoming sexually involved with adults, and what effect such involvements may have upon a child's subsequent sexual adjustments. Most parents would like to know whether the sexual responses of a child are similar, physiologically, to those of an adult.... In this study, we have had the excellent cooperation of a great many parents because they are concerned with the training of their children, and because they realize how few data there are on which to establish a sound program of sex education. (*Sexual Behavior in the Human Female*, 1953: 15–16)

One wonders if it is really the case that 'most parents' would like to know about 'the possibilities of their children becoming sexually involved with adults, and what effect such involvements may have upon a child's subsequent sexual adjustments' – this is rather a bizarre assertion. Why would a parent want to know that? In the *Female* volume, Chapter 4 deals with 'Pre-adolescent Sexual Development'. Again, this material deals with adult sexual contact with children. It starts with newborns and states, 'some human infants, both female and male, are capable of being stimulated by and responding to tactile stimulation in a way which is sexual in the strictest sense of term [previously defined as comprising orgasm].... direct observations made by a number of qualified observers, indicate that some children are quite capable of responding in a way which may show all of the essential physiologic changes which characterize the sexual responses of an adult' (p. 102). If this is not sufficiently clear, he then states, 'What seem to be sexual responses have been observed on infants immediately at birth' (p. 103). He is not writing about baby boys with spontaneous erections here. He appears to mean newborn girls being masturbated to orgasm, as he has previously defined, on p. 101, 'a sexual response in any mammal involves...a build-up of neuromuscular tensions which may culminate at a peak...the phenomenon which we know as sexual climax or orgasm'. I would like to be incorrect here, but my reading of this text is that Kinsey is telling us that he knows of people, 'qualified observers', who have masturbated newborn babies. Kinsey also writes about little girls masturbating themselves or engaging in 'sex play' such as 'mama and papa' or 'doctor' with children their own age, which I find morally unproblematic and an entirely separate issue. However, when he writes that 'we can report 4 cases of females under one year of age coming to orgasm, and a total of 28 cases of small girls three years of age or younger reaching orgasm' (p. 105), it seems clear that these can only have been induced by adults.

Later in the same chapter, Kinsey turns to the subject of 'Pre-adolescent Contacts with Adult Males' (p. 116). Here Kinsey is keen to illustrate that such contacts do no harm. He finds that of a sample of 4,441 females, there was 'only one clear-cut case of serious injury done to the child, and a very few instances of vaginal bleeding' (p. 122). He recognizes no other form of harm which might result. In the *Female* volume, which is intended to cover all sexual behaviour and experiences of women, there is no reference to 'incest' in the list of References. There are three references to 'rape', but the first is to dreams of rape (p. 213), the second to a footnote on 'statutory rape' (p. 287) and the third to a footnote on religious attitudes to rape as 'sinful'. As with the *Male* volume, there is no information presented at all on actual rape or other sexual abuse.

The quotations given from *Sexual Behavior in the Human Male* and *Sexual Behavior in the Human Female* are available for anyone to read. There are no revised editions of either the *Male* or the *Female* volume: although these volumes were reprinted a number of times, they were never revised so there remains only one edition of each text. There is no controversy over whether or not this material is as stated. The two published texts were not the only places where Kinsey raised the issue of adult–child sexual contact. Kinsey continued this theme when he embarked on a tour of Europe in 1955, shortly before his death. During this tour he lectured at the prestigious universities of Copenhagen and Aarhus in Denmark and noted, according to his biographer Gathorne-Hardy, how Scandinavians 'have just as insane a horror' of sex between adults and children as Americans. The real danger was other adults making an issue of it, Kinsey insisted. Gathorne-Hardy (1998: 421) reports how Kinsey told his Aarhus audience he 'was amazed to find they were still having inhibitions regarding contact of homosexuality and older persons with children in spite of their great acceptance of most things sexual'. As Gathorne-Hardy notes, 'Kinsey clearly felt able to be much less circumspect abroad.' In Italy, too, we are told that Kinsey applauded the amount of sex he found and commented on 'the harmlessness, indeed mutual benefits, of adult/child sex' (Gathorne-Hardy, 1998: 424).

Thus, in their published works, far from acknowledging that they have been complicit in criminal and abusive experimentation on babies, toddlers and children, Kinsey and his team are proud of their unique data. These are the data which Pomeroy endorsed, in 1977, with his published quotation that 'Girls should learn to have an orgasm as part of their growing up...when they are young – as early as three or four.' These are the data which Gebhard, in 1979, publicly affirms as part of Kinsey's 'major findings'. Pomeroy, Gebhard, and the Kinsey Institute over the decades have had repeated opportunities to retract or apologize for these data. They have chosen not to do so.

4. Challenges, bowdlerizing, and the Kinsey Reports sixty years on

Sexual Behavior in the Human Male, first published in 1948, is now more than sixty years old. Professor Kinsey, an extraordinarily influential man in his time, has been dead for many years. The records on which his work was based remain locked up inside the Kinsey Institute. Do the views propounded in his major works, especially his two Reports on human sexuality, have any continuing validity or relevance today? Certainly some writers think so. Hugh Hefner, the founder of *Playboy*, 'regarded the *Female* report as the foundation of his "philosophy"' and supported the Kinsey Institute financially (Gathorne-Hardy, 1998: 439), thereby establishing an ongoing link between Kinsey's work and the pornography industry.

More significantly perhaps, both Kinsey's admirers and his critics agree that he was successful in influencing major legislation both in the United States and in Britain (see, for example, Reisman *et al.*, 1990; Weeks, 2007). Kinsey was adamant that the great majority of ordinary American men behaved sexually in ways which would make them liable as 'sex offenders' and thus the law needed to be changed to reflect this and to de-criminalize common behaviour. As he insisted repeatedly, men involved in illicit sexual activities comprised, in his view, 'more than 95 per cent of the total male population'. Kinsey then stretched this even further by suggesting that wanting to incarcerate sex offenders is 'a proposal that 5 per cent of the population should support the other 95 per cent in penal institutions' (*Human Male*, p. 392). Here, of course, he is conflating the total population of people (including women and children) with the total population of men, to strengthen his polemic that it is absurd to suggest that '95 per cent' of the population should be locked up. His biographer, Gathorne-Hardy, comments that it is 'possible to argue that Kinsey was decisive' in his influence in both the United States and Britain and he states that the 'American Law Institute's *Model*

Penal Code of 1955 is virtually a Kinsey document.' (Gathorne-Hardy, 1998: 449). The *Model Penal Code* itself stated:

> We deem it inappropriate for the government to attempt to control behavior that has no substantial significance except as to the morality of the actor… It must be recognized, as a practical matter, that in a heterogeneous community such as ours, different individuals and groups have widely divergent views of the seriousness of various moral derelictions. (Quotation taken from Gathorne-Hardy, 1998: 449)

The *Code* was subsequently adopted in a number of states. While its positive impact was to liberalize laws on consenting adult behaviour, such as homosexuality, it also put in place a legal framework which saw adult sexual contact with children as largely a matter of indifference, simply an expression of 'divergent views'. The *Code* based its recommendations in part on the fact that existing legislation undermined respect for the law by penalizing behaviour many people engaged in. As Kinsey remarks in the film *Kinsey* (Condon, 2004), 'Everybody's sin is nobody's sin and everybody's crime is no crime at all.' However, behaviour may be common but still profoundly harmful: domestic violence is an example of such behaviour, and so is child sexual abuse.

In October 1955, Kinsey visited Britain and acted as an advisor and expert witness for the Wolfenden Committee.

> The establishment by the government of the Wolfenden Committee in 1954 was a compromise, between the desire amongst more conservative elements to do something to control homosexuality and rid the streets of overt displays of prostitution, and a wish on the part of liberals to find more modern forms of regulation than prison or the law. Its task therefore was to navigate between the two extremes whilst trying to come up with an acceptable framework. In doing this it took expert advice, including from the already near infamous Alfred Kinsey, the American sexologist. Kinsey's matter-of-fact approach to homosexuality and his implicit moral neutrality pointed to a less punitive legislative framework. Also, for the first time openly homosexual citizens gave evidence to the committee, as did other perceived experts and a host of other interested parties. The result was not so much a compromise between conservative moralists and progressives as a bold new framework, offering the outlines of a new moral economy for the post-war world. (Weeks, 2007: online)

The Report from the Wolfenden Committee was published in 1957 and resulted in the *Sexual Offences Act 1967*, which – as with the *Model Penal Code* – de-criminalized, and ultimately legalized, adult male homosexuality. Again, it is not the impact on consenting adult behaviour which is of concern, but the general attitude, following Kinsey, that in the 'new moral economy' there is no such thing as rape (only false allegations; see both the *Male* and the *Female* volumes), there is no such thing as child sexual abuse, sex is unproblematically good and no-one is or can be harmed. As Gathorne-Hardy himself (with uncharacteristic disquiet) comments on Kinsey's view on adult sexual contact with children, Kinsey is 'very ready to believe they have *not* been harmed and will *not* be forced' (1998: 224, emphases in original).

Kinsey's influence extends also to contemporary scholarly and pop- ular works on child sexuality. As the book *Dares to Speak: Historical and Contemporary Perspectives on Boy-Love* (Geraci, 1997) makes plain, Kinsey's book is 'surely one of the most revolutionary texts on boy- hood sexuality ever written.' (p. 272), and the following chapter will provide information on other authors who have also taken seriously Kinsey's views on 'boyhood sexuality'; but what is extraordinary is that, for many people and for many years, this part of Kinsey's work seems to have been quite invisible. Until the late 1970s the data in 'Chapter 5' were accepted uncritically and without comment and it was still possible for a leading academic on sexuality to write, 'Somewhat surprisingly, his [Kinsey's] revelations about the genital capacities of children have gone virtually unnoticed.' (Robinson, 1976: 117). The biographer Gathorne- Hardy concurs, noting 'It is an interesting reflection on the changing fashion of concern that this chapter is almost the only one that was totally ignored on publication.' (1998: 222).

What changed the 'fashion of concern' was one woman. No public critique of these data appeared until 1981, when a young American aca- demic, Judith Bat-Ada (now Reisman), gave a paper on the topic at the Fifth World Congress on Sexology, in Jerusalem. Her talk was entitled *The Scientist as a Contributing Agent to Child Sexual Abuse: a Preliminary Consideration of Possible Ethics Violations*. Reisman was the first person to analyse Kinsey's work from the perspective of the children rather than the adults, and the first person to recognize publicly that what is being described is rape. None of the many dozens of other reviewers or commentators had noticed (or been concerned by) the description of small children being systematically 'manipulated' and timed with stopwatches, with the apparent permission, or indifference, of those around them. Reisman's talk went down like a lead balloon among the assembled sexologists. Nothing daunted, she has continued to research and publish (Reisman *et al.*, 1990; Reisman, 1998, 2010).

In 1994, an independent documentary film, *The Children of Table 34*, was released by the Family Research Council in the United States and a year later there was a congressional call for a public investigation into Kinsey's research. This came to nothing. In 1998 – fifty years after the first publication of *Sexual Behavior in the Human Male* – a British television channel broadcast *Secret Histories: Kinsey's Paedophiles*, a three-part documentary directed and produced by Tim Tate. This documentary unearthed new details of how the data for Chapter 5 had been obtained and again called for the Kinsey Institute to open its files for public scrutiny. The documentary included key figures in the debate: Paul Gebhard, Clarence Tripp and Vincent Nowlis, all close colleagues of Kinsey's; the then Director of the Kinsey Institute, John Bancroft; his nemesis, Judith Reisman; both Kinsey's major biographers, James Jones and Jonathan Gathorne-Hardy; and a woman, Esther White, who claims that her sexual abuse as a child may have provided some of the data reproduced in Kinsey's work.

The documentary centres on a man known as 'Mr Green', 'Rex King' or Kenneth S. Braun. This is the man whose handwritten diaries Mrs Kinsey had spent many years typing up into a leather-bound manuscript (now closely guarded within the Kinsey Institute). Braun worked as a US Government Land Examiner (a form of surveyor) in Arizona and New Mexico. Braun kept detailed records of all his sexual acts, including sexual contacts with 605 pre-adolescent males and 231 pre-adolescent females. A fictional account of the meeting between Braun and Kinsey in 1944 is shown in Condon's 2004 movie *Kinsey*, in which Kinsey tells Pomeroy excitedly 'I've waited years to meet this man!' before proceeding sternly to tell Braun off for having had sexual contact with children. The account given in Tate's documentary is more factual and more horrific. Braun was in fact part of Kinsey's circle for many years, from 1943 probably to Kinsey's death in 1956. He was a friend of Kinsey's friends Gershon Legman and Robert Dickinson, who both later collaborated with Braun in compiling a definitive monograph on 'the penis', apparently never published (Gathorne-Hardy, 1998: 211).

In Tate's documentary, Paul Gebhard recalls how Dickinson taught Braun 'how to measure things and time things'. Gebhard continues:

> He encouraged him – he knew he was going to do his ordinary behaviour anyway. Dickinson couldn't have stopped him being a paedophile but he said 'At least you ought to do something scientific

about it, so it won't be just your jollies, it'll be something worthwhile to science.' So he gave him some training by letter and correspondence. (My transcription of recorded interview from Tate, 1998)

Braun's 'jollies' included documented sexual experiments with babies, now – with Dickinson's training – carefully measured, timed and recorded in copious diaries. Braun did not work alone: Gathorne-Hardy mentions in passing that there was 'a Dr Werner, Braun's companion in many sexual jaunts' (1998: 345). Again, like Gebhard, Gathorne-Hardy – having read Braun's diaries in the Kinsey Institute – is fully aware as he writes this that Braun's sexual 'jaunts' included the rape of small children.

By the time Kinsey met Braun face-to-face in 1944, the abuse had been continuing for over twenty years and, according to notes at the Kinsey Institute, the abuse continued for another ten years, all the time when Kinsey was collecting data. Gathorne-Hardy notes, but does not make the connection, that Kinsey was in touch with Braun from late 1943 and that 'the most interesting development in 1944 was Kinsey's increasing concentration on children. . . . By 1944 he had realized how extraordinarily early – three, four or five years old – sexual attitudes and responses. . . start to develop. He decided they must investigate little children *directly*' (1998: 214, emphasis in original). Kinsey and Braun corresponded for at least three years, and Kinsey sent Braun the proofs of Chapter 5 to check prior to publication. The result, according to Gebhard, was that Braun 'contributed a fair amount to medicine's knowledge of sexuality in children'. As Gebhard summed up, 'It was illegal and we knew it was illegal but it was very important for people to study childhood sexuality.' (My transcription of recorded interview from Tate, 1998.)

Kinsey's close colleague Clarence Tripp also saw nothing wrong in using a predatory paedophile to collect information on 'childhood sexuality' and appeared baffled at any notion of harm:

Here was this man with hundreds of contacts – there was never a charge against him, never arrested for anything. The children thought he was wonderful. The mothers thought he was wonderful. There are two instances in which – a young girl – didn't complain – they agreed to the sexual contact – but they found it very painful and yelled out. This was because they were very young and had small genitalia and 'Green' was a grown man with enormous genitalia, and there was a fit problem.

...

Pedophilia is an almost non-existent kind of crime. And the thing that he [Kinsey] hated most about it is that people used words like 'child molestation'. 'Child molestation'! What is that? No-one knows. Abuse of children? Are they talking about boxing them against the ear or hitting them with a stove-pipe? Or are they talking about tickling them? Are you talking about fondling? Are you going to put fondling and death attacks in the same group? As Kinsey said, by this kind of paranoia, you do the child more damage for life than all the pedophiles in the world would do. (My transcription of recorded interview from Tate, 1998)

One point Tripp does not mention in his eulogy is that Braun, as a qualified professional Government official, presumably had quite a level of authority over the rural families he visited. I have never been to the United States and am ignorant of much of American history but I do recall a Great Depression happening in the 1930s and 1940s when Braun was working in the impoverished rural farming states of Arizona and New Mexico. To whom might these vulnerable children and their families have complained, after an influential State official had abused them? More details on these issues are doubtless available in Braun's diaries but these are safely tucked away in the Kinsey Institute and 'confidentiality' prevents their ever being released. Given the Institute's use of 'confidentiality' as their reason not to provide documents, it is morbidly humorous to find the following footnote in Gathorne-Hardy's biography:

These forty-odd pages [written by Kinsey] are written on the back of old sex histories.... [I found] something endearing in the way that, despite their paranoia about confidentiality, the [pages] were partly written on a long list of histories identified by name against their history numbers. On another sheet backing something else I found Kinsey's own history number. It is safe with me. (Gathorne-Hardy, 1998: 431n)

Other commentators might find such behaviour unethical at the very least, rather than 'endearing' but nothing fazes Gathorne-Hardy.

So far, therefore, there is written and spoken evidence that, of the key members of Kinsey's research team, Kinsey, Gebhard, Pomeroy and Tripp not only expressed no strong statements on harm to children from adult sexual contact but, to the contrary, expressed impatience at any notion of harm. Of Kinsey's research team, only Vincent Nowlis is on record as expressing qualified disapproval of the data in Chapter 5.

Braun was not the only paedophile involved in supplying data. Gathorne-Hardy reports, 'The earlier the orgasm the better leads logically to infant orgasm. Kinsey had similar accounts for little girls as for little boys (but not from Braun as far as I can gather)' (1998: 244). Gebhard mentions obtaining data from 'a pedophile organisation in this country', which may have been the Rene Guyon Society, and Gebhard also mentions 'a man in Germany' with whom Kinsey 'carried on quite a correspondence and we were learning some interesting things about pedophilia in Germany'. This man was Dr Fritz von Balluseck, a Nazi who was involved in the occupation of Poland during the war and with whom Kinsey apparently carried on a correspondence from 1936 to 1956, according to German newspaper accounts (Reisman *et al.*,1990). The correspondence came to light when von Balluseck was convicted of thirty counts of child sex abuse in 1957, shortly after Kinsey's death.

To date, Reisman's remains the only sustained critique of Kinsey's work. Her work, situated firmly within the intellectual compass of the American political right, is distinctly unappealing to more liberal academics. This is a pity, because Reisman raises serious allegations about the work of Kinsey's team and the Kinsey Institute which in turn require serious refutation. Instead, Reisman has been the target of contemptuous derision while the charges she raises have been ignored and trivialized (for example, in postings about her on the Wikipedia website). The voices on the political left, the voices of lesbian, gay and bisexual academics and activists, are all surprisingly quiet (or mumbled) on this question. The only reference given to her work in Gathorne-Hardy's detailed biography is an ill-tempered footnote on p. 223, where he dismisses her investigations as 'scurrilous', 'shoddy', 'ludicrous' and 'idiotic'.

Even though her allegations concern the wellbeing of children, no-one at the Kinsey Institute has troubled to discuss them in any detail, or categorically refute them, although, for example, John Bancroft, as Director of the Kinsey Institute, felt compelled to address 'particular controversies and political attacks' in a foreword to the re-issue of *Sexual Behavior in the Human Male* in 1998. Indeed, over the years, as a response to Reisman's persistent investigations, the Kinsey Institute has, reluctantly, had to issue several explanations on where they got their 'child sexuality' data from. It is noticeable that their explanations vary, and they have never issued any evidence in support.

Kinsey's original explanation, as noted earlier, was that the information was taken from '9 of our adult male subjects', some of whom were 'technically trained persons' who kept diaries or other records (*Human Male*, p. 177). Gebhard, then Director of the Kinsey Institute, wrote a refreshingly honest letter to Reisman in 1981, failing to mention any 'technical training' of persons but revealing for the first time that sexually explicit photographs and film of children were apparently taken. His letter states, in part:

> Since sexual experimentation with human infants and children is illegal, we have had to depend upon other sources of data. Some of these were parents, mostly college educated, who observed their children and kept notes for us. A few were nursery school owners or teachers. Others were homosexual males interested in older, but still prepubertal, children. One was a man who had numerous sexual contacts with male and female infants and children and, being of a scientific bent, kept detailed records of each encounter. Some of these sources have added to their written or verbal reports photographs and, in a few instances, cinema. We have never attempted any follow-up studies because it was either impossible or too expensive. The techniques involved were self-masturbation by the child, child-child sex play, and adult-child contacts – chiefly manual or oral.
> (in Reisman *et al.*, 1990: 223)

In 1998, the then-Director, John Bancroft, had forgotten about the photographs and cinema and even the manual and oral techniques. He recalled only that there was one paedophile, Kenneth Braun, who was responsible, conveniently, for absolutely everything. He 'found that, without any doubt, all of the information...came from...one man.' (Bancroft, 1998: page k). More recently, Gebhard who, after all, was there all the time the data was being collected and who should therefore know authoritatively, has decided that actually the data came from interviews, mainly with paedophiles in prison:

> In these more recent attacks, in the last ten years or so, they've been outright accusations that first of all, we did experiments with children...accused us of terrible acts, which of course did not occur.

We did not experiment with children. Kinsey interviewed some children, but it was always in the presence of the parents. He was the only one that interviewed them, the rest of us didn't have the patience required. And so that accusation is without any foundation. Now they're saying, you hired people to do it. We never hired anyone to do it. We got our data from pedophiles, most of whom were in jail, especially in California, where they have a sexual psychopath statute, there were a fair number of pedophiles, and we interviewed them about their activity and the response of the children, according to what they said, you know. We took it with a grain of salt. (Paul Gebhard in interview, Wattenburg, 2000: online)

It therefore seems clear that the Kinsey Institute has colluded with those responsible for the data in falsifying information about how the data were collected. It cannot have been by 'one man' nor can it have been from prison-interviews. When Gebhard carefully chooses the words 'experiments' and 'hiring', I am reminded of President Clinton's statement that he did not have 'sex with that woman', and also of Kinsey's ruse, all those years ago, when he hoodwinked faculty at Indiana University by claiming that he was only filming 'animal' sexual behaviour when what he meant was the human animal. Gathorne-Hardy also gives the example of Kinsey using the word 'conference', which 'remained a euphemism for sex history, and sometimes more, for many years' (1998: 127n). Kinsey set a precedent for secrecy and deception. As he himself said, there is a 'delicate adjustment between things that are acceptable in the home and things that other people outside the home "just don't understand' " (*Sexual Behavior in the Human Male*, 1965: 506).

The Kinsey Institute has loudly claimed that, if it were ever asked to disclose its records, it would prefer to destroy them first. The Institute seems to have retained into the twenty-first century the same attitude to adult sexual contact with children which Kinsey promulgated in the 1940s. The discourse on child protection seems to have entirely passed it by.

5. Conclusion

The aim of this chapter has been to demonstrate beyond doubt what Reisman had the intellectual courage to first point out, back in 1981, that the most important and influential work on human sexuality in the twentieth century was based on the rape of children. This is a startling and profoundly shocking assertion to make, which is why an entire chapter has been devoted to carefully documenting the evidence for this statement. Kinsey's work, likened to the H-Bomb when it was published and the source of innumerable citations, references, comments and even popular songs, jokes and cartoon strips, has formed the bedrock of all subsequent academic studies on human sexuality: it would be almost impossible to find an English-language book on human sexuality published since the 1950s which did not mention Kinsey. No other academic in the field of sexology (and precious few academics in any field) have been featured on the front cover of *Time* magazine or have sold so many copies of an academic textbook. As will be seen in the following chapter, Kinsey's work has been continued and developed by other researchers and writers, and his views on children's sexual nature from birth have been taken up with gusto in certain quarters. As well as sexological studies, Kinsey's work influenced legislation, the gay rights movement and the field of sex education. It is possible therefore to state without equivocation that Kinsey's work has been the most important and influential work on human sexuality in the twentieth century. Kinsey's two reports on human sexuality have deeply influenced science, the media, the law and public opinion.

It is also possible to show, from the evidence provided in this chapter, that his work was based on the rape of children. Kinsey denied, in both the *Male* and *Female* volumes, the reality of even the concept of rape (the only references are to false allegations, dreams and religious proscriptions) and, as Clarence Tripp makes plain, he believed paedophilia was 'an almost non-existent kind of crime' in which he claimed he had found *one* example in his sample of 4,441 females. The central thesis of his work, as I understand it, is that the only 'abnormal' sex is no sex; that the 'human animal' needs orgasms; and that the earlier boys and girls have orgasms, the better for them throughout their life. He based his two Reports on human sexuality on these assertions and he backed up his claims with the documentation of copious data. He regarded Chapter 5 in *Sexual Behavior in the Human Male*, on 'Early Sexual Growth and Activity', as central to his argument and referred frequently to the data in it throughout the rest of his work. The data for his assertions were obtained to some small extent by adult recall during the taking of sex histories. However, substantial parts of the data were obtained from the records and observations (apparently, according to Gebhard, photographed and filmed) of adults 'manipulating' children, aged from birth to adolescence. Under both national and international legislation, this is (and was at the time) child sexual abuse. Where it involves penetration, as it clearly did in some cases, it is (and was at the time) rape.

The work for which Kinsey is rightly valued, on the recognition and tolerance of masturbation and consensual adult sexuality, emerges from this central thesis and his work cannot be addressed without recognition of this central thesis. Far from an 'implicit moral neutrality', as Weeks (2007) describes it, Kinsey's moral position is abundantly clear, and his biographers, particularly Gathorne-Hardy, are equally clear: there is no such thing as rape, and there is no such thing as child sexual abuse; the worst one can say about adult sexual contact with children is that there is 'a fit problem', as Tripp phrased it.

One might say that a difficulty with Kinsey's work, particularly in the American context, is that so much is wrapped up together and this accounts for the hostility to which Reisman has been subjected. Kinsey's point on sexual variation and the fact that one person may experience a very much stronger and more continuous sex drive than another person is a plea for understanding and tolerance which we can all share. Similarly, a view that young people should not be taught to hate and fear their sex-drive but to be accepting of the urge to masturbate and to develop their sex-life as they grow into adulthood is a positive interpretation of Kinsey's data. The difficulty arises from the apparent inability to draw together the discourses of sexual liberation and of child protection, producing cognitive dissonance. One result is the inability to see that someone respected as a scientist is endorsing adult sexual contact with children, leading to the absurd bowdlerization indulged in by Kinsey's biographers and by the film director Bill Condon. In such a view, Kinsey can only be either an admirable scientist who perhaps had a few forgivable peccadilloes, or he has to be a sinister, conspiratorial monster orchestrating evil experiments. The individual, reading Kinsey (or, more typically, reading *about* Kinsey at second- or third-hand) feels that they either have to reject all that he did as evil or, if they support some of what he did (for example, his role in championing alternative sexualities), that they need to rush to his defence and protect him loyally against 'scurrilous' or 'idiotic' claims.

In these actions we are reproducing on a grand scale the dramas played out in microcosm every time an allegation of child abuse is made. Even when provided with abundantly clear evidence of the attitudes of Kinsey's research team to child sexual abuse, many people will still claim to see nothing wrong. The sanitized and bowdlerized version of Kinsey's life and work portrayed in Bill Condon's biopic *Kinsey* (2004), with Liam Neeson playing Kinsey as a sympathetic hero, makes us feel comfortable, even though the more reassuring scenes (in which Kinsey, Pomeroy and Mrs Kinsey are all shown as appalled by Braun's contacts with children) were deleted from the main movie presumably because they are too fanciful even for Condon. The reactions to Reisman's critique, and to Tate's and Condon's highly divergent film versions of Kinsey, provide evidence of how, even when we know child sexual abuse has occurred, we reject that knowledge because we cannot psychologically bear to associate it with anyone we admire.

The following chapter continues to explore Kinsey's impact on views of children's sexuality and its links to how we make sense of paedophiles in society today.

5
Studies on Adult Sexual Contact with Children

Introduction

The previous chapter concentrated on the work of one author, Alfred Kinsey, and his view of 'children's sexuality', a view based not on children's experiences of their sexuality but on adults' experiences of their sexual interactions with children, using the one criterion which Kinsey found important and to which everything else became subservient: the orgasm. Kinsey wished to argue that children have a sexuality which is not harmed by being used for adult gratification, and thus he saw adults 'manipulating' children to orgasm as synonymous with children's own authentic and autonomous sexuality. His views on childhood sexuality have continued to shape understandings of paedophilia and child sexual abuse up to the present day. In particular, Kinsey articulated a view of sex in which the only 'abnormal' sex is no sex and therefore, by extension, paedophilia does not exist as a pathology or even as a separate concept. Children – like animals, adults or wet dreams – are simply another 'sexual outlet' which may be used for orgasm. Kinsey also argued persuasively that 'sex offenders' do not exist and so should not be criminalized. Neither of his two encyclopaedic books on human sexuality deals with the reality of rape and nowhere is the concept of non-consensual sex addressed. According to Kinsey, therefore, it would be absurd to prosecute anyone for such an offence as 'paedophilia' or 'child sexual abuse', and indeed, his work has been used to argue for leniency and, more fundamentally, to revise legislation to make it less vigorous in prosecuting sexual offences. The only reference Kinsey makes to 'child sexual abuse' is to the situation of elderly men wrongly accused by hysterical females (*Male*, pp. 237–8). Relying on Kinsey as a scientific resource on which to base legal and public opinion bolsters the 'sexual liberation' discourse

126

discussed in this volume (Chapter 3) while cutting away any support for a 'child protection' discourse, since from Kinsey's perspective there is nothing harmful from which children, however young or vulnerable, would need to be protected.

When I first began researching the issue of child protection and child sexual abuse, I naively assumed that 'everyone' agreed that adult sexual contact with children harms those children. I was astonished to discover how wrong I was. As with the rhetoric of heated condemnation of paedophilia compared to the reality of how those who sexually offend against children may be treated (see earlier chapters), there seems to be a similar dissonance in the rhetoric of 'child protection' compared to the reality of how people actually behave when a child is at risk of potential or actual sexual abuse. Indeed, the question of harm to children in relation to adult sexual contact remains a topic of lively debate and one of the most vexed areas of this entire subject and it is therefore to this topic that this chapter turns.

This chapter contains four sections. Section 1 presents a brief overview of the question of 'age of consent' as a basis for understanding harm to children from adult sexual activity and follows this with an introduction to a study (well-known and often-referenced in the literature) by a Dutch psychologist, Theo Sandfort, who reported on interviews with a sample of boys on their sexual contacts with men. Section 2 goes into some detail to examine the Sandfort study and Section 3 then widens the discussion to include a selection of other prominent academic texts on paedophilia and adult sexual contact with children.

1. The Sandfort study and 'age of consent'

Although, as suggested above, lip-service is paid to the idea that child sexual abuse is wrong, it is surprising how quickly consensus collapses when the question of age of consent comes up, and this issue will therefore be addressed in this section. For many people, the question of the harm of adult sexual contact with children is related directly to the age of the child, or the disparity between ages, and there is little consensus, for example, on the harm caused by mutual sexual experimentation between 14-year-olds, or the risks from a 15-year-old having sex with an adult a few years older, or the pathology of an adult being sexually attracted to young people under the age of 16 (or 18 in the United States). Indeed, some adult men seem to see it as unproblematically normal and acceptable to be sexually attracted to 'nubile' teenage 'schoolgirls' of 'sweet sixteen' or under. Well-known examples include

Edgar Allen Poe who, in 1836, married his cousin Virginia Clemm when he was 27 and she was 13 (although a sworn affidavit given at the wedding stated that she was 21); John Ruskin, who fell in love with the 10-year-old Rose la Touche when he was in his 40s; Charlie Chaplin who, at 29, married 17-year-old Mildred Harris, at 35 married 16-year-old Lita Grey, and at 54 married 17-year-old Oona O'Neill; Jerry Lee Lewis who, at 22, married his 13-year-old cousin Myra Gale Brown, in 1957; and Elvis Presley who, in 1959, aged 24, started a romance with his future wife, Priscilla Beaulieu, when she was 14.

The legal age of consent varies across the world but an overview of the global age of consent laws shows that most countries cluster around 16 years old as the average age at which people may legally consent to begin heterosexual sex (homosexual sex tends to have separate legislation and remains illegal in some countries). In order to understand a little more about the confused and shifting definitions of 'age of consent', it is helpful to look at the legal history of this concept in one particular country, for example in England. In England, the legal age of consent was first introduced in 1275 and set at 12 years. By 1576 it was assumed that a girl could consent to sex from the age of 11. In 1875, in the *Offences Against the Person Act*, the age of consent was raised to 13 years. In 1885, the age of consent was raised again, to 16, but sex with a girl aged 13 to 16 was legal provided the man was aged under 24. The *Sexual Offences Act 1956* made sex with a girl aged under 16 punishable by up to two years' imprisonment and sex with a girl aged under 13 punishable by a maximum sentence of life imprisonment, with the age of the adult perpetrator largely irrelevant. Following the Wolfenden Report, the *Sexual Offences Act 1967* set an age of consent of 21 for male homosexual acts, with legislation in Scotland following suit in 1980, and in Northern Ireland in 1982. In 1994 new legislation in England reduced the age of consent for homosexual acts to 18 and in 2000 this was lowered again, to 17 in Northern Ireland and to 16 in England, Scotland and Wales, bringing it largely into line with the age of consent for heterosexual acts. The changes in legislation, from 1275 to the present day, have come about on each occasion because of changes in how sex is conceptualized (as property-right, as fornication, as sodomy and so forth) and how children are conceptualized (as property, as corruptible, as vulnerable and so forth).

Today, in contemporary England, there is no concept of legal consensual sex below the age of 16 years and, since the *Sexual Offences Act 2003*, all sexual acts – not just penetrative sex – are now a criminal offence if at least one of the people involved, male or female, is under the age of 16. The *Sexual Offences Act 1956* still applies, although the Home Office has stated that 'the law is not intended to prosecute mutually agreed teenage sexual activity between two young people of a similar age, unless it involves abuse or exploitation'. A more recent amendment to the Act involves the 'abuse of trust provision', designed to protect those aged 16 and 17 who, even though they are over the age of consent, are potentially vulnerable to abuse from people in authority or positions of trust, such as teachers, carers, prison officers, youth counsellors or sports coaches. Non-consensual sex remains technically illegal (but frequently unreported and unprosecuted) at any age.

The legal age of consent, while dependent on social attitudes to young people's sexual activity, also relates to the biological factor of the physical onset of puberty and to the sociological factor of the age at which a significant proportion of young people first engage in sexual acts with others. Over the last 150 years, the age of onset of puberty in the UK has dropped by approximately four years, from an average 16.5 years for girls and 17.5 for boys in 1840, to 11.9 and 13.1 years respectively in the 1990s. At the same time, the average age of first sexual experience in the UK is now 14 years for girls and 13 for boys, with almost 35 per cent of girls and more than 55 per cent of boys having had some form of 'sexual experience' short of intercourse before they reach the age of 16 (Wellings *et al.*, 1994). At the same time, a 1999 NOP [National Opinion Poll] opinion survey on the age of consent suggested that the majority of young people do not want the age of consent to be lowered or removed (Brook, undated, online). This legal marker still provides some form of protection from unwanted sexual attention. It indicates the distinction recognized by society between those who are physically and psychologically ready to experience sexual intimacy with another person, and those who do not yet have the required maturity.

However, as can be seen from this brief overview, the age at which one person can legally give their consent to sexual acts with another person is both historically and geographically varied. While the legal age of consent bears a relationship to the onset of physical sexual maturity (puberty) and thus, arguably, to emotional and mental maturity, the relationship is by no means straightforward or necessarily logical. The variance over time, country, regions or states within countries, and context (whether the sexual act is with a peer or someone older, younger or in a position of authority; heterosexual or homosexual; within marriage or not) all adds to the confusion. This confusion certainly works to the advantage of those who view adult–child sexual contact generally as non-harmful, since it is easy to point to, and disparage, the seemingly arbitrary and illogical bases of legal ages of consent, thus throwing doubt on the whole question of legal 'consent' itself and hence, in turn, any division between people who are 'old enough' and 'not old enough' to have sex. This has led to calls, for example by the well-known British gay rights activist Peter Tatchell, for a reduction in the age of consent to 14 (Tatchell, 2002). A more thoughtful response, and one which acknowledges the agency of young people while also recognizing the existence of exploitation and coercion, particularly by adults against both girls and boys, is that of Matthew Waites (2005) who discusses the current UK legislation and alternative proposals on the age of consent and comments that they:

> ... [focus] excessively on what is legally defined as consensual, rather than recognising that the law has a limited but legitimate role in constituting social norms of behaviour, and a legitimate role in protecting children collectively as a vulnerable group by facilitating state intervention in their lives where necessary. [The proposal to abolish 'child sexual offences committed by children or young persons'] tends not to recognise the existence of consensual but abusive or excessively risky behaviour among young people ... [we should] draw a distinction between what is recognised as consent in law and what we believe is a desirable standard of consent. (Waites, 2005: 238)

Waites' suggestion is for an amendment to the UK law which would introduce a two-year age-span provision applying until the age of 16, as is already current in some other jurisdictions.

> This would mean that 14-year olds could legally have sex with those aged 14–16; 15-year olds with those aged 14–17; and 16-year olds with anyone aged 14 or above, including all adults. The age of consent would thus remain 16 in relation to adults over 18... [This provision] should be accompanied by redoubled efforts to extend and improve the provision of sex and relationship education, sexual health promotion, and skills, resources, and support of many kinds to young people, to enable them to make decisions about whether and how to have sex more confidently and effectively.
>
> My solution implies a conception of young people's citizenship which repudiates the prevailing stark dichotomy whereby children's sexual citizenship is equated entirely with 'protection', understood as legal prohibition, and defined in stark contrast to adult sexual citizenship, defined by sexual 'autonomy' (understood as the absence of legal prohibitions). (Waites, 2005: 238–9)

Waites and other authors (for example, see Levine, 2002) are concerned that age of consent legislation may patronize children and deny them agency and decision-making skills. However, they remain aware, as Waites emphasizes, that many young people do look back and regret early sexual experiments. This confusion over our need, as a society, to protect young people from harm (whilst simultaneously not criminalizing or morally condemning them for sexual experience or denying them agency in exercising their right to bodily autonomy and integrity) leads to uncertainty over how best to revise or reform current age of consent legislation. This confusion has been used by some individuals and organizations to argue for liberalization of age of consent laws which would at the same time relax legislation against adult sexual contact with children.

One example of the use of this confusion to argue for greater liberalization and indeed the complete removal of the legal concept of an age of consent, to be replaced by a system of individual negotiated agreement, is provided by the book, *Boys on their Contacts with Men* (Sandfort, 1987), published within the context, and as part of, a Dutch campaign for greater sexual freedom. *Boys on their Contacts with Men* is written as an accessible text for the general reader and an explicit and major part of its *raison d'être* was to inform the debate in the Netherlands in the late 1970s and early 1980s on lowering or abolishing the age of consent, much as Kinsey's work in the 1940s was written to inform and influence the debate on relaxing sex offender laws. The book is based on an investigation carried out by Sandfort as a research assistant in 1980–81 at the Sociological Institute of the State University, Utrecht, in the Netherlands. Sandfort wrote two books, in Dutch, from his investigation, published in 1981 and 1982. In 1986, when the Dutch legislature was actively considering revising the age of consent laws, Sandfort summarized his work in a paperback book aimed at the general reader, first in Dutch and then, in 1987, in English. Section 2 now looks in some detail at this book and the arguments it puts forward for the benefits of adult–child sexual contact.

2. 'Boys on their Contacts with Men'

Theo Sandfort is something of a hero to many paedophiles. He is, for example, on the NAMBLA list of recommended reading – always a good indication! (see http://www.NAMBLA.org/readings.htm, accessed 1 April 2008). His writings are widely referred to (although, like most academic texts, perhaps not actually so widely read). Dr Sandfort, now a research scientist at Columbia University, is regarded as a notable academic in the area of sexuality: he has been President of the Dutch Society of Sexology, President of the International Academy of Sex Research, and serves on the board of various academic journals on sexuality. In 2000, Haworth Press published his *Childhood Sexuality*, billed as 'one of the first books to present facts about the normal sexual behavior of children under thirteen'. Coyly, Sandfort does not mention his work on paedophile relationships in the list of publications on his web-page (http://www. hivcenternyc.org/people/theosandfort.html, accessed1 April 2008).

The investigation on which *Boys on their Contacts with Men* was based was part-funded by the NVSH, the Netherlands Society for Sexual Reform, a campaigning organization which still thrives, calling itself 'the most comprehensive site about sexuality'. Its web-page on paedophilia portrays views negative to paedophilia as being hysterical, illogical and 'primitive'; it shows pro-paedophile images including the cover of a pro-paedophile magazine; and it also contains a brief interview with Martin de Jong, chair of the Dutch Paedophile Association. It does not contain any views which are not supportive of paedophilia (http://www.nvsh.nl/variants/paedophilia.htm, accessed 2 April 2008).

Why is *Boys on their Contacts with Men* a significant book? It is one of the few books (indeed, perhaps the only book) to which paedophiles can point and say, 'Look, a scientific study has been done which proves that adult–child sexual relationships can be positive for the child.' The English-language edition contains a glowing Foreword penned by Dr John Money, the doyen of sexology, who acclaims the book as 'One of the most valuable works of research scholarship on the topic of pedophilia that has ever appeared in print.'

Sandfort has two points to prove in this study. Firstly, he wants to provide evidence that children do enjoy sex and are sexually active and therefore that age of consent laws which limit the extent of their sexual expression below a certain age do not reflect reality and should be altered or removed, thus de-criminalizing consensual sexual contact at any age. His second point is that people generally regard all adult–child sexual contact as harmful. Therefore, if he can prove any counterexamples, the harm argument will be shown to be logically flawed. He has therefore gone out to find a sample of boys who will tell the researcher, convincingly, that they enjoy their sexual relationships – or 'sexually expressed friendships' – with men and that they find it 'pleasant' and therefore not harmful.

He was able to recruit this sample because, as well as part-funding Sandfort's research, the NVSH also provided the entire sample on which the study was based. Sandfort explains on p. 37, that the men were found through the NVSH and especially through the 'pedophile and youth emancipation groups'. He then says, 'It was the men, the older partners, who asked the boys to participate.' He does not, in this book, say what his own role in the NVSH may have been, or whether any of the 'older partners' were in fact Sandfort himself, or his friends. In any case, he does not discuss the fact that, to the boys, he himself, as a well-educated professional adult man and possibly one already known to them as a member of the NVSH (we are not told), he must have seemed not dissimilar in status to the 'older partners'. In the interviews, Sandfort presents, entirely appropriately, as non-judgmental, but again – from the perspective of the young boys (23 of whom were aged 14 or younger) – this positive and supportive attitude towards adult–child sex might in fact have made it more difficult for them to deviate in their answers from any NVSH 'party line'. For example, it is interesting to read how, when asked explicitly about negative factors around their sexual relationship, the boys provide examples of men over-riding their wishes and 'pestering' them for sex but then repeatedly deny that this is significant or insist that it only happens very infrequently. It would be interesting to read the full transcripts and certainly this is a point which could be sensitively explored in any follow-up study.

Sandfort also remains silent on how exactly the boys were chosen to participate in the sample, and how many boys may have been selected out as 'unsuitable', although he does tell us that:

> [the] possibility cannot be excluded that only the 'better' relationships were here investigated. Although we made absolutely no effort to 'select' a favorable sample, it is undoubtedly true that men and boys will be more willing to participate in a project like this if what is being studied does not cause problems in their relationship and so create a bad impression of it. (Sandfort, 1987: 35)

This rather convoluted sentence seems to mean that, although 'we' (that is, Sandfort) may not have deliberately selected only a 'favorable' sample, it is more than likely that the men (who actually recruited the sample) did.

In the book, Sandfort tells us that he interviewed 25 boys aged between 10 and 16 years old, all of whom were having a sexual relationship with men aged between 26 and 66. In all, then, he tells us 25 boys were involved, and 20 men (because five of the men were each having relationships with two of the boys in the sample). However, it is rather odd that, when the names used in the book are counted up, he actually refers to 27 boys and to 25 men (whose ages also seem to vary). This seems extremely careless for such a ground-breaking study. There are also two Simons aged 12 given in the book, one having a relationship with Ed (aged 32), and one with Maarten (aged 32). Thus, as well as being sloppy with detailing numbers of respondents and ages, Sandfort seems to have been quite surprisingly careless in allocating pseudonyms to distinguish between the respondents in this very small sample. In addition to the 27 names, he also seems to confuse one child as being either Bert or Bart and another child as John or Johan, so there are in fact 29 names in total for the children. If Sandfort is so offhand with basic details of names and ages one wonders what other information from the research is being treated equally casually. (All quotations in this section are from Sandfort, 1987 unless specified otherwise. The ages given are the ages of the children *at the time of interview*, which is usually older than the age at which sexual activity had commenced.)

The overall impression from this book is rather sad. The boys, particularly the younger ones, come across as affectionate, caring and eager to please, working hard to conform to the ideal of the 'nice', 'pleasant', 'considerate' young boyfriend. They remind me oddly and unexpectedly of the stereotype of the 'mail-order bride', aware that her tenuous position can only be maintained as long as she adheres to the idealized model of meek and obliging, submissive femininity (Robinson, 1996). In this regard, it was intriguing to catch hints of how the boys seemed on some level to identify with their mothers. It would be helpful to see the full interview-transcripts to explore this in more depth (three transcripts are provided in an appendix to Sandfort's book). It is not surprising that if the main model of sexual companionship which the boys had was that of their parents, and they identified their 'older partners' as similar in some ways to their fathers, then they might in some sense identify themselves with their mothers' experiences. Thijs (aged 10) describes his sexual experience as, 'I think it's exactly like a woman going to bed with a man – it's nice. And I feel the same things they feel.' (p. 111). Rob (aged 12) explained:

> Through sex with Chris, I learned how my parents relate to one another.... Chris explained what was really going on at home, because sometimes I just don't understand what they are talking about. [TS: But what does that have to do with your sexual relations with Chris?] Well, my father sometimes sort of teases my mother,

flatters her and stuff. I didn't used to have the faintest idea why he did that, and now I know. (pp. 79–80)

For much of the time, however, the experiences seem to be, as one would expect, less about identifying with their mothers and more about sharing some complicated masculine social network where various individuals have sex with various others, both adults and children, in a kaleidoscope of complex interactions. For the boys caught up in this network, this is regarded – by some of them at least – as 'normal'. As one child, Lex, aged 13, states about his parents' knowledge of his own sexual relations, 'Oh, they think it's okay, as far as I know.... [TS: They're not opposed to it?] No, they do that kind of thing themselves, so... [ellipses in original]' (p. 102).

All 20 of the men involved in this investigation, Sandfort tells us, had had previous paedophile relationships, and 12 of the 20 were known to the authorities, with three of the men actually still on probation for sexual offences at the time of the study. Sandfort notes (p. 37) that 'In the 25 friendships which are the subject of this book, 20 men were involved: five of them had two younger friends, each of whom participated in this investigation.' As we have seen, this claim is problematic, because in fact 27 boys' names are used and 25 men's names, with only one name (Maarten) used twice. We therefore cannot know which of the men had 'two younger friends'. Neither is this aspect given much attention in the book. Teasing it out, however, it seems that, far from this being a study of 'normal children' living in an everyday community, a number of the boys were living in a context in which the adults around them either actively endorsed adult–child sexual contact or held a neutral opinion on it, and in which a tangled web of current and past sexual relationships intertwined.

To give a flavour of this strange environment and its links with the NVSH, there is the example of Erik (aged 10) who has a mother in the NVSH, where he had first met his 'older partner'. Erik explains, 'I was there. And so, of course, were a whole lot of pedophiles, and so was Edward [aged 57]. He was very nice, and he had brought a car race game with him' (p. 47). Sandfort describes how, 'Lex [aged 13] was brought by some of his age-mates to Richard who immediately started telling him about pedophilia... Within an hour they had sex' (p. 66). In Lex's words, 'he showed me some films. Sex films.... There were four of us looking at the film and then they started pulling my pants down... and so Richard said, "Now, will you let me...?"...I got used to it.' (p. 66). The 'older partner' Richard may also have had a previous sexual relationship with Theo (aged 13) who is shown as now having a relationship with Bert (aged 35). Rob (aged 12) had a similar experience:

> a week or so after I met him...We'd been making ['half-naked'] photos...And then he started to explain things to me...how you really *got* to jerk off and other things like that....I didn't have the faintest idea about any of that....Okay, every so often I saw I had a hard-on, but I didn't know anything more than that. (p. 65)

Gerrit (aged16) had an older brother who had a sexual relationship with Gerrit's 'older partner' for two years, overlapping with Gerrit's relation-ship (Gerrit's brother appears not to have been included in the sample). Gerrit described how his 'older partner' Barend (aged 39) started the sexual activity:

> the three of us [Barend, older brother, and Gerrit] were lying here on the bed and Barend had a sex book on the table. So my brother and I began to read it and I began to sort of jerk off and so on. From then on we had sex with one another....Barend started to jerk off a little, and my brother too....Barend did it a little bit to my brother, but not to me. Because I was a bit embarrassed – my brother not. He went around with Barend for two years. (p. 162)

Gerrit himself was then active in involving his friend Harrie (aged16) in a paedophile relationship. Similarly, Rob (aged 12) was now having sex with the 'older partner' who had previously had sex with his brother (who appears not to be included in the sample). Both John (aged 13) and his brother Jantje had a sexual relationship with the same man (again, Jantje appears not to be included in the sample). The brother of Jos (aged 13), and possibly his sister as well, may also have been involved with a paedophile – it is not clear from the text. Both Maurits (aged 10) and Simon (aged 12) were having a sexual relationship with Maarten. Willem (aged 13) is described as 'already experienced' when he starts a relationship with his 'older partner'. Rene (aged 12) met his 'older partner' when 'I went to his home to meet a man I'd known for six years, also a pedophile, who'd just got out of prison.' Hans (aged 13) met his current 'older partner' through another paedophile, and Simon (aged 12) had previously had a relationship with another paedophile, Ton. This is more complicated than a soap-opera!

Within this sample, therefore, a picture emerges, not of an aver-age neighbourhood as Sandfort seems to want to imply, but of a group of men – all connected to 'pedophile and youth emancipation groups' of the NVSH – having sex with clusters of siblings and their friends; of paedophiles introducing children to other paedophiles and of children subsequently introducing their brothers and schoolfriends to paedophiles. It has reached the point where Bert / Bart (aged 14) claims:

> that's the way it always is; one quarter of all boys do it, thus in my class of 16 there are four, including me, who have relations with a pedophile. [TS: That seems to me a bit too many.] Well, it just goes on an awful lot, but you'll have to ask Albert about that – he knows the figures a lot better. (p. 107)

In addition, Paul (aged 14) had previously 'had a sexual relationship with' (or been sexually abused by) his step-father – we are not told at what age this occurred. Is this then an example of a free-and-easy sexual paradise in which children are at last 'emancipated' to express their full sexual natures without unnecessary social inhibitions? Or is it an envi-ronment in which the sexual decisions made by the children are shaped by the dynamics of the secretive clique in which they are being brought up? (The study is of course silent on the experiences of those children who may have been offered sexual 'emancipation' by eager adults but yet declined their kind offers.)

This may well be an environment in which the children can feel 'spe-cial' – admired, pampered, cuddled, indulged and attended to (at least until they reach adolescence). But this is also a clique which is protec-tive of the men far more than of the boys: the major concern seems to be with keeping the men out of prison, not with ensuring the children have genuine autonomy. Rob (aged 12) has clearly been taught to feel very protective of (and responsible for) his 'older partner'. 'What really frightens me is what Chris has already gone through, and that, thanks to me, he might have to go through it all over again. That he would have problems with the police and such. And also my mother.' (p. 88) Walter (aged 15) also innocently repeats the justifications he has heard from his 'older partner', 'We're not hurting each other, are we? If you murder somebody you only sit in jail a few months; but if you go to bed with somebody you get punished more severely – that's what Steven says.' (p. 88). More unpleasantly, John / Johan (aged 13) discloses that his 'older partner' has threatened John's parents into silence, 'One good thing, though, is they'd never turn Marcel in. My mother is on disability but she works black [illegally]. Marcel said, "If she turns me in, the next day I'll turn her in." ' (p. 99).

The boys also seem to feel responsible for their 'older partners' sexual pleasure. 'Pedophiles ought to be able to enjoy themselves', says Marco (aged 12, p. 79). Little Ben (aged 10) has been told that sex is 'doing nice things for children', apparently: 'Sex with Herman is, uh, love for children and, uh, doing nice things for children, that sex is not bad.' (p.78). Ben also commented that Herman says, '"I want to do something nice but you don't want to do it." So then I think he's mad at me.' (p. 78). Poignantly, he also tells us, 'I think it's wonderful to sleep together. Then I don't have to lie in bed alone. Sometimes I'm a little bit scared to go to sleep if I've seen a movie.' (p. 54). Jos (aged 13) felt pressurized, 'When I don't want to do it and Bas [aged 35] keeps pestering me.' (p. 84). Martin (aged 12) also expressed that pressure – but then quickly backtracks: 'I ask him not to do something, I say I don't like it, and then he doesn't stop. But that doesn't happen so much.' (p. 82). Johan / John (aged 13) had hidden his pain: Sandfort reports that 'Marcel (45) said that he had anal contact one time with Johan (13), who found it painful. Johan, however, had not admitted it had hurt and said that he wanted to do something nice for Marcel.' (p. 71). On p. 80, Johan bravely denies there is anything wrong, 'There's nothing unpleasant about it [sex] ... I haven't any trouble with it. I like it and he likes it, so I think why should we make problems about it?' Lex (aged 13) also felt he owed his 'older partner': 'Well, you ought to have sex, because he does so much for me. He takes me out a lot. So I should pay him back somehow; that's what he thinks, but I think so, too, so I'm not against it.' (p. 94). Hans (aged 13) also felt responsible and anxious not to 'let the other guy down':

> if I'm doing something and, uh, something he likes but I, well, don't like it so much. Sometimes every so often you can say no, but other times you really shouldn't. ... you tell him no and he gets mad. ... If you say no you're letting the other guy down. ... you got to find a solution, and that's not easy. (pp. 83–4)

Sandfort's apparent incapacity to understand the power-dynamics of what he is studying is at times ludicrous. Theo (aged 13) attempts to negotiate with his 'older partner' while feeling guilty that he is 'telling a fib': 'he wants to suck me off and I tell him it hurts, and so I'm telling a fib [because it doesn't really]. ... I'll say "If the TV stays off I'm going to sleep alone", and then I get to watch the TV a little longer.' (p. 95).

Sandfort ponderously asserts, 'From this answer it can be seen that the boy realized he could withhold sex from his partner and so use it as a power tool.' (p. 95) A 'power tool'?? No doubt this is affected by the translation from the Dutch, but what is truly amusing is that over the page Sandfort then feels compelled to conclude his discussion on 'power' with a lengthy quotation (p. 96) – on a man's ability to ejaculate 'to the ceiling'! Yes, Professor Sandfort, very exciting no doubt, but that is not actually the kind of power we were expecting you to analyse! (It is also notable that this anecdote about a man in his fifties ejaculating 'to the ceiling' emphasizes an image of paedophiles as highly potent, virile and masculine, counter perhaps to more popular but less flattering notions of them.)

This quotation is also revealing for another reason. Sandfort introduces this quotation as 'an example from the interview with Ben (10) of how he often cheered on his partner Herman (55) when they had sex'. Sandfort wants the child to be talking about 'cheering on' his 'partner' when he ejaculates, but what the little boy is actually talking about is how absurd it all is and therefore how it makes him laugh. Sandfort is quite unable to hear this, and keeps steering the little boy until he says something positive about ejaculation:

> Ben (aged 10): Oh, when he wants to come I say, "Come! Come!"
>   (*Bursting out laughing*)
> TS: Does it make you laugh, or is it also serious?
> Ben: Yes, I always start laughing (*Again laughs*)
> TS: But you mean it seriously, you're encouraging him?
> Ben: Yeah, I laugh my head off.
> TS: You laugh your head off? Why do you find it so funny?
> Ben: (*Still laughing*) All of a sudden, psssst! Up to the ceiling!
> TS: Do you also think that's sort of strange?
> Ben: Uh, no.
> TS: You don't think it's strange?
> Ben: Later I'll be able to do it, too.
> TS: Do you think it's too bad that you can't yet?
> Ben: Yes, but when I'm eleven or twelve I will.

The younger boys of 10 and 11 years old especially seem somewhat baffled by what is going on. Ben, for example, does not seem to derive any enjoyment from the sexual contact which he describes as an 'unpleasant tickling' (p. 78). Why a 10-year-old child would want, on a daily basis, to 'cheer on' a 55-year-old man ejaculating is something that doesn't seem to occur to Sandfort.

At no point does Sandfort distinguish between the experiences of the younger or older boys in his sample. This omission is almost certainly driven by Sandfort's belief that age is irrelevant to consent – in fact, consent as a concept is not addressed. It is enough for Sandfort that some of the boys describe themselves as 'initiating' sexual contact and that they find pleasure in their experiences. For example, regarding Jan (aged 11), Sandfort reports that 'Sander said [to Sandfort] that it was really he who had taken the initiative, and that he had been very careful how he began: "You get a response to something you do, and that determines whether you go any further or not. The whole process lasted three months."' (p. 67) We are not told how old Jan was at that time, but we are told that it was 'a long time ago', presumably therefore Jan was aged no more than 9 or even younger. In Britain today, there would be no hesitation in naming this behaviour as 'grooming'.

So, does this book tell us about 'sexually expressed friendship' between boys and men? Is it reassuring in its message that such friendships can be positive and not harmful? To what extent are they 'friendships'? To what extent are they 'sexually expressed'? And to what extent is the sexual expression integral to the friendship, in the views of the boys? It seems clear from what the boys say that some of these relationships are indeed regarded as friendships. Here it is difficult to be precise, because Sandfort has not been precise and has given us 27 names of boys while telling us that he studied 25 boys so there is a certain amount of confusion to be taken into account. At least one boy (Andre, aged 14) is clear that it is not a friendship, he does not love his 'older partner', he was in it for the sex and now he has a girlfriend he is finishing his contact with the man. With some of the other boys, for example Marco (aged 12), from whom we hear only once (p. 79), there is no clear evidence either way and, for others, what seems to matter are the incidental benefits of time with an adult. Lex (aged 13) talks about the activities he is able to do, to which Sandfort responds, 'You're pretty lucky, eh?' and Lex replies poignantly, 'Yeah, that only happens if you go around with a pedophile, or you're the only child at home, of course,' (p. 52). Harrie (aged 16) explains that he gets treats like French fries whereas otherwise, 'There are seven of us in the family, so you just can't do that sort of thing' (p'53), and for Willem (aged 13), it is the lack of parental discipline, 'At home you can't do as much as you can here at Roel's. Like smoking – they don't let me smoke at home. Here I can do just about everything.' (p. 53); while, for Wouter (aged 12), he could escape from an unpleasant home situation, 'I feel at home... I can hide from my dad.' (p. 54).

For some of the other boys, for example Gerrit (aged 16), it is fairly clear that his friendship with his 'older partner' may be providing him with space to think, away from his family, and encouragement of his dreams of living in the countryside, and his hobbies such as sketching. Gerrit did not initiate the sexual aspect of this friendship and it is likely that, had it not been initiated, he would still have enjoyed the company of his friend.

For a number of the other boys, too, what they seem to value most in their friendships with the adult men is the attention, the treats, and the physical warmth of hugging, cuddling and back-rubbing. Peter (aged 14) is clear that what he likes is being cuddled (p. 56). Sandfort makes the comment, which everyone in this culture should take to heart, that boys in this age-bracket, once they are no longer little children, are unlikely to receive much physical affection. If the only person who is going to provide cuddles is a paedophile, then for some lonely and affection-starved children that alone may be sufficient reason to spend time with him. The answer is not that 'sexually expressed friendships' are positive: the answer is that those of us who care about children and adolescents must feel comfortable to offer them that bodily touch and warm, comforting physical affection that we all crave throughout our lives – the hugs, back-rubs and cuddles – while never crossing the boundary into inappropriate sexual contact. The boys also felt more relaxed and freer in their behaviour in the homes of their 'older partners'. They felt they could talk to these adults and perhaps escape from a stressful situation at home. Again, this is not something on which paedophiles have a monopoly: any adult could potentially befriend a young person and play a valuable role, offering support without any sexual element. It is a sad comment on our culture that so few children and adolescents have adult friends outside the family to whom they can turn when their own family situation is difficult.

It seems therefore that some of these relationships were indeed perceived as friendships by the boys but – far more often than Sandfort would like to admit – even in this carefully selected, and arguably brainwashed, little group the sex is likely to be something the boys feel obliged to take part in rather than experiencing it as an integral and necessary aspect of their friendship.

Sandfort's work has been reviewed and criticized (as described in Bauserman, 1990) on the grounds of method (for example, biased sampling), speculation (for example, assuming that the boys were lying throughout their interviews), and moral or ethical concerns (for example, the fact that the relationships studied were illegal). Bauserman refutes these critiques, essentially by decrying them as 'ideological' and 'dogmatic', in other words, as based on a moral position which differs from Bauserman's own. In turn, his analysis of the critiques has been addressed by two of the original reviewers, David Finkelhor and David Mrazek (both published in Sandfort, Brongersma & Naerssen, 1991). Finkelhor's response is particularly interesting. He is a key author and researcher in the field of child sexual abuse and his model on paedophilia is widely used. Finkelhor comments, 'Sandfort's findings are probably valid and could be (and need to be) replicated by other investigators' but he also states, 'it is probably an extremely unrepresentative sample. It is impossible to make policy on the basis of such a sample' (1991: 313); and he goes on to say that:

> [W]e are talking about an experience that has a very high risk.... The public policy priority to protect children from unwanted and coercive sexual approaches by adults seems justified given the evidence of its wide prevalence and the high risk for serious effects. The (now grown) children who have had such experiences are very active in lobbying for such protection. I have encountered very few individuals with self-defined positive experiences who are lobbying for legal protections for their kinds of experiences. Mostly it is pedophilicly oriented adults who argue for such rights.... Some types of social relationships violate deeply held values and principles in our culture about equality and self-determination. Sex between adults and children is one of them. Evidence that certain children have positive experiences does not challenge these values, which have deep roots in our worldview. (Finkelhor, 1991: 314)

In order to understand Sandfort's book, it is important to bear in mind its wider context (the drive by the NVSH to reduce or abolish age of consent laws and to de-criminalize adult–child sexual contact) and also to read carefully the quotations from the boys which, even in the limited form in which they are presented, still cannot manage to paint the picture of positive sexual enjoyment that Sandfort and the NVSH wanted to portray. According to Bauserman (1990), Sandfort had intended to follow up this study, and had obtained permission from all the boys to conduct such a follow-up. This never happened. The boys in the sample must now be aged in their 30s and 40s – it would be of great value if they can be traced or would be willing to get in touch, so that a researcher could re-contact them and allow them to speak, in their own words as adults looking back, about how they found the sexual relationships, the research, and their views now.

3. Other studies on adult sexual contact with children

The value of Sandfort's work is that it offers us a uniquely candid insight into how paedophiles may behave in society. In distinction to the many clinical or prison-based studies of paedophiles, Sandfort's is almost the only one which actually positions paedophiles in society, within a social context where they are permitted extreme leniency in their sexual behaviour (as will be remembered, at least three of the paedophiles were on probation at the time of the research and the book makes clear that, even when arrested, most of the paedophiles were effectively only 'cautioned' and allowed to continue). Although his expressed purpose was to interview the boys, at the same time he cannot help but show us the paedophiles themselves, in his descriptions, in their own comments and through the words of the boys.

This is a highly atypical setting. For example, Sandfort tells us that, when Robert (aged 42) invited Rene (aged 12) to start a relationship with him, Rene replied 'I'll see. If they think it's okay at home, then it would be fine.' (p. 44). In many ways, this is the great paedophile fantasy come true: the paedophile able to have a sexual relationship which is ignored or even approved of by the child's family. And, unlike Hollywood movies such as *Long Island Expressway, Leon* or *Man on Fire* (see Chapter 3), no-one gets to die either: the worst that seems to happen is that the paedophile goes to prison but comes out again and carries on as before. This, then, is the paedophile fantasy which is counterposed to the popular cultural fantasy of the 'evil pervert'. In Sandfort's book, the paedophile is well-integrated into society and able to offer boys valuable resources such as knowledge, affection, outings and treats – a 'value-added paedophile', one might say. In Sandfort's book, as with Kinsey, no-one is harmed, there is only good sex, and sexually active paedophiles have a place and a positive role to play in society.

As noted in Chapter 3, Sandfort's is by no means the only text which treats the subject of adult sexual contact with children in this positive light. Crawford *et al.* inform us that there are a 'plethora of publications that are positive' on this topic and that 'Intergenerational Studies has just begun, and ... there are shades of grey and white in the discussion that do not appear in the literature of abuse' (1997: 255–6). This section now turns to look at a small sample of those texts which treat adult sexual contact with children in 'shades of grey and white'. These texts tend to derive from the fields of sexology, pathopsychology, evolutionary psychology, criminology, sociology, sociobiology, anthropology, ethnology and human ethology. It is important that there is an awareness of these books and the arguments within them. The reader may be surprised at the influence of these books, the authorities involved in creating them, and the bodies of data on which they draw. Unless such literature, and the arguments within them, are clearly understood and addressed, and thus challenged, their subtle but powerful influence remains.

A noticeable fact about these texts is that they emphasize male-with-male paedophilia and scarcely touch on male-with-female paedophilia or paedophilia by women. Regrettably, as a mono-lingual, I am not able to comment on work available only in languages other than English, although it is clear that there is, for example, a body of Dutch- and German-language work which is relevant to this discussion but not available in translation (for example, the work by Sandfort available only in Dutch; the studies in the 1980s by the social worker Monica Pieterse on paedophiles, again published only in Dutch). It would be all but impossible to provide a thoroughly comprehensive bibliography of all the relevant works, as work on paedophilia and paedophiles *per se* will shade off into the wider areas of sexual 'variation', 'deviation' or fetish; children's rights, children's sexuality, children's development and sex education; social work and healthcare; moral and legal discussions and other cognate discipline-areas. I do not pretend that the titles given below provide a scientifically rigorous sample of available English-language material; the intention is that they should simply provide the reader with a flavour of some of the relevant texts. Book-length works include Gagnon & Simon (1970), Rossman (1976), O'Carroll (1981), Cook & Howells (1981), Taylor (1981), Sandfort (1982), Wilson & Cox (1983), Brongersma's two volumes (1986), Feierman (1990), Li Chin-Keoung, West & Woodhouse (1990), Sandfort, Brongersma & van Naerssen (1991), and Geraci (1997).

In addition to work which seems mainly concerned with the adult experience, there are also a number of books on children's sexuality written by authors who have published statements which endorse adult sexual contact with children (Pomeroy, Yates, Constantine, Martinson, Sandfort) or who are closely related to and have defended the work of Kinsey in this area (Pomeroy, Bancroft). Examples of these include Yates (1978), Constantine & Martinson (1981), Martinson (1994), Sandfort & Rademakers (2001) and Bancroft (2003).

The following four reviews are again not intended to be comprehensive but to illustrate to the reader that such texts exist and are
easily obtainable through libraries and booksellers. The views contained
in them (drawn from academic and popular discourse and using the
kinds of historical, anthropological and biological arguments discussed
in Chapter 3) are able to influence the 'sexual radicalism' discourse by
providing a resource arguing for the legitimacy and normality of adult
sexual contact with children. When we attempt to understand the place
of paedophiles within contemporary society, and how society responds
to paedophiles, books such as these help us to understand the arguments
for tolerance which exist and how they are developed and transmitted.

Adult Sexual Interest in Children (1981), edited by Mark Cook and
Kevin Howells. This book is part of a series entitled *Personality and
Psychopathology*. It is compiled by two British lecturers (one at University College Swansea and one at the University of Leicester) and arose as
a result of a major conference on sexual behaviour organized by Mark
Cook, the *International Conference on Love and Attraction*, held at Swansea
in 1977 and subsequently written up as a series of conference papers
published by Pergamon Press in 1979 as *Love and Attraction: An International Conference*, edited by Mark Cook and Glenn Wilson. At the
conference, Kevin Howells had convened a symposium on paedophilia,
at which Tom O'Carroll, a well-known paedophile activiist, had been
invited to speak but which was disrupted when Judith Reisman (see
the previous chapter) brought this to the attention of ancillary staff
at the University who then threatened strike action if O'Carroll was
given a platform. At the same conference, Floyd Martinson convened
a symposium on Child and Infant Sexuality.

This book therefore arose from the authors' experiences of controversy surrounding the conference, and they write: 'We began planning
this book with the intention of assembling a body of information about
the various aspects of adult sexual interest in children, which might
provide a factual basis for a cooler and more reasoned approach to the
issue' (p. viii). The collection includes chapters by the sociologist Ken
Plummer and the forensic criminologist and Director of the Institute
of Criminology at Cambridge, Donald West (see below). The tenor of
the book is liberal in the sense that sex with children is generally seen
as something not to get too excited about, although there are various
provisos about the possibility of harm.

A sample chapter is that by Thore Langfeldt on 'Sexual development in children'. Langfeldt, a psychologist from Norway who has a

clinical practice with children with 'deviant sexual behaviour' (Cook & Howells, 1981:112), appears to share an interest similar to Kinsey's in masturbation and early childhood sexual experience. Like Kinsey, he discusses how, 'at the neonatal level' 'an orgasm is easily produced' (p. 102), and he makes use of reports 'from pedophiles' on 'erections in small boys' (*ibid*.). He also states that 'observations are confirmed by reports from sexual interactions between young boys and adults' (p. 104) and by '[i]nterviews with men and boys having sexual relations' (pp. 104–5). Looking at childhood sexuality, he discusses how 'sexual activation may occur as a result of active manipulation by the child itself or by its caretaker' (p. 105) and expands this by stating how an 'uncle or some adult friend of the family might in some cases tell the child how to masturbate' (p. 106). These interventions are implicitly approved. There is a confusing but rather disturbing discussion of 'muscular oriented therapy' on 'young children' (pp. 116–17) which seems to be aimed at causing 'an increase in the pelvic bloodflow which gives rise to erection and lubrication' (p. 117). The overall tenor of the chapter is to suggest that touching children sexually is positive and helpful and connotes with 'liberation', 'pleasure' and being 'liberal', whilst not touching children sexually connotes with being old-fashioned and ashamed and having an 'anti-hedonistic attitude'.

Pedophilia: Biosocial Dimensions, edited by Jay Feierman and published in 1990 by Springer-Verlag. My attention was drawn to this book because it is frequently cited and recommended by those within the paedophile community. As with the Cook & Howells book, this collection arises from conference papers, this time a symposium in 1987, organized by the International Society for Human Ethology, on understanding paedophilia from cross-cultural, cross-historical and cross-species perspectives. An emphasis of the collection is on the contribution of evolutionary biology to contemporary human behaviour and, since the collection was published in 1990, some aspects of the more specialized work on neuro-endocrinology, for example, are likely to be somewhat out-of-date. This is an odd collection in some ways, with contributors going into great detail on the sexual behaviour of Japanese quail, laboratory mice and so forth without always clearly linking it to any implications for understanding why some men find children or adolescents sexually attractive. Nevertheless, it remains a fascinating work, even for the non-specialist. There are contributions by social scientists Vern Bullough and Paul Okami, but the majority of contributions are from the physical sciences. In some ways the most interesting part perhaps is the final concluding chapter by Feierman himself, which is essentially a heartfelt plea for tolerance, although it is noticeable that while there is clear empathy for the men caught up in the dilemma of paedophile sexual attraction (and who may find themselves sentenced and publicly disgraced for offending behaviour), there is no such clear empathy expressed for the children involved if the men do act on their attraction. Feierman refers sensitively to the cost of being a paedophile as 'an indeterminable sentence of never to be discussed inner turmoil and pain' (1990: 553).

Children's Sexual Encounters with Adults, written by Li Chin-Keung, Donald West and T. P. Woodhouse, was published by Duckworth in 1990 and then reprinted in 1993 by Prometheus as *Children's Sexual Encounters with Adults: A Scientific Study*. (The edition reviewed here is the earlier, Duckworth, edition.) This book contains two reports of research conducted by the authors. The first study, by West and Woodhouse, is a survey of male students which asked about their sexual experiences with people older than themselves before the age of 11 and when aged 11 up to 16 years. They received 182 completed questionnaires and undertook 23 interviews with respondents who had a history of relevant sexual experience and 13 interviews with respondents who hadn't. Forty-five students reported experiences between the ages of 11 and 16 years and 22 reported experiences aged under 11 years. The majority of the experiences were with male non-family members, often a one-off encounter with strangers, and the respondents reported these as embarrassing but otherwise 'indifferent'. For example, one respondent told how a friend's father had touched him in bed at night:

> I was almost wholly indifferent, it was bloody embarrassing, but I was almost completely indifferent to the whole thing. I don't seem to recall having – I mean it was a nuisance that I was being kept awake. Other than that it was slightly embarrassing I seem to remember. (1990: 53)

The authors then attempted to expand the data-collection using electoral registers in London and Cambridge, contacting respondents through telephone and postal questionnaires and visits to randomly selected addresses to ask men about their childhood sexual experiences. Not surprisingly, they encountered some difficulties! Nevertheless, they collected 298 questionnaires using this method, of which 60 (20 per cent) reported some sexual experience with adults or with someone older than themselves at the time, before the age of 16. Allowing for bias in non-response, the authors suggest a prevalence rate of around 10 per cent. They found that whilst some respondents had found their experiences very distressing or disturbing, some had not. Some experiences, mainly those when the respondents were aged around 15 years, and particularly those involving women rather than men, were regarded positively. There were no instances of parental sexual abuse reported in this study. The authors conclude that 'whereas the early sexual experiences of girls tend to be regarded as violation, those of boys are considered initiation' (1990: 127). This relatively relaxed attitude is echoed in the second part of the book, which comprises Li's doctoral thesis, supervised by West. During the early to mid 1980s, Li found and interviewed 20 self-defined paedophiles, contacting them through psychiatric clinics, an un-named paedophile organization (presumably the Paedophile Information Exchange, PIE), and *Forum*, a 'soft porn' magazine. The backdrop to Li's analysis of his research findings was the Cleveland investigation in 1987, in which, within a five-month period, 121 children were diagnosed as having been sexually abused and were taken into care by social services, thus provoking a sustained national debate about the nature and prevalence of child sexual abuse. Against this backdrop, Li sets out a careful analysis of the issues and cautiously posits a 'middle ground' on the 'continuum of adult–child sexuality, bearing in mind that there is considerable grey area in this continuum.' (1990: 314, emphasis omitted).

Male Intergenerational Intimacy: Historical, Socio-Psychological and Legal Perspectives, edited by Theo Sandfort, Edward Brongersma and Alex van Naerssen, was published in 1991 by Harrington Park Press (a subsidiary of The Haworth Press). This book was published simultaneously under the same title as a special issue of the *Journal of Homosexuality*, volume 20, numbers 1/2, in 1990. Sandfort is of course well-known for his *Boys on their Contacts with Men* (see previous section), and Brongersma has been referred to affectionately in an online discussion as one of the 'grandfathers' of the paedophile movement and by Plummer, in this volume, as a 'committed paedophile' (p. 320). This compilation brings together contributions from Ken Plummer, the British sociologist and a leading theorist on sexualities, David Thorstadt, the outspoken boy-love campaigner and the public face of the North American Man-Boy Love Association (NAMBLA), and Li Chin-Keung, writing on his study on adult male sexual experiences with boys (as discussed in *Children's Sexual Encounters with Adults*). Also contributing are a number of others, including Edward Brongersma himself, on 'Boy-lovers and their influence on boys'. The book is written mainly from a Dutch perspective and therefore displays a social attitude strikingly at odds with the North American or British model. This is shown, for example, in the two chapters dealing with the treatment of paedophiles, in which the aim of treatment is to increase self-esteem and 'social autonomy' and explicitly not to reduce sexual contact with children, contact which is assumed, on the word of the paedophile, to be consensual.

I hesitated for months to open this book, once I had taken it out of the library, because I expected I would find it too disturbing to read. In fact there is much of interest here and the historical chapters on 'pedogogical Eros', the 'Uranian movement' and the history of tolerance in the Netherlands are informative. The polemics in favour of 'loving boys' are silly rather than disturbing (or perhaps by now I'm getting inured to them). The near-total absence of any reference to family or parents is remarkable and Brongersma's quotation on how a relationship with a paedophile will help a boy to 'burst the gates of the family cage' (p.169) sums up pretty succinctly what seems to be the view on the contribution of the family and the relative importance of 'the boy-lover' to everyone else in the boy's life. Similarly, Jones' remark on 'the man-over-boy power imbalance typical of so many father/son' relationships (p. 287), as distinct from good old boy-lover relationships, of course, seems to betray a real hostility to the family, perhaps a jealousy? Overall, one is left with a sense that the vision of male intergenerational intimacy being portrayed in this book is a self-serving fantasy of educated middle-class men finding themselves pursued by sexually rampant working-class young adolescents eager for their attentions, whom they can then altruistically liberate from their repressive and stultifying parents in order to educate and prepare them for manhood. Strange that they don't find their services more in demand.

As well as these books, which together build a vision of paedophiles in society acting sexually but harmlessly with children, there are also those texts which relate even more precisely to Kinsey's work on 'children's sexuality'. As we saw, Wardell Pomeroy, Kinsey's close colleague, went on to write popular lay books on children's sexuality, and to insist in print that incest can be pleasurable for children and that girls (Pomeroy was less interested in boys) should have orgasms from an early age (Arnow, 1977). John Bancroft, one-time Director of the Kinsey Institute (who can be seen in interview in Tate's film, *Kinsey's Paedophiles*, defending Kinsey's position on using paedophiles to research 'children's sexuality') also went on to edit a collection of papers, *Sexual Development in Childhood* (2003). Bancroft's book, with contributions from Philip Jenkins, David Finkelhor and others, does contain some useful discussions, but there appears to be little or no discussion of the ethical implications of researching children's sexual development and overall it does not reduce my concern at the manner in which Kinsey's legacy is still treated.

Some of Kinsey's previously unpublished data, obtained from adults having sexual contact with children and babies, may also have been used directly in other publications. Floyd Mansfield Martinson's book, *Infant and Child Sexuality: A Sociological Perspective* (1973), is still available online and in this Martinson states that, alongside his own observations and interviews:

> I have also read and incorporated data from Alfred Kinsey's interview notes on a sample of children two to five years of age, data which have not been previously published. Permission to utilize these data was granted by the Institute for Sex Research (the Kinsey Institute), Indiana University, Bloomington, Indiana. (Martinson, 1973, Preface: online)

It is possible that these may be the interviews Kinsey conducted with children in a nursery-school in California in 1949 (Gathorne-Hardy, 1998: 327) but it is unlikely that this will ever be verified.

Martinson also explains:

> Recall of sexual encounters is possible from about age three. For earlier ages one cannot rely at all on subjective data as such. One must utilize the observations of mothers, researchers, and others who have been particularly close to the infant and young child. Among others, Larry and Joan Constantine have graciously offered me the use of data on a small number of child sexual experiences that they gathered incidental to their study of multilateral marriages.(*ibid.*)

Apparently a 'multilateral marriage' involves three or more people, but what relevance that has to 'child sexual experiences' in the under-3s is opaque. Constantine and Martinson later edited a book together (1981) called *Children and Sex*. Like Sandfort and others, Martinson is something of a hero in this field. He was the fourth recipient of the Kinsey Award (which has also been awarded to Gebhard, Pomeroy and Bancroft, among others) and received an obituary in the *Journal of Sex*

Research when he died in 2000. The obituary enthused that, 'More than anyone else in sociology has done, Floyd made us knowledgeable about sexuality in children.... He was recognized as one of the world's authorities on child sexuality and he received many awards.' (Reiss, 2000: 391). Martinson's 1994 book on *The Sexual Life of Children* is described by its publishers as tracing:

> the development of sexuality in the child from the prenatal, through birth and up to puberty and adolescence.... Western society has been slow to recognize sexual experiences and conceptualizations as an important part of a child's development. This is the only work that has been written in a frank and open manner about the many sexual encounters that children have on a daily basis as part of their normal psychological development. (Greenwood Publishing Group, undated: online)

In fact, as we have seen, it is not the only work written on children's 'many sexual encounters'. Another significant text in this field is titled *Sex Without Shame*, by Dr Alayne Yates, a psychiatrist. Her book, first published in 1978, is, like Martinson's book, now available online. Like Martinson also, Yates refers repeatedly to the Kinsey data on childhood sexuality. She also quotes with apparent agreement, in Chapter 6, the slogan, 'Sex before eight or else it's too late', attributed to the René Guyon Society. Her book includes a great deal of rhetoric on both incest and on developing an 'erotic' relationship with your child from birth, which appears to be related to her own professional practice as a child and adolescent psychiatrist at the University of Hawaii. Yates had a relatively prestigious career, for example being a guest editor of *Sexual and Gender Identity Disorders, for Child and Adolescent Psychiatry Clinics of North America*, published by W. B. Saunders in 1993.

Yates goes on at great length and with a high level of detail. A flavour of the text can be conveyed by the following excerpts on incest:

> There is one event that occurs in all strata of society and that provides youngsters with intense erotic stimulation – incest. While incest can lead to serious problems, it is not always harmful.....Mutual sex play among siblings does not prove harmful, and could foster a robust, healthy, nonincestuous stance later in life.... Incest does not necessarily produce damage.... The girls I have evaluated who were young, uncoerced, and initially pleased with the relationship remain emotionally unscathed, even after protracted incest. However, they may

be devastated by the social consequences after discovery. They are fully orgasmic... When these girls move out into school and the community, they swiftly form gratifying liaisons with more appropriate males. They retain a taste for older partners, such as foster fathers, male teachers, doctors, and policemen.... There is an important lesson to be learned from noncoercive father-and-daughter incest. Early erotic pleasure by itself does not damage the child. It can produce sexually competent and notably erotic young women. Childhood is the best time to learn, although parents may not always be the best teachers. (Yates, 1978: online)

Notice Yates' emphasis that girls who experience incest are 'fully orgasmic' – this is the point repeatedly made by Kinsey and later by Pomeroy. In other words, following Kinsey, orgasm is reified as the highest good: it trumps any other good, such as the security and psychological well-being a child receives in a non-incestuous environment. Incest or other early sexual experience is presented as benefitting the girl by readying her to be 'sexually competent and notably erotic' in her 'gratifying liaisons with more appropriate males'. The list of these 'more appropriate males' which Yates produces – 'foster fathers, male teachers, doctors, and policemen' – sounds more like a recipe for serial abuse from precisely those adults who are given the greatest responsibility by society to protect vulnerable children.

Yates goes into quite extraordinary detail when she is looking at the 'erotic' involvement between parents and very young children, particularly babies. She notes her experience of 'the hundreds of births in which I either officiated or observed', although it is not in any way clear why a psychiatrist would 'officiate' during labour or delivery. Again, the following excerpts can only give a flavour of her approach, which includes 'exercises' which she, as a psychiatrist, recommends from birth and for babies up to one year of age:

Mothers who are erotically involved with their infants raise sexy children.... The application of delicately scented and delightfully creamy lotions to the genitals isn't just for hygiene or, as the label indicates, to protect against harmful bacteria. Lotions and oils are highly sensuous and the genital contact distinctly erotic. What difference does it make anyway to call a spade a spade? After all, good mothers have always patted and powdered the penis and swabbed the clitoris.

...There are certain exercises that enrich the experience of body intimacy – for both mother and child. These are designed for use in the first six months of life. The first exercise may be begun on the delivery table... Mothers on the delivery table who have the chance but avoid looking at the penis or clitoris are dealing with significant sexual inhibitions.... Mothers who retreat from the sight of infant genitals need to pay close attention to the next exercise. There's time to concentrate at the first feeding.... Look at the arms, the legs, the belly, and the genitals. All deserve careful attention. The clitoris may be hidden or covered with a mucous jelly. Two fingers spread the labia to reveal the contours. The newborn girl is still affected by your hormones so that the labia are flushed and the clitoris enlarged and glistening. Can you touch it?... If the penis is uncircumcised slide back the foreskin to reveal the glans.... Are you reluctant to touch it? Some mothers are so frightened that they never retract the foreskin. Eventually it adheres to the glans and often becomes infected.

...More advanced exercises involve your reactions to your infant's secretions.... The glistening modicum of saliva or the dab of mucus which slips from the baby girl's vagina are bits of a cherished being, until recently a part of you. Full acceptance of these secretions is the same as the ability to savor your mate's sexual perspiration, semen, and saliva.... If infancy passes without an abundance of these intimate sensations, then the sexual response will be limited. Thus all forms of licking, washing, tickling, and sniffing contribute to the growth of the eroticism....

Breast-feeding is a potent gratification, for both mother and child. Rhythmic sucking, scent, warmth, and closeness combine to produce the optimal erotic congress. Genital pleasure is enmeshed in the total experience. Direct genital stimulation occurs as the mother presses the child's hips against her body....

...The genitals are ordinarily stimulated, if only under the guise of hygiene.... Diapering is prime time for the enhancement of genital eroticism.... Genital manipulation is often an accepted method to calm an irritable infant. Although statistics aren't available, sexual dysfunction seems far more likely in countries where diapers are employed. Certainly the parent who conceals the baby's genitals beneath a tightly pinned diaper assumes a huge responsibility. This parent becomes the infant's main source of genital pleasuring.

...During the second six months the infant develops a separate self and recognizes the parents as distinct individuals.... The infant with a background of pleasure knows what he likes and now begins to seek that which feels good.... Some little girls rub against a pillow or squeeze thighs together to create erotic feelings. The father becomes a playmate with a bouncy knee.... More advanced exercises include the provision of large soft or fuzzy dolls and pillows of various shapes. The session can be extended to include play with mud or finger paint in the backyard or tub....

The infant in the second half year needs to develop reciprocity.... Teaching the infant to swim has been in vogue for a number of years. Initially these programs were sold to the public as the stylish acquisition of an essential skill.... The real payoff from infant swimming has nothing to do with skill. A wet, wriggly, naked body, ecstatic in the sensuous delights of water and the defiance of gravity, is hard to resist. Make the most of it.... The child can scarcely contain her joy; she's done something great. As she clasps her thighs about her mother's waist, clitoral impressions add to her gusto.

Can the infant receive too much stimulation through these activities? Will eroticism take over the child? Data from many cultures yields an emphatic 'no.'... By nature children have catholic tastes.... If they've observed or participated in oral sex they may devise a game with this as the central focus.... Sex play is certainly healthy.

... In cultures where children are sexually active, sex play continues uninterrupted. Unfortunately, in our culture, there's a sharp decline in all sexual activity by the end of the oedipal phase.... Parents who have followed the suggestions in these chapters, or who have in other ways communicated acceptance and enjoyment of sex, have promoted a solid erotic foundation. (Yates, 1978: online)

Any parent who has raised small children understands the importance of accepting and loving every aspect of their dear baby – smelly faeces, urine escaping everywhere, vomit, dribble, snotty noses and all. Many parents also recognize the importance of close and sustained skin-to-skin contact, breastfeeding, snuggling and sleeping together to build the child's sense of security and subsequent self-assured independence (Liedloff, 1986; Kitzinger, 2008). None of those considerations, however, need ever involve the kind of genital fixation and violation advocated here. One wonders what the publisher, and Yates' employers at the University of Hawaii, thought of these recommendations and 'exercises'.

4. Conclusion

Overall, as can be seen, this review of a small selection of books, chosen more or less at random from those available, present a vision of paedophiles in society as acting sexually but harmlessly with children; a vision which is entirely consonant with the work of Kinsey in the 1940s. Kinsey was not the originator of this view by any means. He himself drew on earlier and contemporary theorists and researchers such as the anthropologist Clellan Ford (1909–1972) and the psychologist Frank Beach (1911–1988), whose main work on cross-cultural sexual customs, *Patterns of Sexual Behavior*, published in 1951, is still referred to in current studies (for example, see Green, 2002). The key contribution of Kinsey was not to instigate but to popularize the idea of adult sexual contact with children and, within that, the notion that children, from birth, are sexual agents who have the capacity to be willing participants in sexual encounters with adults. This approach can be easily identified in the work of Langfeldt, Sandfort, Brongersma, Martinson, Yates and others. Together, these authors have produced a powerful strand within the 'sexual liberation' discourse which has been taken up by other 'sexual radicals' or 'sexual dissidents' who would arguably not otherwise have sympathy with paedophilia but who are convinced by its association with, for example, gay rights or queer politics.

It is noticeable that a number of these books are from reputable academic and Establishment sources (for example, Donald West was the Director of the Institute of Criminology at Cambridge University, and Edward Brongersma a senator in the Dutch parliament). These are not self-published rantings by neurotic loners on the margins of society (although there are of course also examples of those within this genre). Often, the books and articles are peer-reviewed and produced within contexts which have national or international standing: they cannot be dismissed as irrelevant or merely subcultural. The impact of such texts has been, and continues to be, profound on the development of the discourse of 'sexual liberation'.

Those of us who naively had no idea that academic and popular texts genuinely do exist which promote adult sexual contact with children, including newborn babies, need to realize the significance of these works. Kinsey's *Reports* were published in the late 1940s and early 1950s. A generation later, Pomeroy, Yates, Constantine, Martinson and Sandfort were publishing their texts from the early 1970s to the early 1980s. A generation on and we now appear to be experiencing what even sceptics such as Philip Jenkins (2003) have identified as an epidemic of child pornography. Child sexual abuse remains at epidemic levels in every country in the world in which statistics are gathered. For example, a United Nations report in 2006 found that 150 million girls and 73 million boys aged under 18 experienced forced sexual intercourse and other forms of sexual violence involving physical contact in 2002 and that in 21 countries, most of them industrialized, as many as 36 per cent of women and 29 per cent of men said they had been the victims of sexual abuse during childhood, with most of the abuse occurring within the family (Usborne, 2006).

Books are also now being made available online, or coming back into publication, which have been unavailable since the 1970s. For example, Tony Duvert (1976) was an author who, like Kinsey again, was fascinated by masturbation and by the notion of a child's right to sexual exploration with adults. As with Sandfort's work, Duvert also used his book to argue for a lowering of the age of consent. He combined his interest in the sexual life of young boys with a passionate loathing for parents and families, describing the paedophile (especially the well-off, middle-class, homosexual paedophile) as 'the father's rival'. The publisher's synopsis of the book includes the following:

This title offers a scathing view of sex manuals for children and society's hypocrisy of over [sic] sex that argues for the rights of children to their own bodies and their own sexuality. Written in the wake of May 1968 and Deleuze and Guattari's *Anti-Oedipus*, Tony Duvert's *Good Sex Illustrated* (*Le Bon Sexe Illustré*) was part of the miraculous moment when sexuality could turn the world upside down and reveal social hypocrisy for what it was. Bitterly funny and unabashedly anarchistic, *Good Sex Illustrated* openly declares war on mothers, family, psychoanalysis, morality, and the entire social construct, through a close reading of sex manuals for children. Published in 1973, one year after Duvert won the prestigious Prix Médicis, it proved that accolades had not tempered his scathing wit or his approach to such taboo topics as pedophilia. (Posted as product description on Amazon, 2007, http://www.amazon.co.uk/Good-Sex-Illustrated-Foreign-Agents/dp/1584350431, last accessed 10 December 2009)

As a society, we seemed to have learned little between that 'miraculous moment' in the 1960s and the present day in our capacity to distinguish between the self-indulgent pleasure of privileged adults to publish scathingly witty, taboo-busting diatribes against 'hypocrisy' and the rather more sober requirement to protect actual flesh-and-blood children from sexual abuse. Rather than averting one's gaze and hoping that these sorts of books will go away or will have no effect (or that publishers will take more responsibility in what they choose to publish), it is better to understand what the arguments are, how they are used, who is citing and quoting these authors, and overall, something of what the contemporary impact may be. Sandfort's research, for example, continues to be used by a number of writers as evidence that man-boy sexual contact can be positive rather than harmful. Work published over the last few generations continues to reverberate in that cultural space within which individual and legislative decisions are made. When we seek to understand the issue of paedophiles and their place in society, we need to take cognisance of, but not be blinded by, texts – from however lofty a source – which are based on a model of 'childhood sexuality' derived from the rape of small children by paedophiles with stopwatches.

6
Paedophiles and Adult Male Sexuality

Introduction

This book has argued that society has rather an odd attitude to paedophiles – simultaneously both intensely hostile and remarkably tolerant. Mainstream Hollywood 'nymphets' (Shirley Temple, Brooke Shields, Dakota Fanning or even Macaulay Culkin) act out fantasies which can seem very close to NAMBLA's porn, and senior Establishment figures in Europe join with celebrities in the United States to protect a convicted child-rapist from justice. British MPs, international footballers, J. K. Rowling and the Pope all publicly share the horror and distress of Madeleine McCann's disappearance – while in Portugal the law is carefully watered down ahead of the Casa Pia orphanage trial (in a scandal said to have 'shaken the very foundations of Portuguese democracy'; Tarvainen, 2004) and the trial itself then peters out into obscurity. On the web, the owner of a site termed 'the largest online child pornography-oriented videotheque' (quoted in Leurs, 2005: 32) contemptuously brags that he knows 'many of the best [internet] security people in the world, and none of them work for the British police' (Clarke, 2009, online).

Chapter 3 introduced some tentative figures on the prevalence in the general population of adult sexual attraction to children. These figures may help to explain to some degree why child sexual abuse is so prevalent and also help us become aware that paedophilia is not a rare or even necessarily a remarkably aberrant form of sexuality. Sexual attraction to children can be conceptualized as part of a continuum of normative human (male) sexuality. Fantasies of being able to identify and remove all paedophiles from contact with children through bureaucratic schemes of 'vetting and barring' or Criminal

Record Bureau checks (as the British Government has wished to do) or even, in darker moments, of rounding up and executing them all, are patently absurd, however tempting they may be when faced with the horror of child sexual abuse – and it may be this (subliminal) awareness which fuels the powerful anti-paedophile rhetoric in contemporary culture.

Chapter 3 concluded that we can make sense of the paradoxical responses to paedophiles through the recognition that there are two parallel and conflicting views on paedophiles, based on a differentiated conceptualization of sexuality (and child sexuality) and therefore of the harm or harmlessness of adult sexual contact with children. It is these two discourses, swirling like oil and water, which produce such an unpredictable and paradoxical cultural environment.

One discourse offers the view that 'children's sexuality' can be seen as 'dissident', 'radical' and 'alternative' to normative heterosexuality, much like homosexuality or sado-masochism, for example. In this view, the antonym of 'sex' is 'sex-negative' 'anti-sex' or prudishness. There is no conceptual space for 'innocence' as a positive quality or experience and there is no point at which a child is regarded as too young for sex. This view draws on historical and cross-cultural examples of adults having sex with children, and also, more recently, on (misrepresented) primatological research on bonobos, to assert the universality and thus normality of adult sexual contact with children. Any negative consequences are seen as primarily to do with 'anti-sex' attitudes in society. As Gathorne-Hardy (in a discussion on the *Female* Report) summarizes Kinsey's view on the impact of men's sexual contact with girls:

> Since in Kinsey's view there was nothing *inherently* unpleasant about male genitals, and the only thing inherent in genitals being touched was pleasure, adverse reactions had to be learnt. It was these (inappropriate) learned reactions that caused distress. Similarly, he was irritated by the way the hysteria surrounding the tiny minority of violent cases... spread out to the vast majority of cases where it was not just inappropriate but was what did the damage. There is a considerable body of fairly recent research to suggest he may be right. (Gathorne-Hardy, 1998: 377, emphasis in original)

This quotation neatly, accurately and succinctly sums up the 'sexual radical' position. For the 'considerable body of fairly recent research', Gathorne-Hardy appends a footnote to four pieces of research, which are by Professor David Finkelhor (whose research does not support this view), Professor Diana Russell (whose research does not support this view), Paul Gebhard and colleagues (whose research is in fact Kinsey's so, by circular logic, does support this view) and Professor Theo Sandfort (whose research on 'boys on their sexual friendships with men' was explicitly supported by a pro-paedophile organization, the NVSH).

The second discourse on sexuality (and on child sexuality) is in fact the one supported by the empirical research of Finkelhor and Russell and is the one propounded by them as well as by other researchers and theorists. This discourse often contains a political analysis which suggests, as with the first discourse, that there is indeed something problematic, difficult and oppressive about normative or 'compulsory' heterosexuality. Overlapping with the 'sexual radical' discourse, it also often suggests that human sexuality in all its forms is distorted and impoverished by a lack of imagination, a reluctance to tell new and more honest sexual stories (Kincaid,1998). Again, it shares with the 'sexual radical' discourse a critique of the subordination of children and an increasing sensitivity to the concept of children's rights. Where it differs fundamentally is in its understanding of the qualitative distinction between adult and child sexuality, its awareness of the developmental stages of childhood and its emphasis on 'least harm' and respect for autonomy as ethical goods which balance or outweigh the good of 'genitals being touched'.

Identifying and disaggregating these two discourses begins to permit an exploration of the culturally mediated relationship between paedophiles and society, but in order to go further it is necessary to examine in more detail what lies at the heart of both discourses – this 'sexuality' which both the 'radical' and the 'child protection' discourse so repeatedly problematize. This chapter therefore sets out some of the ways in which human sexuality can be seen as shaped and constructed. This is by no means a comprehensive overview of every aspect of human sexuality but is intended to draw out some salient points.

Section 1 focuses on some of the difficulties in our relationship with children in contemporary society and the ways in which children become ciphers freighted with our postmodern anxieties. Section 2 goes more deeply into those aspects of adult male sexuality which are most problematic, the links to dominance, violence and denial of empathy, and Sections 3 and 4 provide some examples of the impact normative adult male sexuality has had over the centuries on the lives and the bodies of women and children. This leads into the final discussion and conclusion provided in the Epilogue.

1. Finding children sexy

In the introduction to this chapter I suggested that paedophilia may not be a rare or even necessarily a remarkably aberrant form of sexuality. Some readers may be offended and angered at this suggestion that paedophilia is not categorically different from ordinary sexuality: others may find this a comforting thought, helping to explain moments of involuntary arousal when around children. It is this secret – hiding in plain sight – that a 'sizeable minority of men' may find children sexually attractive (Hall *et al.*, 1995: 692) which provides the motor for the confusion and conflicting messages within contemporary society. Roman Polanski, attempting to downplay his conviction for child-rape, shrugged it off with the comment, 'But ... [sexual intercourse], you see, and the young girls. Judges want to [have sex with] young girls. Juries want to [have sex with] young girls – everyone wants to [have sex with] young girls!' (cited in Cohen, 2009, online). By 'everyone', of course, Polanski is not referring to the human population in general but to adult men like himself. However, it is nevertheless the uncomfortable truth within his statement which arguably provides the energy to drive both child sexual abuse and irrational (and ineffectual) reactions to paedophilia.

What is relevant in this debate, therefore, is in no sense children's own authentic and autonomous sexuality but only the desiring gaze of the adult – and, in fact, the adult male. As one commentator has phrased it:

> Society needs the pedophile: his existence allows everyone else to view sexy children innocently ... Why does the American national psyche need the pedophilia of everyday life? .... Were society to allow itself to articulate that it does have sexual interests in children ... society would have met the enemy and seen that he is us.
>
> ... Childhood – the social concept – cannot do the moral work society has created it to do. In a century whose distinguishing marks are depression and Depression, genocide and the prospect of omnicide, life can look pretty damn nasty, brutish, and short. And so to serve both as ethical prop and security blanket, we have created a moral museum of innocence and purity – our Eden – and we have labeled it childhood. But then the paradox of everyday pedophilia is this: once we have made over childhood into purity and innocence, we naturally enough want to have it, but to have it would make it what we no longer want. (Mohr, 1999: online)

Of course Mohr, like Polanski, also assumes that 'society', 'everyone else', 'the American national psyche' and 'we' are all ungendered, implicitly male. He suggests that 'everyday pedophilia' has been created through a social need to see childhood as pure and innocent and then subsequently to 'want' it. However, this would not in itself lead to sexual arousal to children since there is no straightforward or inevitable relationship between 'innocence' and being 'sexy': this may be one social construction of 'sexy' but there are others. Mohr exaggerates but he does have a point: the 'pedophilia of everyday life' contains the truth that, if it is indeed correct that paedophilia is simply one point on a continuum of sexuality, then there are not 'them and us', 'paedophiles' and 'everyone else'. In many ways, there is only 'us'. If this is indeed the case, what is to be done? The author James Kincaid has a suggestion, that we should simply accept the fact:

> [That] children are devised by our culture as erotic and that we are bound to find them so.... the erotic is, after all, a large territory in which we move all the time; that our being there seldom surprises us or makes us likely to assault the nearest thing in sight... For me (and you too) it is no hardship to live with a scale of erotic responses and to find pleasurable even the sort of low-grade, background erotic hum we experience at a cafeteria or on a bus. Feeling erotically buzzed or even highly charged does not mean entering automatically into a different order of being. Human beings do not have a rutting season, do not spray or howl at the moon or start humping the legs of guests at parties. (Kincaid, 1998: 287)

Kincaid does not disagree that children have been sexualized or made an erotic focus in contemporary society but his level-headed view is that this need not lead to any injurious behaviour. His prescription for sanity around children is:

> If you find yourself getting too excited, going too far, wanting to incite or not to stop – then stop. If you are hard-pressed, then indulge in voyeurism... Take the model of Joe Gargery in Dickens's *Great Expectations*. Joe's love for Pip is so powerful that he knows when he must leave.... he tears himself away...
>   Not wishful to intrude I have departured fur you are well again dear Pip and will do better without
>   Jo
>   P.S. Ever the best of friends

Not wishful to intrude, we should all departure while the kids are well, maintaining our friendship as distance, even if an erotic distance. I think this stoic story is also available to us, once we wash away the hysteria. (Kincaid, 1998: 289)

What commentators such as Mohr and Kincaid are essentially proposing is that human (male) sexuality is plastic: it can be moulded to fit social and cultural norms, and that contemporary society over the past 150 years or so has 'devised' childhood as innocent and children as erotic, thus shaping how adults perceive them. While there is much evidence, from Freud onwards, that sexuality is indeed plastic, it seems highly unlikely to me that the 'sexy child' is really only a modern invention. What has changed, rather, is not the eroticizing of the child but the (attempted) protection of the child from adult male sexuality. In my view, the shift has been towards a greater valuing of the child and thus a greater awareness of her or his potential exploitation and harm.

Children have long been both beloved and denigrated, idealized and feared. Increasingly from the Enlightenment and into the Romantic period, children were cherished as almost sacred, angelic, noble, Apollonian, closer to God than disenchanted adults ever can be; in Wordsworth's phrase, even 'trailing clouds of glory' as infants descended from heaven to impure Earth. At the same time, an older but still continuing tradition sees children as intrinsically evil, Dionysian, wild, untamed, asocial and anti-social, needing wickedness beaten out of them and goodness beaten in. Thus the child is deviant, threatening, anarchic but also beloved and dependent, calling forth self-sacrifice and altruism on the part of adults, especially the parent (Jenks, 1996). Having to embody these conflicting images, the child moves from being an authentic individual to a symbol, a cipher containing and re-presenting adult anxieties back to us. Perhaps this explains in part the huge public distress at the inexplicable disappearance of one little 3-year-old, Madeleine McCann. Madeleine came to represent, for many of us, all the children, known and unknown, whose lives are lost, whose security and happiness is destroyed and perhaps also that part in our own adult selves which feels threatened, insecure and overwhelmed by human evil. If Madeleine came home, then perhaps the world would really be okay after all.

It seems to me that this shift in valuing and concern is likely to be linked to the current social climate in Western societies of high divorce rates, the prevalence of step- or 'recombinant' families (Giddens, 1993), and cultural anxiety over the role of men and, in particular, fathers.

As families disintegrate and adult relationships collapse – often into acrimony and despair – conceptualizations of children have correspond-ingly shifted. As part of a slow process over the last two hundred years, which witnessed first the rise and now the agonizing, slow-motion, explosion of the nuclear family, children have moved from the mar-gins of adult social concern to centre-stage, to a position where they have arguably overtaken other adults as the primary love-object. We see in children both our hope for the future and our link to a nostalgic, warmer and more loving past (Jenks, 1996). To children are handed the emotional burdens which we as adults can no longer carry. Where adult relationships no longer offer reliable love and trust, the adult–child bond becomes a primary source of love and stability. As the sociologist Ulrich Beck expresses it:

> The child is the source of the last remaining, irrevocable, unex-changeable primary relationship. Partners come and go. The child stays. Everything that is desired, but not realizable in the relationship, is directed to the child. With the increasing fragility of the relation-ship between the sexes the child acquires a monopoly on practical companionship, on an expression of feelings in a biological give and take that otherwise is becoming increasingly uncommon and doubt-ful. ... The child becomes the final alternative to loneliness that can be built up against the vanishing possibilities of love. It is the private type of re-enchantment, which arises with, and derives its meaning from, disenchantment. (Beck, 1992: 118)

The child, then, contains and expresses our anxieties in an increas-ingly fragile and risky world. But what of gender? As adult relationships decompose, do women turn increasingly to boys (or girls) for erotic com-fort? There is no evidence of this. Polanski, Mohr, Kincaid and others, when they speak of the adult desiring the child, mean the man desiring the girl – or, at times, the boy.

The adult male fetishization of young girls was shown in Chapter 2 where men celebrated the 'splendor of little girls' and reminisced for decades over a few innocent moments spent together. This fetishization is also perhaps shown in the portrayal of the 'Hollywood nymphets' as both sexualized and innocent, both vulnerable and powerful – Lolita seducing Humbert Humbert, Mathilda singing 'Like a Virgin' to Leon. These children are carefully portrayed as powerful but not too power-ful, sexy but controllable. What is being fetishized is not the girl *per se* but the quality of the relationship. The male role here is part boyfriend, part big brother, father, uncle...all the best, fun bits of men relating to females without any of the difficult bits. It is fun for the girls too, at least at times. There is something here about a structurally powerless but privileged status, a kind of 'court fool' which girls and young women can inhabit and which is not accessible to adult women. It need not be sexual or even erotic; it may simply be about the security of gentle flirting and friendship, a close and cosy dyad where the girl can be powerful, the man can be childlike – and boring old Mummy is excluded. There may not be much written in the professional literature about this dynamic, but it is the stuff of much fiction as well as film. In the *Just So* stories, Rudyard Kipling's famous children's stories first published in 1902, we see this enacted in the two tales of Taffy and her Daddy:

> Once upon a most early time was a Neolithic man....we, O Best Beloved, will call him Tegumai, for short....And his little girl-daughter's name was Taffimai Metallumai, and that means, 'Small-person-without-any-manners-who-ought-to-be-spanked'; but I'm going to call her Taffy....Now attend and listen ! (Kipling, 1902: 123–4)

Kipling weaves a tale of a little girl of about 5, perhaps, and her cleverness (she invents first writing and then the alphabet) under the close and caring eye of her Daddy and the somewhat more distant warmth of her Mummy (who is a bit silly, and misunderstands things, and stays behind in the cave while Taffy and her Daddy go out together). This triangle is about patriarchy, the allure of the powerful adult male (and to a lesser extent the rejection of the contemned adult female), but it is especially about the times when male power can be big and cuddly and safe and playful. The film *Leon* is brutal in comparison to Kipling's gentle bedtime story, but the dynamic is the same. As with *Lolita*, any possible mummy has been cleared off the scene (and wasn't that nice anyway) and now, with Mathilda, Leon the professional hitman can play with his oven-glove pig and she can make eyes at him and help him with reading and writing. He can be the wounded king and she the little princess (with the wicked stepmother out of the way). The story is repeated with variations in *Lawn Dogs* and *Man on Fire*. There is a price to pay but, after all, what little girl would not opt to be the little princess, the special friend of her wounded king, the big yet vulnerable grown-up man? The heady allure of patriarchy when the powerful man is just a little boy inside, needing her as much as she needs him, is a dynamic that works well for both parties, up to a point.

This may be an example of the Apollonian child (Jenks, 1996) where the girl is idealized into a particular image of femininity. As noted in Chapter 2, she is playful, nurturing, undemanding and paradoxically protective of the adult male. As a research respondent, 'William', reminisced (again, quoted in Chapter 2), when he was unhappy 'this little girl would perceive exactly when I felt most "low" and would come and give me a little hug, or hold my hand – and make me feel so much better'. She lent him her cuddly toy, she sent him an email which 'made me almost die on the spot. I have it printed out here in a drawer by my bed, and it's a rare day when I don't read that particular mail before I go to sleep.' William described to me his feelings about little girls:

> To me, there is simply nothing on this earth as beautiful... subtlety and understated spiritual power.... the incredible power she has to affect and move me, to bring me to my knees in awe and adoration!... The superlatives are not superlative enough.... Lewis Carroll in one of his letters, wrote of experiencing a 'feeling of reverence, as at the presence of something sacred' when he was photographing certain of child friends 'undraped'.... And, probably, most people – or most decent people anyway – would agree up to a certain point: little girls *are* beautiful, cute and charming. So how is this 'paedophilic'? How is it sexual? Well, the point is that the beauty and loveliness of little girls, which I have tried my best – inevitably rather inadequately – to describe above, *is* to me utterly *sexy*. It is erotically appealing.... I am moved *romantically*.... Girl Love is, to me, a 'sexuality – plus'. If that makes sense! It is *everything* to me, the core of my identity as a person, and everything that is most significant and important. ('William', 2007, research data)

Another research respondent also tried to sum up his feelings about little girls:

> Secret, sensual, intensely imaginative, passionate, curious... Their love of glitter and pink and magic wands and fairy wings is a celebration of paganism and extravagance.... Kneeling in the garden mixing up a magic potion of flower petals and water, my feelings are that I am beside a fountain of creativity, and that whatever threadbare image or faded narrative I drop into it will emerge coloured like a Disney feature and glistening with life. ('Tim', 2008, research data)

Both 'William' and 'Tim' devoted pages to attempting to convey the subtlety and nuance they experience. What I have termed the fetishization of the quality of a relationship does not permit straightforward description – or indeed straightforward distinction into 'paedophilic' and 'non-paedophilic' attraction. Perhaps it is not so surprising, given these subtle dynamics, that society finds it difficult to address adult male sexual attraction to girls (the attraction to boys seems to have a different quality, as explored to some extent in Chapter 5). It is not merely the subtlety which obscures. It is also the discomfort of confronting the reality when the 'wounded king', the special friend, becomes instead the abuser. This talk of 'awe and adoration', glitter and fairy wings is all very far from Kinsey's cold-blooded model of 'sexual outlets' and 'genitals being manipulated' but it can end up in the same place.

History shows us again and again the inability of society to hold in the collective mind the notion that adults harm children sexually, and how frequently that painful reality slips out of awareness. Jeffrey Masson (1985) documents how often commentators (typically, medical doctors and psychologists) have identified assaults against children and then denied or misidentified the reality of their findings. When in 1896, Sigmund Freud first gave his paper, *The Aetiology of Hysteria*, at Vienna, he reported what he had uncovered from early analysis of patients, that a significant proportion of his patients had been the victims of sexual abuse within their own families, typically girls from around the age of 8 years old being abused by their fathers. He felt he had made a discovery of the most extraordinary scientific importance. To his astonishment, the response was hostile. Freud wrote afterwards to his friend Wilhelm Fleiss that the lecture:

> met with an icy reception from the asses, and from Krafft-Ebing [who attended the lecture] the strange comment: It sounds like a scientific fairy tale. And this after one has demonstrated to them a solution to a more than thousand-year-old problem, a 'source of the Nile'!...They can all go to hell. (Quoted in Masson, 1985: 9)

Within two weeks of the lecture, Freud was writing, 'I am as isolated as you could wish me to be: the word has been given out to abandon me, and a void is forming around me.' (Masson, 1985: 10). Over the course of the next ten years, Freud systematically retracted the 'seduction theory' which had almost destroyed his career, and proposed instead his theory of the Oedipus complex, that little girls wished to have sex with their fathers and fantasized accordingly.

In an ironic twist, when the psychoanalyst Jeffrey Masson uncovered letters and documents showing that Freud's later disavowal of the existence of childhood rape was motivated not by a search for truth but by discomfort at its implications and a failure of courage, Masson himself also experienced the icy blast of disapproval. Instead of analysing his material, reviewers labelled Masson's book 'comical and self-serving', slanderous and mean-spirited, and described its author as 'monumentally stupid', 'a charlatan' 'filled with motiveless malignity'. As Masson writes, 'My character was attacked, my motivation was attacked, but my arguments... were not adequately addressed.' (Masson, 1985: xv). By reminding people uncomfortably of children's abuse – and the complicity of adults in refusing to hear – Masson became a scapegoat. He was sacked from his post as projects director of the Freud Archives and ejected from membership of the International Psychoanalytical Association.

I have so far argued that, within society, there is a continuum of men, who may or may not be labelled paedophiles and who may or may not act on their attractions, who find children sexually arousing or who are attracted to a relationship with a child which has erotic overtones. All of these possibilities may, for the sake of simplicity, be subsumed into the phrase, 'finding children sexy'. These relationships may be happy and rewarding for both parties. They may also slide into sexual abuse, in which case society finds it a struggle both to acknowledge and to deal with the child's pain. The following sections now turn to look at a more sombre issue: the relationship between adult male sexuality in general and the capacity to cause harm.

2. Culture, sex and the 'Axial Age'

This book has studiously avoided simplistic references to men who have sexual contact with children as being psychiatrically ill or 'deviant', because such explanations can provide only narrowly focused individualized biographical accounts, missing out the wider social and cultural context. Similarly, the book has also avoided terming such people as 'evil' or accounting for them as 'bad apples', since these terms suggest that we need look no further than essentialist categories or the random nature of life. Instead, in order to analyse why men sexually abuse children, we need to understand 'the values underpinning society', as Pope Benedict XVI expressed it in his homily on paedophile priests (Arch Diocese of New York, 2008).

In order to understand sexual abuse, this book contends that we need to place such behaviour within its cultural context and ask what it is about human culture, apparently universally, which permits or enables men to sexually abuse children. Culture in its widest sense can be defined as the way in which a society controls women's reproduction, for example by 'classifying women according to the types of sexual relationships they are to have with men' (Brock & Thistlethwaite, 1996:82). All aspects of a culture can be understood as part of this overall process of controlling women and, through women's reproductive bodies, the process of controlling a formalized set of rules for inheritance of property and titles. Thus there is an immediate and intimate relationship between sexuality and culture.

Within any cultural system, religion – as an over-arching belief-system – plays a central role. Religion speaks about the key moments in life – birth, marriage, and death – and thus about reproduction as a central element in human existence. Its focus on reproduction provides the justifications which make the control of women (through concepts of virginity, chastity, modesty and honour) ideologically inevitable and therefore invisible in any particular culture. It is thus to religion that we turn in order to make sense of what culture has to say about sexuality. The major universal religions (those that make universal claims about reality and human life, including Buddhism, Christianity, Confucianism, Hinduism, Islam and Judaism) all stem from a particular revolutionary moment in human thought which took place during the end of the Bronze Age and the start of the Iron Age two and a half thousand years ago. This revolution has been termed the Axial Age (Eisenstadt, 1978, 1986) as it formed a great axis on which human civilization shifted, moving from a world-view based fairly unproblematically on material reality to an understanding of transcendence and ultimately a division between two spheres of existence: the illusory world of matter and decay, and the true world of spirit and the mind. Gradually, over the centuries from 800 to 200 BC, societies across India, China, Persia, Israel and Greece developed religious, philosophical, moral and legal systems based on the ethical values of compassion, justice, wisdom, righteousness and the 'virtuous man'. As the historian Karen Armstrong has described it, the most significant qualities of the Axial Age thinkers were compassion and empathy:

> The greatest Axial teachers all taught a spirituality of empathy. Not only was it wrong to kill another person; you must not even speak an unkind word or make an irritable gesture. Nor could you confine your benevolence to your own people: your concern must somehow extend to the entire world. In fact, when people started to limit their sympathies, this was another indication that the Axial Age was

coming to an end. Each of the Axial sages developed his own formu-
lation of what has been called the Golden Rule, which they insisted
was the essence of religion: do not do to others what you would not
have done to you. (Armstrong, 2006: online)

The role of the sage, the wise man or the saint then becomes to tran-
scend the mundane and to grasp spiritual truth. The thinkers of the
Axial Age laid the groundwork for the ascetism and renunciation found
in Hinduism and Jainism, the monastic and contemplative tradition
in Buddhism (which later significantly influenced early Christianity),
the monotheistic and dualistic principles of Zoroastrianism which contributed to the Abrahamic traditions of Judaism, Christianity and Islam,
the transcendent 'mandate of heaven' within Confucianism and the
Way of Tao, and, centuries later, the rise of philosophy and rationalism
within European thought.

This pivotal moment in human thought produced effects which still
have an impact on all our lives today, and by understanding the similarities at the origin of these religions and philosophies we can untangle
some of the cultural processes which, over the last two millennia and
more, have tended towards the social construction of a sexuality which
denigrates and abuses women and children while preaching love and
compassion (Brock & Thistlethwaite, 1996).

The ideology of the Axial Age split the universe into two segments:
the temporary physical world and the true world of ideas or spirit. It is
this split which has had particular – and profoundly damaging – consequences. The ideology of transcendence was born into a cultural context
in which women were already socially devalued. Those great thinkers
of the Axial Age, who came to define and dominate the formation of
cultures affecting billions of people for the next two millennia, were
all men. They developed truths which they held to be self-evident and
which others took to be universal. Taking the perspective of the world
in which they lived, they believed it to be axiomatic that women were
inferior to men and that their function was to serve men. The 'way of
virtue' for the sage and the virtuous gentleman was by definition a way
of manliness.

The ideology of transcendence shaped religious and intellectual
thought from China to Europe. As the dominant ideology at the point
when all the major religious and philosophical texts were first written
down, its impact is not confined to one particular historical moment but
has continued to this day. Four key ideas in particular can be identified
as significant to the ideology of transcendence: these are the ideas of

hierarchy, discipline, rejection and contempt (developed from the work of Brock & Thistlethwaite, 1996).

The new religions, as put forward for example by the Buddha or the Hebrew prophets, challenged the absolute power of worldly kings but did so by setting up alternative hierarchies which emphasized obedience. Moving the realm of absolute power from the material to the non-material realm did not dissolve hierarchy but ultimately reinforced it and sanctified it, making it even harder to speak out against, or even acknowledge, stratified and gendered power imbalances. Secondly, linked to narratives of hierarchy, power and submission, was the development of the concept of self-discipline as one strives towards the goal of salvation or enlightenment. While female monastic traditions existed on a small scale, it is the male monastic tradition, particularly in mediaeval Europe and in contemporary East and South-East Asia, which – with the distinctive robes of the monk, *bhikkhu* (or 'renouncer') – has provided its surrounding communities with a visible daily reminder of religion and of religious attitudes towards discipline and the body. However, self-denial sets up inevitable psychological processes that play themselves out both individually and on a larger scale, affecting entire cultures. The denial of bodily pleasure and sex within monastic traditions – particularly when the conscious awareness of that denial is itself suppressed or denied – creates a sense of anxiety and disconnection. In response, it is a common human reaction to disparage or hate what one desires but cannot have.

In psychological terms, renouncing the world and striving for perfection can lead not only to denial but also to dissociation and splitting. In Freudian terms, the rational and moral superego is at war with the instinctual id and unbearable pressure is liable to build up unless some form of release can be found (Freud, 2001 [1927]). In spiritual traditions, this release is intended to come in the form of ecstasy: the joy, grace and harmony in which oneness is found. But, regrettably, a more common outcome is dissociation. Dissociation is the fragmentation of the self and the splitting off of feelings that connect and integrate the self. Instead of *yoga*, the union of oneness, there is fragmentation. In the unconscious psychological process of dissociation, we deal with trauma or anxiety by dividing it up into bits and 'projecting' some of those bits away from ourselves, out into the world. Parts of the world are now 'good' and other parts are 'bad', evil and hateful (Gomez, 1997). In this way the psyche again regains control, reduces anxiety and resolves the dilemmas of wanting and not having, but the cost of that reduction in anxiety is heavy. It is a loss of self-awareness and a distorted perception of the world, in which evil is now seen as existing outside, in what one desires but cannot have. For many men in the monastic traditions, evil existed in women.

This leads to the third main idea within the ideology of transcendence, which is that of hate and violent rejection. It is perhaps a surprising assertion that these rational philosophies and these religions of love and peace have violence as a central idea, especially given the explicit importance of *ahimsa* (non-violence) within Hinduism, Jainism and Buddhism, for example. Nevertheless, no doubt imported into the new ideology from the prevailing climate of warfare, violent concepts and images are endemic. The religion of Zoroastrianism, for example, is predicated on the idea of a battle between the opposing forces of good and evil. Military iconography abounds in other religions too, with images of soldiers, weapons, and struggle. Focal concepts such as power, hierarchy, obedience, discipline, endurance and overcoming all lend themselves to a sense of antagonism and the belief in an 'enemy', whether that enemy is regarded as being located externally – in the world, the Devil, or unbelievers – or is found within oneself – in one's own will, temptation, the flesh, or in one's sensual or sexual desires.

This stress on rejection, hatred, violence and warfare leads to the fourth main idea of the ideology of transcendence, which is to regard the earthly world as sinful and polluting, a place of temptation and illusory pleasures. The physical world is seen as a shadow or reflection of higher truth, as illusion (Maya) or as a fallen state which is no more than a temporary way-station on the path to our true home, which is paradise, 'suchness', nirvana or heaven.

There are many ramifications to this view of the physical world. One is that it sets up a duality between culture – the disciplined, restrained, scholarly, spiritual or virtuous life – and nature, regarded as chaotic, soiled, depraved or simply irrelevant. It also sets up a duality between the mind and the body. As one Zen master, Kyong Ho (or 'Empty Mirror') has expressed it, following traditional Buddhist thought: 'To discover Mind, one should understand that one's body is no more than a dead corpse and that this world is, for good or bad, nothing but a dream.' (Kwan Um School of Zen, 1997, online). Traditional meditation themes in Buddhism include meditation on the foulness of food and on ten different kinds of corpses, from murder-victims to bloated, putrefying or worm-infested corpses, to skeletons. In Indo-European language there is a relationship between the words for 'mother' and the words for 'earth' ('matter', 'material', 'mud' and 'muck' are all related to 'matrix' – the base of all life, the source, origin, the mother, the womb). While this conceptual relationship may have stemmed from a reverential acknowledgement that no life exists without the sustaining mother, as the ideology of transcendence took hold, both the physical earth and the mother herself became no more than dirt. Platonic thought gradually identified the body (soma) as 'the prison, the cage, the tomb' in which the soul (psyche) is 'bound and buried' until liberated by death (Ferwerda,1986: 124). This disquiet or disgust with the body is a recurrent theme, expressed in its most recent manifestation as cyber-culture's rejection of the physical body as mere 'meat' and the pleasure taken in manga (Japanese cartoon) characters or computer avatars who are made of gleaming, perfect materials such as chrome.

At the same time, the valorization of the life of the mind has successfully created an important social space for the sage, the philosopher, the rabbi, the scholar, the teacher and, in some contexts, the scientist. However, in all the societies in which literacy has historically been valued, its attainment has been differentially available – with boys being encouraged to learn to read and girls often strongly discouraged. (This is particularly ironic given the finding that, in societies where universal education is provided, it is girls who out-perform boys in literacy and who, as adults, are known to read more for pleasure: Norris, 2007).

It is not just women's minds which have been disparaged. An ideological view of the natural world, including human bodies, which emphasizes and devalues their corruptible, decomposing, messy nature, lends itself easily to an attitude of suspicion and contempt towards those aspects of everyday life which are painful but also to those which are pleasurable. For many men, a source of great pleasure is sexual activity and, for a heterosexual man, that desire for sexual pleasure is intimately linked with the desire for union with a woman. To desire but not to be able to have is uncomfortable and, as described earlier, to reduce the discomfort and strain, the human mind may make use of the unconscious mechanism of projection, projecting the desire out of the self and into the other. This process is not in itself a gendered process, but because of the gendered differences in life-experiences, with militaristic and monastic discipline a predominantly male experience, the psychological processes of projection and dissociation have historically been more likely to occur among men. Repudiating sexual desire in the search for transcendence, while continuing to experience that desire, has thus entailed for many men repudiating women in the fight to control that desire. Both 'the body' and 'women' become sources of anxiety, hostility and cultural disparagement.

The sociological fact that men, far more than women, have over the centuries been members of large organizations which stress discipline over bodily desires, has led to a situation where the psychology of denial, hostility and projection has entered into men's thinking, found a strong cultural resonance, and hence become a powerful undercurrent in those written records which have laid the basis for so many religious and philosophical concepts still current today. Such cultural assumptions are buried many centuries deep in our collective thinking and are embedded within all the major religions, affecting attitudes towards women's legal status, citizenship, decision-making, and their physical autonomy, their ability to make free choices over their bodies, their reproductive options and their sexuality. The beautiful and powerful yearnings for transcendence, love, compassion, justice and wisdom which found their historical beginning in the writings of the Axial Age were structured in hierarchical, militaristic societies which violently rejected weakness, physical bodies, sexuality and women.

3. The impact on women and children: sexual abuse and exploitation

The previous section has suggested that the ideology of transcendence, as the dominant ideology at the point when all the major religious and philosophical texts were first written down, has shaped religious and intellectual thought through its focus on the key ideas of hierarchy, discipline, and violent rejection and contempt for the material world. This ideology splits existence into two realms, valorizing the spiritual life of the mind while denigrating the fleshly world of nature, bodies, death and sex. It is proposed that the outcome of this cultural and intellectual heritage is a situation in which, for specific historical reasons, male experience has become more prone to the psychological strategies of dissociation, splitting and projection. Men, with a history of military and monastic traditions not commonly shared by women, have built a psychosocial and cultural tradition which projects 'badness' into women, seeing both their minds and their bodies as inferior. Over the centuries, this has produced a painful distortion in human sexual relationships, in which men typically both desire and despise the adult female body.

Not only female bodies but female sexual desire too has been problematized. Men, by splitting and projecting their own frustrated desire out onto women, have produced a terrifying chimera, a cultural stereotype of the 'sexual woman', out of control, anarchic, with an overwhelming lust which threatens to destroy not only individual men but to bring down whole civilizations if not rigidly contained, policed and punished. This can be seen at work in innumerable texts from all the major religions, which emphasize the sexual degeneracy of women and the corresponding moral resolve required of men. From Islam, for example, there are a number of sayings (*ahadeeth*) such as, 'I am not leaving behind me any *fitnah* [temptation] that is more harmful to men than women': in other words, women are the source of the most harmful temptation, dissension or test that men can experience. Another saying is: 'This world is fresh and sweet, and Allah has appointed you over it, so see how you will do. Fear this world and fear women, for the first *fitnah* faced by the Children of Israel had to do with women.'

Repudiating sexual desire in the search for transcendence, while continuing to experience that desire, has thus entailed for many men repudiating women in the fight to control that desire. Both 'the body' and 'women' become sources of anxiety and hostility. The cultural disparagement of women over many centuries has become so invisible that, for example, a contemporary author describing Zoroastrianism in an article entitled 'Gender equality and status of women in Zoroastrianism' is able to write, completely without irony:

> Zoroastrian religion does not discriminate between men and women. Leaving aside the differences with regard to religious observances and role responsibilities, both the sexes are treated equally in the religious texts.... Zoroastrian scriptures suggest that women are prone to the temptations of evil and therefore should be kept under regular watch.... Menstruation and childbirth are viewed as major sources of pollution in Zoroastrianism. Women are advised to maintain seclusion and avoid contact with everything.... [Menstruating women should stay] three paces from the faithful. The women who bring food to such women should maintain a distance of three paces.... If a child touches them during this period, his body and hands should be washed. (Jayaram, 2007: online)

Such powerful yet culturally invisible disparagement of women's sexuality and disgust of women's bodies, over millennia, have profoundly affected the social, sexual and psychological relationships between men and women. This section aims to document some of the impacts of the ideology of transcendence on the lives and bodies of women and children, bringing into greater awareness the distortions we all face when attempting to understand human sexuality and thus particular and specific manifestations of sexuality such as paedophilia and child sexual abuse.

Human sexuality has no inherent requirement to be abusive. The example of bonobo apes, given in Chapter 3, indicated that human development may have included the potential for sex to be always mutually pleasurable and sociable, initiated by females as well as males and never coercive. However, our other closest animal relatives, the chimpanzees, routinely show a form of male sexuality which is coercive, violent and is interpreted by primatologists as rape (Wrangham & Peterson, 1996). Humans, bonobos and chimpanzees all share a common ancestor, a primordial woodland ape. What differentiated the development of sociable bonobo sexuality from aggressive chimpanzee sexuality was not inherent biological difference but social development, as differences in diet and foraging patterns led to changes in social structure (*ibid.*). This suggests that human males may have the biological capacity to follow either path, and that the choice of path is determined by the social and cultural context. This therefore suggests that there is no biological imperative for men to rape, only a cultural conditioning to do so.

It is in this context that we can begin to explore and make sense of the experience of human sexuality over the past millennia since the rise of the ideology of transcendence. We can begin to see that, whether we are considering normative sexuality (penetrative heterosexuality) or non-normative forms such as 'pederasty' or child sexual abuse, all these forms have developed within a cultural framework in which specific myths about male sexuality and female sexuality have been propounded and specific expectations (that women tempt, that men rape, and so on) have structured the experience of sexuality and sex. We cannot divide off the sexual abuse of children from other forms of sexual abuse, principally against women. They are not separate and distinct categories but are part of the same cultural construction of adult male sexuality.

In Chapter 1, I suggested that we 'have got ourselves into a pickle sexually'. That is putting it rather mildly. For example, in the Democratic Republic of Congo, what is occurring at present has been graphically described as 'a war against women' in which, in the last ten years, hundreds of thousands of women have been raped, most of them gang-raped, in a situation horrific not only in its scale but in its systematic nature and brutality. This is not rape because 'soldiers have got bored and have nothing to do'. On the contrary, it is a deliberate strategy, a way of ensuring that communities are forced to accept the power and authority of particular armed groups through terrorizing women and girls. It is using rape as a weapon of war (*CBS News*, 2008).

As with other rape situations, there are no distinctions made for age: rape-victims admitted to hospital have ranged from 3 years old to 75 years old (*CBS News*, 2008). A report for the BBC described one meeting:

> As we walked forward to meet the tiny 16-year-old, she doubled over, clutching her stomach and trying to cover her feet with the faded cloth she had wrapped around her body. She averted her eyes. Urine covered her feet. Vumi suffers from incontinence, and cannot sit down because of the pain, the result of a horrific rape incident last October.
>
> 'The attack happened at night, and we were forced to flee into the bush,' she said, in a voice barely more than a whisper. 'Four men took me. They all raped me. At that time I was nine months pregnant. They gang-raped me and pushed sticks up my vagina – that's when my baby died – they said it was better than killing me.'
>
> The men then stole her few belongings and her community, unable to live with the smell, shunned her. (Martens, 2004: online)

The rapes, often involving attacks on pregnant women, include violent sexual assaults with sticks and other implements, resulting in permanent injury, pain and the humiliation of incontinence and social rejection for survivors. As one reporter explained, 'Many have been so sadistically attacked from the inside out, butchered by bayonets and assaulted with chunks of wood, that their reproductive and digestive systems are beyond repair' (*New York Times*, 2007).

And yet, in the Congo, the raped women sing. An online article on their agony and their endurance ends by commenting on the extraordinary atmosphere of hope even in the midst of such terror, recording how rape survivors congregate each morning in the hospital in Panzi to raise their voices, singing at a religious service. Our sufferings on earth, they sing, will be relieved in heaven. Relief in Congo, it seems, is just too much to ask for (*CBS News*, 2008). The ideology of transcendence provides both the underpinning cultural rationale for their violent and repeated rape, in its vicious hatred of the female body and specifically the sexual parts of the female body, and also the comfort and the expectation of heaven to relieve their intolerable pain.

In order to occur on such a scale, rape requires indifference in the wider society. Again, the invisibility of all but the most extreme abuses against women is shown in the indifference of governments to the trafficking and forced sexual exploitation of women. For example, US military bases in South Korea are surrounded by brothels. A report in *Time* (MacIntyre, 2002) describes how the area outside a military camp in Tongduchon is off-limits to Koreans, while 'Filipinas and Russians in micro miniskirts idle in the doorways, trying to coax G.I.s inside'. The journalist notes how, speaking with one sergeant:

> He is proud to be up here, 'protecting democracy' from North Korean aggression. But that concern doesn't extend to the Russian and Filipina women who work the bars where he spends his free time: they're just part of the landscape. 'The women are here because they've been tricked,' he says, nonchalantly. 'They're told they're going to be bartending or waitressing, but once they get here, things are different,' he adds, with a knowing look. (MacIntyre, 2002: online)

Both the US military and the Korean government collude in allowing the prostitution and trafficking to continue, despite the protests of NGOs. It seems that the South Korean government, complicit in failing to take seriously the human rights abuses and international law crimes against Korean 'military comfort women' during the Asia Pacific War with Japan, is now repeating its disregard for trafficked women forced into sexually servicing military personnel, and that this disregard is widely shared. As the sergeant in the *Time* article comments, 'We're here to protect democracy. We're not here to practice it.'

Other armies have used similar institutionalized military brothels. One example is the British army in Tripoli, where each of the army's different ranks and racial groups had its own brothel. One soldier, describing the militarized prostitution system in the early 1940s, remembered how a pavement in Tripoli 'held a long queue of men, four deep, standing in orderly patience to pay their money and break the monotony of desert celibacy. The queue was four deep because there were only four women in the brothel.' (quoted in Yoshimi, 2000:186). These examples of sexual violence, including institutionalized sexual abuse, serve to emphasize the gruelling impact of normative adult male sexuality, as shaped by centuries of the ideology of transcendence, on the lives and bodies of women. What of the experiences of children?

When we analyse a gun, we do not analyse it in terms of what it might shoot but in terms of what the gun itself is like. The gun may be used to shoot white men, black men, small girls, animals. It is the same gun. Similarly, adult male sexuality may express itself by focusing on women, men, girls or boys but it is essentially the same cultural and psychosocial model of sexuality which underpins all forms of male sexuality, whether those are expressed violently or lovingly, in rape or with tenderness. For many, male sexuality has become a gun in contemporary culture. It need not be.

Contemporary child sexual tourism draws on the same ideologies as the sexual abuse of women, ideologies which see children and women as of less value than men, able to be exploited without empathy, treated as commodities rather than fellow humans.

Alongside ideologies of sexuality and gender, the ideological hierarchy of ethnicity also plays its part. Children and young people from certain ethnic groups are more vulnerable to recruitment into the sex industry. In Thailand, hill-tribes in the north and north-eastern regions are lighter-skinned than lowland Thais and are thus seen as more desirable. Girls sold into prostitution by their impoverished families are able to earn significantly more than they would as labourers or subsistence-farming peasants. Girls may regard it as a duty owed to their families to earn such money. For the entrepreneurs from the city, the ethnic-minority children are seen as simply another exploitable resource. Within Thailand generally, there is widespread denial of the economic reality of these transactions: the families may wish to believe that the girls are simply doing bar-work rather than prostitution; and middle-class commentators salve their consciences by pointing the finger at the 'greed' of the peasants in selling their children, rather than acknowledging the harsh conditions of extreme poverty under which they live (Brock & Thistlethwaite, 1996).

In Nepal, similarly, economic conditions of great poverty, political instability and a religious and cultural setting which values boys and sees girls as a burden also combine to create a situation in which young girls are vulnerable to being trafficked into sexual abuse. Girl trafficking occurs through kidnapping and the direct selling of children into prostitution by their families under the guise of false employment and marriage brokers. Young girls are sold across the border to brothels in India, where prostitution is legal. It is estimated that between 5,000 and 7,000 girls, between the ages of 7 and 16 years old, are trafficked each year from Nepal to India and that more than 200,000 Nepalese girls are involved in the Indian sex trade (Burba, 2006).

Escape is almost impossible except in cases where the young child contracts HIV: in that case, they may be sent back to Nepal but, once there, they are often forced to live in hospital camps or return to prostitution after being shunned by their families and communities. Even as young, terminally ill, desperate children, they are not welcomed home. Traditionally, once females leave their family home, they cannot easily return. A Buddhist nun working with the children explained:

> I have talked to many girls in the [hospital] camps [in Nepal], and they say the same thing — 'I would like to go back home', but because of the culture, parents don't want to keep the girls for a long time in the home, so when they come back from India, they don't want them. (quoted in Burba, 2006: online)

Another nun described how:

> One girl came back [to Nepal] four years after she disappeared. She went to her home and when her mama saw her, her mama asked, 'Why [did] you come back?' And the girl had tears [running] down her face. I spoke to her mama and she said to me, 'Inside, I love my daughter, but I cannot accept her in my house,' and she cried. (*ibid.*)

Ethnicity also affects the situation in Taiwan, where the aboriginal inhabitants now constitute 2 per cent of the population but account for one-third of underage sex workers (Brock & Thistlethwaite, 1996: 64). It is reported (*Pravda*, 2006) that the non-governmental organization ECPAT (End Child Prostitution And Trafficking) estimates there to be 100,000 children working in the sex industry in Taiwan. As with the situation in Thailand, these are tribal hill-people whose traditional living has been disrupted by environmental degradation of the land by logging companies and whose children are offered a 'good job in the city' by agents working for brothels. As in many other contexts, the intertwining of racism and destruction of once-fertile land has its greatest impact on vulnerable children. Once the land has been raped, it's the children's turn.

4. The impact on women and children: bodily mutilations

The foregoing section gave some examples of the actual everyday reality for women and children around the world of the impact of an ideology of transcendence which has split human thinking into the two realms of spirit and body, valuing those aspects which are transcendent, spiritual and non-material and despising the reality of earth, death, suffering, bodies and sex.

This ideology has created a situation where someone is prepared to kidnap a 7-year-old girl and traffic her to another country. There, sufficient numbers of men to make it economically worthwhile are prepared to force their penises into her so that they can orgasm. At some point, she may contract HIV. At some point, she may die. Her physical and psychological agony, her very life itself, are regarded as of less value than the men's wish to relieve themselves sexually. This happens to something like 200,000 Nepalese girls. This is one example from one country.

There is no biological imperative which makes the behaviour of these men necessary. Neither do we need to draw on a rhetoric of human evil, comforting though it might be. Human sexuality is unitary: we are joined by a shared human sexuality and, in order to make sense of what these men do, we need to look to culture and ideology to explain it. These practices are abhorrent but they are not aberrant. Both in terms of the numbers of people affected and in terms of the ideologies used to justify them, these practices are normal: they are a normal, everyday part of sexuality around the world.

The ideologies which have distorted sexuality and resulted in the normalization of such abusive practices as rape, forced prostitution, trafficking and child sexual abuse have also had other impacts. These other impacts are directly on the body. They are cultural practices which alter the body of girls or women, in order to control (reduce) female sexual pleasure and enhance male sexual pleasure.

An example of this is the historical practice of 'footbinding' in Chinese culture. It has been estimated that over the last one thousand years, somewhere between three billion women (Ross, 2002) and four and a half billion women (*BBC*, 2003) had their feet bound. That is, a minimum of three thousand million women – roughly the equivalent of the entire population of girls and women alive on Earth today. In China, the female foot, not in its 'natural' state but when 'civilized' by modification and elaborate clothing, became highly erotically charged for men (Jackson, 2000; Ko, 2002, 2007). Feet may carry a particular nationalist meaning for Chinese people: many Chinese have an inherited extra toe or toe-nail (Chi & Wang, 2004) and this recessive genetic trait is seen as specifically linked to pure Han ancestry. It is possible that this has relevance in the emphasis on women's feet as symbolizing both culture and nation.

According to tradition, the custom of footbinding began during the Southern Tang dynasty (907–923) when the Emperor had one of his favourite consorts bandage her feet to make them pointed in order for her to dance more beautifully. The parallel here is with high-heeled shoes in Western culture and with the exaggeratedly 'feminine' hip-movements which wearing high-heeled shoes encourage (think of Marilyn Monroe in *Some Like It Hot* [Wilder, 1959] – the cross-dressing men in the film, by contrast, wear flat shoes). Similarly, ballet-shoes permit a specific form of 'feminine' dance – *en pointe* – where the weight of the dancer's body is taken on the toes, supported to some extent by stiffening the body and toe of the *pointe* shoe. This move, first introduced into ballet around the 1830s, is a specifically female dance movement: there is no routine use of *en pointe* among male ballet-dancers. Footbinding, however, unlike the later *pointe* shoes, did not remain restricted to elite forms of courtly dance. Over the centuries the custom spread from the court to the upper class and then to the majority of the population.

Small feet became synonymous with beauty, so much so that it was difficult for a woman with large feet to find a husband. The perfect foot was, according to a well-known expression, one that was 'thin, small, pointed, crooked, perfumed, soft, and symmetrical' (Ross, 2002, online). The practice of footbinding involved bandaging both feet with the foot bent and the smaller toes strapped to the heel so tightly that the bones of the foot gradually broke over a period of several years, as the weight of standing on the feet slowly crushed them. A form of club-foot – known by names such as the Golden Lotus or Three-Inch Hook – was produced, only three to four inches in length. Women could walk only by tottering, falling from foot to foot (Chang, 1993). Pregnancy increased the pressure and therefore the pain. Medical consequences of footbinding included chronic pain, inability to move freely, fractures, circulatory problems and osteoporosis (Cummings & Stone, 1997). During the Cultural Revolution, footbindings were forcibly removed, but where the feet were already broken the release of the bandages only harmed the women more. It is extraordinary that the same culture which embraced reflexology as part of its traditional medical practice could also produce the cultural practice of footbinding.

In Chinese culture, as with other cultures with an ideology of transcendence, nature and the feminine were both subordinated to culture and the masculine. Like the art of bonsai, footbinding took the 'natural' and made it aesthetic through the imposition of 'culture'. The following extracts are taken from an interview with a Taiwanese surgeon and expert on footbinding, Dr Ko Chi-sheng:

It is the longest lasting and most widespread fetish custom in history.... Binding usually began when the girl was four and took about five years to complete. If started too late the feet would be too large and not supple enough to bend, but starting too soon carried the danger that the girl would be crippled for life and unable to walk.... There were sexual reasons behind binding... After binding the feet the lower legs atrophied [the muscles weakened], so when they walked... they used their hip muscles to move... with resulting hypertrophy [enlargement] of the hip muscles... and also the perineum muscle.... When the Japanese took control of Taiwan in 1895 they outlawed foot-binding, but studied it. Japanese doctors took X-rays of women with bound feet and compared them with those with normal feet. They found the skeletal structure was identical. The difference was in the muscles. Binding increased the shrinkage power of the vagina. (quoted in Ross, 2002: online)

In other words, one of the main consequences of footbinding was that the vaginal muscles became more developed and could grip the penis more tightly (an effect which can be produced by general health and vigour, and specifically by pelvic floor muscle exercises, far more easily than by crippling the feet). Men also used the bound foot itself as a sexual object: a man could put the foot in his mouth; he could put his penis between the woman's feet. It is possible that he also pushed his penis into the tight space created where the arch of the foot had been broken. The feet often remained wrapped even during sex, however, as the wrapped foot was regarded as highly erotic, with the decorative 'lotus shoe' seen as perhaps the most sexually arousing item in Chinese culture, because of its connection to the sexualized and hidden foot. A nineteenth-century French scholar in China explained:

All the Celestials whom I have interrogated on this point have replied unanimously: 'Oh, a little foot! You Europeans cannot understand how exquisite, how sweet, how exciting it is!' The contact of the genital organ with the little foot produces in the male an indescribable degree of voluptuous feeling, and women skilled in love know that to arouse the ardor of their lovers a better method than all Chinese aphrodisiacs is to take the penis between their feet. It is not rare to find Chinese Christians accusing themselves at confession of having had 'evil thoughts on looking at a woman's foot' (quoted in Ross 2002: online).

At an individual level, footbinding restricted women's movements around the house and locality. Walking could only be done mainly on the heel of the foot, supported by the shoe. When not wearing shoes and supported by a walking-cane, women could scarcely walk at all. In everyday life, this disability could be accommodated by a lifestyle where most work (childcare, food-preparation and cooking, spinning, sewing and making clothes and shoes) was conducted sitting down, but in emergencies, just as with contemporary wheelchair-users, bound women were far more vulnerable than those able to use their legs to run away. During famine, they could not walk to reach food; during military invasion, they could not flee; and in a house-fire, they were far less able to escape (Ross, 2002).

Footbinding had an impact not only on the individual woman but also on the woman's family, community and ultimately on the whole of Chinese culture and society. Dr Ko Chi-sheng claims:

The maximum distance [women with bound feet] could walk was about three or five miles, so it shrunk their world, made them conservative, they needed care and support, needed large families. It also had an important influence on architecture – Chinese houses have a single floor, two at most, because women couldn't climb up stairs. Everything was small, villages, narrow lanes, and so on because women needed support to walk, a man's help, a rail, or a wall, or they carried umbrellas to use as walking sticks. The women couldn't travel. So while the West was able to explore the world, to colonize the world and send settlers out to America, Canada, South America, New Zealand and Australia, the Chinese were restricted by both the physical and mental consequences of foot-binding. They couldn't take their women. The Chinese stayed in China. The Chinatowns you see in America, the overseas Chinese were all from Guangdong in southern China, because they didn't practise binding. (quoted in Ross, 2002: online)

Another practice which, like footbinding, has had a powerful effect on the individual bodies of girls and women and has affected many millions of women over periods lasting many hundreds, perhaps thousands, of years, is the cultural practice of 'female circumcision'. Like footbinding, this has traditionally been carried out on young girls – often by their mothers or other female relatives – as a way of ensuring their marriageability. Unlike footbinding, this practice is both continuing and expanding.

The first historical reference to it can be found in the writings of Herodotus, who reported its existence in ancient Egypt in the fifth century BC (Lightfoot-Klein, 1991). Around the middle of the twentieth century onwards, the practice began to die out in a number of countries, but that trend has now been reversed and the practice is expanding. It currently affects around 130 million women and girls in the world today, with prevalence rates in Egypt, for example, running at around 96 per cent (Unicef, 2006).

Like footbinding, female genital cutting or 'circumcision' also results in chronic pain and incapacity. While male circumcision (from the Latin, *circum*, around, and *caedere*, to cut) involves cutting around the foreskin, leaving the glans or head of the penis intact, the equivalent (cutting off just the prepuce or hood of the clitoris) rarely happens in female 'circumcision'. In this case, therefore, the word 'circumcision' is a misnomer, and the terms 'genital modification', 'genital cutting' or 'genital mutilation' are more accurate descriptions of what takes place. Commonly, part or all of the clitoris itself is cut away completely, which is equivalent in sensory and functional terms to cutting off the head of the penis. Additionally, in some countries the procedure further includes the cutting away of the small labia, the large labia, or both. The most drastic operations are found along the Horn of Africa, in Northern and central Sudan, Southern Egypt, Djibouti, Somalia, parts of Kenya and Ethiopia. Here all of the above surgeries are carried out and, in addition, the skin of the outer labia is scraped clean of its inner tissue and is then sewn together over the wound, so that only a tiny opening, intended to be barely adequate for passing urine and menstrual fluid, remains. This widely practised procedure is called infibulation or Pharaonic circumcision. The majority of these operations are still carried out in a situation where people do not have access to anaesthesia or antibiotics, and the instruments typically used are unsterile razors, scissors or kitchen knives. Broken glass is also used (Seisay, 2008). The death-rate among girls subjected to this procedure is estimated to be between 10 and 30 per cent (Lightfoot-Klein, 1991).

Depending on the amount of flesh removed from the girl's pubic area in the genital 'modification', consequences are likely to include chronic infections and pelvic inflammatory disease, difficulty in urinating and passing menstrual fluid out of the tiny opening remaining, pain in intercourse, and scar-tissue affecting the ability to give birth. Girls subjected to this procedure are more likely to contract HIV infection and more likely to die in childbirth.

It is not easy to hear from women themselves who have undergone this procedure. Anecdotes tend to be used either to argue for or against the practice. Descriptions are often couched in medical terminology and leave out the lived, everyday reality. As with women's experiences of having bound feet, the direct experiences and views of 'circumcised' women are seldom available for those outside the culture to hear. It is therefore important to take time to read the following accounts, which are from oral histories collected in Cairo in the late 1970s from five women, four Muslim and one Christian, ranging in age from early 20s to mid-60s (Atiya, 1984). The women gave narrative accounts of their daily lives including everyday concerns and successes, illnesses, deaths, marriages and work, and in among these accounts each woman told of her experience of being circumcised:

> **Om Gad**: Circumcision is absolutely necessary. I don't know why, but it is a tradition. These parts in a woman grow bigger the older she gets. They are ugly and deface her.... I was nine years old when I was circumcised... We are told it's a big event.... When my cousin came to call me I was overjoyed. I got up and ran with her. It was a feast! Although I'd heard a child scream when being circumcised I wasn't afraid. Some of our cousins had already been circumcised when we arrived at the house. They were sitting there laughing. It only hurts the moment the razor hits, then the stinging goes away... So they got hold of me, and my maternal uncle's wife sat behind me and held my legs apart. I was sitting on the floor on a piece of rug. The barber stood in front of me and did the operation. I cried out once, then they made a bandage of cotton and gauze and placed it between the 'sisters' [labia] and said, 'Don't bring your legs together or the wound will heal over. If this happens, when a woman gives birth she is torn.'
>
> **Alice**: I was eight years old.... The night before the operation they brought us [the cousins] together and stained our hands orange with henna. All evening the family celebrated with flutes and drums. We were terrified. We knew what to expect. Each would ask the other, 'Are you afraid?' and each would answer, 'I'm very afraid.' This went on all night like a refrain. We couldn't sleep. I heard the midwife come in about five o'clock the next morning. I was to be the first because I was the eldest. They did the operation and then pounded an onion and salt mixture to put on the wound to cauterize it. When it was all over, they carried me and put me to bed.... On the seventh day we got up. They had new dresses made

for us.... Our mother told us to tie our severed clitorises to the hems of our dresses. The family then paraded us through the streets like brides and took us for a picnic by the river. We were told to throw our clitorises to the Nile. This would bring us happiness. Words! At sunset we went home. It was all over. This operation makes it harder for a girl to enjoy sex, and as sex is all important to men, then where is the happiness this custom brings?

Suda: [Circumcision is] a must. It's the first taste of suffering a girl ever has. I cried for a week before I was circumcised. I was twelve, but I knew what to expect from the time I was eight years old. I learned from the talk of the older girls. People say that the older a girl is when she's circumcised, the less chance there is of these parts growing back [sic]. I don't know if that's really true. But that's why some people keep this ordeal until a girl is twelve or thirteen. I was told it would hurt a little, but it was hell. The midwife puts alcohol on you afterward, and you're on fire. I knew I had to go through this operation. I knew there was no getting around it. It's as sure a thing as having to get married or give birth.... The midwife gave us each the bit she cut from our bodies. She said, 'Take this. Keep it with you all the time for a month.' This is to prevent us from becoming sterile should an ill-wisher put the evil eye on us. My mother put mine in a piece of cloth and pinned it to my dress. After a month, I went to the river with my cousins and threw it out.

Dunya: [I was circumcised at six years old.] I remember the circumcision clearly, and when the knife hit, it was as if someone had built a fire under me. Then they twist a length of clean sheet or gauze which is soaked in disinfectant and sulphur powder, and they bind the child with it. My heavenly days, it's worse than fire, and you stay in bed, unable to move, with legs apart, for days! I wouldn't do it to my daughter. I wouldn't want to hurt her.

Om Naeema: When I was about seven years old, my mother had me circumcised. We circumcise girls in summer... Girls are circumcised to keep them cool and able to control their sexual urges. Boys are circumcised because it is believed that they cannot copulate or beget children if they are not. Most often in the villages, a group of girls is circumcised at the same time. Afterwards, the women wash them in the river, each in turn. Then they bind them with a clean cloth dipped in oil and iodine.... I didn't feel anything when the knife hit, but later when feeling came back and the medicine wore off, about noon that day, I thought the sky would come crashing down about my head from the pain. I cried.... My mother wept with me and said, 'Never mind, my darling, this is your day. It will pass.' She boiled an egg for me and fed me grapes and dates to keep up my strength, saying all the while, 'When you eat this you will be well.' She also dissolved some sugar in water and gave it to me to drink, comforting me with her words, 'Drink this, mama's little heart. It will relieve the stinging you feel and cool your wound.' She went on this way until I got better, and then she stopped worrying over me.

(Quotations from Atiya, 1984)

In many countries where female genital mutilation is practised, women who do not undergo the operation are regarded as unclean, contaminating and stinking. People may refuse to associate with them, or buy food from them, as they claim they can smell their genitals. (An ironic fact, given that female genital circumcision makes urination and the passing of menstrual blood and faeces more difficult. After giving birth, circumcised women are more likely to become incontinent – and thus rejected by their community because of the smell.)

This revulsion at female genitals is seen in other countries also. Surgical removal of the clitoris (for the treatment of masturbation or 'excessive' sexual desire) was practised in Europe and the United States in the nineteenth and early twentieth centuries; in a paper published in 1866, Isaac Baker Brown, president of the Medical Society of London, wrote that the only permanent cure for diseases such as nymphomania was to remove the clitoris – the 'source of evil' (Vergnani, 2003).

Today, surgical 'labial reduction' and 'vaginal tightening' are increasingly popular in the West (Elliott, 2008). Women who have had the surgery have enthused, 'now I love the way I look; nice and neat and new. My vagina looks perfect', while plastic surgeons commented, 'The most common reason we hear [for the surgery] is that they have had a negative comment made by a male sexual partner. Women are made to feel that they are not perfect the way they are' and that there is 'often pressure from a man who tells them they need it. I assume that their standards for labial beauty were set by a combination of the porn industry, sex-oriented magazines and the Internet.' (Kobrin, 2004, online). While these operations are voluntarily chosen by adult women, in stark distinction to traditional female genital cutting, their existence may be used to provide some justification for the tradition. Far from dying out, the traditional practice is spreading to new areas and the most extreme form, referred to as 'scraping the girls clean', is becoming more popular, as it is considered that 'this is the modern and hygienic way that educated people do it' (Lightfoot-Klein, 1989: 48).

Footbinding and female genital mutilation are examples of cultural practices which control women's sexuality: footbinding by restricting girls' and women's physical autonomy and by turning their bodies into passive and eroticized objects on which a specific male sexual fetish could be played out; and genital cutting by physically reducing the female capacity for orgasm and by socializing the girl to see her vulva and vagina as something which is not her own private property but which is a family and communal possession over which others exercise control. The concept of *izzat* (usually translated as 'honour') sums up the communal nature of the ownership of the girl's or woman's sexuality: it belongs primarily to her father and other male relatives and then to her husband, but not to her.

Atrophying the leg muscles to tighten the vagina, or cutting away the labial flesh to tighten the vagina, are not the only practices used. In contemporary societies, a phenomenon called 'dry sex' has been reported in South Africa, Senegal, Zaire, Cameroon, Malawi, Zambia, Kenya, Zimbabwe, Saudi Arabia, Haiti and Costa Rica (Kun, 1998), with prevalence rates of around 46 per cent (Beksinska *et al.*, 1999) to 86 per cent (Baleta, 1998) of women in South African community samples reporting this practice, especially among younger groups.

'Dry sex' involves the use by the woman of a wide range of substances which might include herbs, salt, methylated spirits, vinegar, bicarbonate of soda or bleach to dry out her vaginal secretions prior to sex. The substances irritate and inflame the vaginal membranes, making the vagina swollen, hot and dry. The result resembles an allergic reaction or chemical burn (Kun, 1998). It increases the friction and therefore pleasure for the man, but results in bruising and tearing for the woman, especially if she is adolescent, causing pain and bleeding. However, as one report quoted, 'Men love dry sex. If you're wet, they think it's not normal.' In Zambia, for example:

> girls are made to believe that they are supposed to be dry. There is even a name given to girls who are too wet – Chambeshi River, referring to a river in Zambia. Some men tell girls that being wet means that they have been with too many men. (*Human Rights Watch*, 2003: online)

Another report explains:

> In parts of sub-Saharan Africa, to please men, women sit in basins of bleach or saltwater or stuff astringent herbs, tobacco or fertilizer

inside their vagina. The tissue of the lining swells up and natural lubricants dry out. The resulting dry sex is painful and dangerous for women. The drying agents suppress natural bacteria, and friction easily lacerates the tender walls of the vagina. Dry sex increases the risk of HIV infection for women, already two times as likely as men to contract the virus from a single encounter. The women [selling sex] can charge more for dry sex, 50 or 60 rands ($6.46 to $7.75), enough to pay a child's school fees or to eat for a week. (McGeary, 2001: online)

The practice has now begun to be studied because of the link to HIV infection. One wonders whether this practice, causing pain to millions of women on a regular basis for most of their life, would have ever been discussed in the literature, even to the marginal extent that it has been, if it were not for the relationship to HIV transmission. This practice, so important in the daily lives of millions of women, has continued almost unspoken, as yet another example of the invisibility of women's and girls' experiences.

5. Conclusion

The aim in this chapter has not been to set out the quaint, exotic or historical customs of those who are 'Other' than us – customs at which we can squirm in titillated disgust before turning away and forgetting. These cultural practices are in absolutely no sense irrelevant or marginal to understanding contemporary Western understandings of paedophiles in society. On the contrary, the argument here is that examining and theorizing such cultural practices is central because these examples show us, in an un-moderated and unflinching form, what normative adult male sexuality looks like and has looked like for thousands of years. Far from the world of privileged Western 'sexual radicals' in their fetish-gear, or the rarefied intellectual sphere of academics quoting scathingly witty and taboo-busting French cultural theorists to defend sex with boys, these examples go some way to show us the lived experiences of many millions of ordinary people in the world today.

The contention of this book is that human sexuality is unitary, it is holistic. It cannot be broken up into obscure nineteenth-century pseudo-medical taxonomies – such categorizing may please those with a stamp-collecting mentality but does not reflect a reality in which human sexuality, as with any other aspect of being human, is nuanced, socioculturally produced and fundamentally about relationship not biology.

All the examples cited here illustrate the painful nature of men's sexuality, a sexuality which treats with contempt what is desired. The focus of the cultural practices is the vagina – raped, ripped apart inside, used to relieve British soldiers' boredom (a long queue standing four deep 'because there were only four women in the brothel'), tightened by destroying leg muscles, tightened by slicing away flesh with razors or glass, tightened by burning with bleach. In order to understand the problematic nature of men's sexuality, we must not bracket out those experiences which 'only' affect non-Western women or children. Humans are one species, and human sexuality is universal within our species. If we wish to understand paedophiles in society, we need to confront the dilemmas at the heart of human sexuality.

Writing on the trial of Adolf Eichmann, Hannah Arendt analysed the moral context within which the Holocaust took place and identified five cultural processes. These processes involved 'language rules'; having a system of 'bearers of secrets'; co-opting victims to participate in their own destruction; focusing on meticulous attention to rules; and the use of 'privileged categories' – exemptions to the general rule. Together, these five processes produced a situation of which Eichmann could later say, 'Nobody came to me and reproached me for anything in the performance of my duties' (Arendt, 2006:131). No-one had challenged Eichmann as he went about his business of mass-murder on a vast scale. Arendt is particularly scathing about the acceptance by non-Nazis of the 'privileged categories' established early in the process by the Nazis. She states:

> the acceptance of privileged categories – German Jews as against Polish Jews, war veterans and decorated Jews as against ordinary Jews, families whose ancestors were German-born as against recently naturalized citizens etc. – had been the beginning of the moral collapse of respectable Jewish society. (Arendt, 2006: 131)

She contrasts this acquiescence to such categories with the attitude of the French Jewish war veterans who were offered the same privileges by their Government and refused them, replying with great courage and humanity, 'We solemnly declare that we renounce any exceptional benefits we may derive from our status as ex-servicemen.' (p. 132). Arendt makes clear that 'What was morally so disastrous in the acceptance of these privileged categories was that everyone who demanded to have an "exception" made in his case implicitly recognised the rule' (*ibid.*), thereby agreeing implicitly with the notion that while some Jews might be worth saving, the majority of Jews were not worthy and could be murdered *without protest*. She concludes her discussion:

> In Germany today [1963], this notion of 'prominent' Jews has not yet been forgotten. While the veterans and other privileged groups are no longer mentioned, the fate of 'famous' Jews is still deplored at the expense of all others. There are more than a few people, especially among the cultural élite, who still publicly regret the fact that Germany sent Einstein packing, without realizing that it was a much greater crime to kill little Hans Cohn from around the corner, even though he was no genius. (Arendt, 2006: 134)

The deep moral corrosiveness involved in setting up categories of privileged versus non-privileged, worthy and unworthy, the protected versus the abandoned, is at root the same moral corrosion that can be seen when the US Army ignores the abuse of trafficked women on its bases, or when men travel abroad to sexually abuse children from impoverished countries. It is also, painfully, the same moral corrosion that privileges celebrities such as Roman Polanski over their child-victims, or privileges a discourse of adult sexual radicalism and liberation over a discourse which foregrounds and emphasizes the need of the vulnerable to be protected.

Epilogue

Living with Paedophiles in Society and Finding Hope

The material presented in this book has ranged from the current day to the Bronze Age, from the glittering celebrities of Hollywood to the remote jungles of the Congo and the brothels of northern India, from Wikipedia to the darknet, from the familiar and expected to the hidden, obscure, ignored and invisible. The aim has been to uncover connections which can help us make sense of human sexuality and thus, through that, to make sense of adult sexual attraction to children and adult sexual contact with children. The book argues that these phenomena are not 'outside' society but are embedded deeply into how people think about sex.

Returning to the examples discussed in Chapter 1, we now have a clearer understanding of why society's responses, for example to Jackson and Polanski, have been so ambivalent. There is no consensus on how we should respond. The messages received through popular culture are confused and contradictory. News stories and 'misery lit' offer us a moral world of clear distinctions, of good and evil, a world peopled only by victims and monsters; a world in which the face of Madeleine McCann looks silently out at us, a forlorn cipher for all the heart-wrenching suffering of childhood. At the same time, Michael Jackson, whom some regard as having been a predatory paedophile who abused a series of young boys, is buried with great pomp in a golden casket with much fulsome praise and scant reference to his 'sad fall', 'troubling stuff' or 'attendant problems' (Niven, 2009). Online, paedophiles put forward manifestos and argue for the benefits of 'child grooming', Kevin Brown and his peers discuss civil rights, and a whole world of alternative discourse is opened to any enquirer with internet access. In the movies, each decade provides its offering of 'NAMBLA porn' whether Shirley Temple, *Lolita*, *Pretty Baby*, the pubescent Natalie Portman making eyes at Jean Reno in *Leon*, or the delights of the young Dakota Fanning – and Bill Condon and Liam Neeson dollop on the charm in spadefuls to show us that Kinsey may have been a little socially awkward at times but by golly he was an all-American hero.

Serious peer-reviewed tomes from Cambridge University and other academic institutions add to the mix. Scholarly studies of pederasty, of historical and anthropological research, lend weight to the suggestion that sex with children (or, at any rate, with boys) can be acceptable and harmless. The radical critiques of patriarchy and heterosexuality emerging out of the 1970s have found themselves diverging to such an extent that there is now a total disconnect between those discourses which promote sexual liberation and those which focus on child protection. Neither side speaks to the other. It seems that academics either find the notion of paedophiles irritating and irrelevant – or else titillating and deliciously naughty (Newman, 2009).

We have now reached the point where the confusions, contradictions and disconnections need to be strongly challenged. It is no longer enough to argue that because Kinsey was instrumental in bringing gay rights and sex education, it doesn't matter that his work was based on the abuse and rape of children. Nor is it acceptable to argue that because Kinsey's work was based on the abuse and rape of children, we should therefore repeal legislation on homosexuality and teach only abstinence in schools. Both arguments are simplistic and fallacious. What is required is a careful and sensitive, but thorough, disaggregation of the discourse on 'sexual liberation' (acceptance of sexualities alternative to the norm of penetrative heterosexuality) from acceptance of child sexual abuse. Children are indeed sexual, and may indeed be sexually active, but that does not supply an excuse or a justification for adult sexual contact with children.

This book has drawn attention to the small number of studies available on the prevalence of adult sexual attraction to children in the general population. We need far more (and larger) studies on this crucial aspect, but the studies so far undertaken suggest tentatively that such attraction may be more common than we had thought. However, realising that adult sexual attraction to children is not necessarily rare or even particularly aberrant helps us make sense of some of the more paradoxical responses to paedophilia in society, both the violent rejection and the indifference and tolerance. It also makes more sense of the figures on child sexual abuse.

We know that most sexual abuse of children takes place within the family or by someone known to the family. We also know that most of those who sexually abuse children do not self-define, and are not clinically defined, as paedophiles. However, in order to sexually abuse a child, the perpetrator typically would need to be sexually motivated and find the experience sexually arousing. Using the concept of a continuum of sexual arousal to children (rather than a dichotomous categorization into 'paedophile' and 'non-paedophile') helps to make sense of those situations where those who are not 'paedophiles' sexually abuse children. It also begins to bring into awareness the experiences of those who are sexually aroused but do not act on their attractions. As one study found, there may be 'a sizeable minority of men who do not report engaging in pedophilic behavior [but who] exhibit sexual arousal to pedophilic stimuli.' (Hall *et al.*, 1995: 692).

This book therefore, paradoxically, agrees with the Kinsey studies on human sexuality on two main points. First, Kinsey may have been right when he put forward the view that paedophilia is not pathological, in the sense that it is part of ordinary life. Those who have argued for paedophilia to be removed as a category of mental illness point, as Kinsey did, to the widespread prevalence of adult sexual contact with children, noting that sexual arousal patterns to children 'have been common and accepted in varying cultures at varying times...Do they constitute a mental illness? Not unless we declare a lot of people in many cultures and in much of the past to be mentally ill.' (Green, 2002: 470). This comment points up the absurdity of trying to make 'paedophilia' no more than a clinical or psychiatric label: it is far more than that. By attempting to restrict our understanding of a complex cultural phenomenon down to a simplistic medical diagnosis, we lose sight of what matters – the harm caused to children. Far from locating the problem of 'paedophiles' within the specific psychopathology of any particular individual, this book has argued that the problem is instead about all of us, about aspects of human sexuality, human society and human culture in general. Regardless of the numbers of people who have sexually abused children, it remains wrong and harmful. The focus should be on the act of harm to the child, not the mental state of the adult.

This leads to the second point from the Kinsey studies, which is that Kinsey may be right in suggesting that a large proportion of men are 'sex offenders'. This view may be correct if we take the definition of an offence as involving harm to the victim of the sex act, which was not Kinsey's approach. Kinsey did not discriminate between offences that were mainly to do with indecency (such as consensual oral sex between adults in private), or which caused mainly psychological distress (such

as exhibitionism or obscene phone-calls) or which could cause physical and severe psychological harm (such as sexual assault and rape):
he simply wanted the whole gamut of 'sex offenses' removed from the
statute book. In his view, the fact that, as he saw it, 95 per cent of men
were 'sex offenders' meant that sex *offences* should be reduced, not sex
offending. It is very odd, given that Kinsey interviewed so many male
prisoners, that not one of his sample disclosed rape to him, or, given
that he interviewed several hundred male prostitutes, not one apparently had ever been sexually attacked. For Kinsey, as we have seen, rape
and sexual abuse did not exist, even theoretically. Therefore, for him
and for his followers, finding that 'sex offending' is common leads to
the conclusion that it should be tolerated. In contrast, my conclusion is
that if a particular form of 'sex offending' is indeed common (and the
statistics on child sexual abuse suggest that it certainly isn't rare), then
tolerating such actions simply means that we collude in the abuse, we
are complicit. It is time to develop a new strategy.

If human sexuality were a fixed, immutable biological drive, then
we would just have to put up with rape and child sexual abuse. But
human sexuality is not like plumbing; it is like language. We inherit the
grammar but we develop the vocabulary and we speak our own words.
We learn it, we share it and shape it. As Kincaid reminded us, 'Feeling
erotically buzzed or even highly charged does not mean entering auto-
matically into a different order of being. Human beings do not have a
rutting season, do not spray or howl at the moon or start humping the
legs of guests at parties.' (Kincaid, 1998: 287). Sexuality, sex, eroticism,
romance, love, desire, attraction . . . all these are shaped by our own individual biographies, by the communities around us, by the wider culture
and by the social, economic and political context.

Normative male sexuality is to a significant extent predicated on a
denial of empathy. I suggest that this has come about as part of the
fall-out from the ideology of transcendence. Just as our early autobio-
graphical experiences shape us, for good or ill, throughout the rest of
our lives, so the historical accidents of the Axial Age, by becoming cod-
ified into sacred and immutable texts, have shaped cultural experience
ever since. This ideology stressed the concepts of hierarchical power,
self-discipline and a rejection and hatred of the material world. Over
centuries, many millions of men found themselves caught in religions
which taught that the highest good was transcendence of the mundane
world and control or denial of temptation – temptation which was often
in the form of sexual pleasure with women. These men responded to the
stress of denying temptation by using the unconscious psychological

process of dissociation, as we all do to some extent when we deal with trauma or anxiety (Gomez, 1997). Dissociation splits off the anxiety-provoking 'bad' bits of experience and projects them out. This reduces anxiety and resolves the dilemmas of wanting and not having, but the cost is a loss of self-awareness and a distorted perception of reality.

This process is also shown, as in the example in Chapter 1, in the projection of hostility away from 'us' (which in this case was well-liked figures such as Polanski or Jackson) and onto the Other, the scapegoat figure of the 'evil paedophile', often faceless and scarcely known but loathed. By splitting the world into 'good guys' and 'bad guys' anxiety becomes controllable, even though one's grasp on reality is diminished in the process. Similarly, for entire cultures, anxiety and longing could become more manageable by splitting the world into 'good guys' and 'evil women', onto whom all the frustrations of lust and desire could be loaded. Women in their entirety became despised, and the particular biological parts of women (vaginas, clitorises) became in many cultures specifically and intensely despised, to the extent of structuring whole lifestyles around governing these body-parts through rituals of virginity, *izzat* (honour), marriage, sex segregation and *purdah* (seclusion), footbinding or genital cutting.

As was noted in the discussion on footbinding:

> The maximum distance [women with bound feet] could walk was about three or five miles, so it shrunk their world, made them conservative, they needed care and support, needed large families. It also had an important influence on architecture – Chinese houses have a single floor, two at most, because women couldn't climb up stairs. Everything was small, villages, narrow lanes, and so on because women needed support to walk, a man's help, a rail, or a wall, or they carried umbrellas to use as walking sticks.... the Chinese were restricted by both the physical and mental consequences of foot-binding. (quoted in Ross, 2002: online)

Not only was the vaginal opening shrunk as an effect of footbinding, the entire social and cultural world of the Chinese population was shrunk and made small and narrow. And yet the impact of this cultural practice would have been entirely invisible to the Chinese during the thousand years in which footbinding was culturally normal. What to many now is a strange and almost inexplicable distortion was simply 'the way it is'.

Despising something, and at the same time desiring it, provokes powerful emotions of fear, disgust and longing. It is the unconscious processes of denial, disassociation, splitting and projection – developed, reinforced and normalized over tens of centuries – which have resulted in a psychosocial context in which men find it difficult to empathise with those around them, particularly those they desire sexually. Masculinity itself, as a cultural construct, becomes predicated on specific forms of self-control and self-denial.

John Stoltenberg, in his collection of essays *Refusing to be a Man*, turns to the question of 'how men have (a) sex' and highlights the relationship between the cultural construction of masculinity and the processes of socialization to deny and repress one's feelings, especially as these processes are played out in the intimacy of sexual relationships (Stoltenberg, 2000a). Masculinity, like femininity, shifts and changes over time. What we have now is different from the masculinity of even one generation ago, but at the same time patterns can be seen which repeat themselves over generations and across countries and cultures. Being a man and having sex in fourteenth-century India, for example, is recognizably similar to a man having sex in second-century Greece or twenty-first century Australia. The same processes of hierarchy, discipline, rejection and contempt run through each encounter, more or less subliminally or powerfully.

In contemporary Western culture, theorists are becoming increasingly aware of how masculinity and male sexuality are linked to violence and emotional disconnection (Garbarino, 1999; Gilligan, 1999; Stoltenberg, 2000a, 2000b). Gilligan, for example, as a practising therapist working with some of the most violent men in the United States, writes that shame is a peculiarly masculine experience (and thus rage and violence become peculiarly masculine behaviours) because masculinity itself is such a fragile social construct, endlessly vulnerable to being challenged, disparaged and shamed. Cultural constructions, since they exist only through social agreement, are by their very nature fragile and open to continual challenge. Masculinity, as a construction in opposition to femininity, is inherently fragile and vulnerable to being exposed – all men feel emotions, feel weakness, gentleness and empathy and thus feel failure as a 'real man'. Paradoxically, it seems that the more a man is sensitive to universal human emotion, the more he fails masculinity. This vulnerability to failure can lead to 'losing face', creating an engine of psychic energy which can be used either to challenge the absurdity of culturally imposed notions of masculinity – and thus start digging a way out of the pit of violence and degradation – or, alternatively, to simply reinforce the construct of masculinity through stereotyped responses of shame, hostility and dominance.

While numerous authors have written on the fragility of the masculine self, one memorable study is by a woman journalist, Norah Vincent. Vincent, a lesbian, lived in drag as a man for over a year in order to research what it feels like in everyday life to be received and treated as a man. A major part of her research was the discovery of how beleaguered men feel. She writes:

> [Getting] into the so called boys' club in the early years of the new millennium felt much more like joining a subculture than a country club.... [being with men was] not a sign of having joined the over-class, for whom superiority is assumed and bucking up unnecessary. It was more like joining a union. It was the counterpart to and the refuge from my excruciating dates, which were often alienating and grating enough to make me wonder whether getting men and women together amicably on a permanent basis wasn't at times like brokering Middle East peace. (Vincent, 2006: 281)

She found the whole experience depressing, unpleasant and restrictive, not because she was attempting to pass as a man but because she was being received and treated as a man.

She concluded:

> I don't really know what it's like to be a man. I never could. But I know approximately. I know some of what it is like to be treated as one. And that, in the end, was what this experiment was all about. Not being but being received.
>
> I know that a lot of my discomfort came precisely from being a woman all along, remaining one even in my disguise. But I also know that another respectable portion of my distress came, as it did to the men I met in group and elsewhere, from the way the world greeted me in that disguise, a disguise that was almost as much of a put-on for my men friends as it was for me. That, maybe, was the last twist of my adventure. I passed in a man's world not because my mask was so real, but because the world of men was a masked ball. Only in my men's group did I see these masks removed and scrutinized. Only then did I know that my disguise was the one thing I had in common with every guy in the room. (Vincent, 2006: 273)

Male violence, including sexual violence, is structured deeply into human culture and into all contemporary known societies. When we attempt to understand paedophilia without recognizing this fact, it remains nothing more than an inexplicable mystery.

But the awareness that femininity, masculinity and sexuality are socially and culturally structured provides the key to the way forward. The sexual and gendered experiences of both men and women are dynamically shaped and are open to revision and change. As the gender theorist Raewyn Connell reminds us, recognizing 'the deeply historical character of gender has an important intellectual and political consequence. If a structure can come into existence, it can also go out of existence. The history of gender may have an end.' (Connell, 2002: 70). So too may the history of abusive sexuality. While this book has shown that currently adult male sexuality is culturally constructed to be abusive and non-empathic, there are signs that this is changing and can change further. Sexuality is shaped by popular discourse (the rise of the more sensitive 'new man' would be one example) and by social factors (for example, a boost in educational and economic status among women leads to more egalitarian relationships).

I propose that what is needed is to take far more seriously the discourse on 'sexual liberation'. At the moment, this discourse remains the elite preserve of the privileged and self-indulgent few in wealthy Western countries. It is seen as relevant only to those who are lesbian, gay, queer or whose sexuality is in some other way alternative to mainstream heterosexuality. But it is mainstream heterosexuality, as the sexuality of the majority of the world, which needs to be liberated and become radically other than it has been.

The dull, corrosive, abusive, unempathic sex endured by so many millions around the world, permeated by a hatred of women's genitals so extreme that it can encompass slicing off the clitoris with broken glass, or expecting a woman to sit in a bath of bleach to dry up her secretions, where 'consensual' sex hardly differs from the routine brutalization of rape or the coruscating contempt and hatred visited on prostituted women and children – this is the sexuality which needs radical transformation. Heterosexuality shapes and has shaped the whole of the project of civilization. A particular form of heterosexuality based on legitimate male inheritance and thus dependent on coercive male control of female sexuality has become normal throughout global society. It is a commonsense, taken-for-granted form of sexuality, a cultural tradition so deeply engrained that other constructions of heterosexuality have become almost inconceivable. The terrible logic of paternity, producing male heirs to preserve past descent and inherit future property, constructs societies based not merely on sexual reproduction but on an exact and unwavering form of legitimate male reproduction. These societies, spread across the world and throughout millennia, are therefore based not on human sexuality in all its diversity but rather on one precise culturally shaped form: the heterosexuality of the patriarch, the father, the inheritor of earlier patriarchs and the progenitor of future patriarchs. Together, each individual sexual encounter based on this sexuality reinforces and perpetuates the disjuncture between sex and empathy, between sex and profound human connection.

What is required is new stories, new imaginations (Kincaid, 1998). As the commentator Judith Levine expresses it, 'a rich imagination is the soul of good sex' (Levine, 2002: 153) and this rich imagination can make room for awareness and empathy.

And we can, if we wish, take advice and inspiration from a very surprising source. The psychotherapist Judith Herman, who revolutionized thinking on trauma, once said, 'Radical ideas are always very simple... They are only radical because of [political] obstacles, not because of their complexity.' (interview with Kreisler, 2000). And in addition, it seems to me that once an idea has been stated, it's no longer radical at all but entirely commonsense. People scratch their heads to remember a time when the idea wasn't obvious, even though it was unthinkable until the moment it was thought. So here's a radical thought: we can look to paedophiles for inspiration. Not, of course, to child abusers, but to that group (we have no idea how large) who are sexually attracted to children and, because they recognize the potential harm, choose not to act. If there are indeed ways in which paedophiles are 'sexual radicals', it may be less about who they desire and instead about how some may choose to contain their desire.

My research on 56 self-defined paedophiles living in the community (Goode, 2009) found that a small number of the sample felt strongly that adult sexual contact with children was to be avoided. These respondents articulated a model of self-controlled chastity, continence and celibacy – concepts completely unfamiliar within the discourses of 'sexual liberation' and indeed even of 'child protection'. Respondents wrote about the importance of the online support they received in holding onto this self-identity:

> I haven't been placed in any 'tempting' situations, but the knowledge that acting on my attractions is not inevitable is great for my peace of mind in case I am ever placed into such a situation.... [Online,] I've learned that I'm not the only one dealing with these issues, and that the other people like me aren't at all like we've been taught to expect

of people attracted to minors. We are in just as much control of our actions as everyone else. We aren't monsters. We are merely human beings, with all the strengths and weaknesses that implies. ('Kristof', 2007, research data)

For those living ordinary lives in the community, experiencing such attraction and choosing not to act on it is typically an intensely hidden secret, never discussed in the professional or academic literature and never mentioned in popular culture. We have no way of knowing how many people may be experiencing this. This is the flip-side of paedophilia. Just as we recognize that adults may sexually abuse children and yet not be paedophiles (not exclusively or primarily sexually attracted to children), so we must recognize that adults may be sexually attracted to children (and may or may not self-define as paedophile) but can choose consciously and deliberately never to act on their attraction.

What can we say about these people (seemingly predominantly men) who voluntarily choose restraint rather than express their sexuality? These men are consciously choosing not to conform to any negative stereotype. Rather than taking on a masculinity which denies empathy or which violently seeks gratification at the expense of the other, such men choose self-control, even when it's a hard struggle:

I have nobody to confide in about my experiences. I do not trust friends or family. I do not know of any online forums run by non-paedophiles that offer support. And I see little use in confiding with other paedophiles online because I don't think they can see things any more clearly than I can. . . . I would like to tell the world what it is like to be a paedophile so people would be more understanding of the horrible life I and others like me have to live . . . [People should know that] it is possible to have compassion for people who are sexually attracted to children without condoning sex between children and adults. . . . I do my best to stay away from children. I don't even talk to children if I can help it. . . . Thank you for giving me this opportunity to share my thoughts and experiences of this most secret and troublesome part of my life. ('Justin', 2008, research data)

Justin has chosen not to embrace a radical, counter-cultural position as a member of an 'alternative sexual minority' (Weeks, 1989). He does not feel a sense of entitlement to express his sexuality regardless of the impact it may have. Contemporary discourses on paedophilia have almost nothing to say to him or about him. We would have to look to depictions of male sexuality outside these traditions, from medieval celebrations of courtly love to early Victorian models of manliness or contemporary work on interrogating normative masculinity and 'refusing to be a man' (Stoltenberg, 2000a), before we can develop a framework within which to understand the experiences of 'non-contact' paedophiles. Justin and those like him seem to offer us an unexpected but hopeful model of gentleness, self-awareness and self-restraint. While it is only a tentative indication, it reminds us that nothing is fixed, nothing is pre-determined. We can change. We can separate attraction from action. We can develop new stories based on empathy.

We are at a crossroads in contemporary culture. We are reaching the end of the 200-year period of human culture based on fossil-fuel-derived energy. Globally, we are running out, not just of fossil fuels but also of fresh water, of fish, of land for agriculture, of metals, of chemicals... of all the myriad resources needed to live and grow. We are fast reaching the point of 'peak everything' (Heinberg, 2007). What will happen to concern over paedophiles in post-peak civilization?

It may be that at least some of the moral panic around paedophilia in the last decade or so has been a way to express (or transfer) some of our guilt at our collective failure to protect children. We have been 'spending the kids' inheritance', as bumper stickers merrily proclaimed in the seemingly carefree '90s. Now we are only just beginning to count the cost. While the substantive issues of credit crunch, economic crisis, population pressure, climate change and the destruction of much of the Earth's ecosystems begin to creep into public awareness, the anxiety engendered about the future for our children may have been expressed through the public scapegoating of paedophiles as those who overtly threaten and harm our children.

As the century of 'peak everything' plays itself out with increasing fury and destruction, systems of child protection in even the wealthiest countries will begin to break down and in impoverished countries and communities children will be, as always, the most vulnerable. The coming century will not be a secure or happy one for the majority of the world's children. The project of human civilization, not only in the form of Western democracy and enlightenment but throughout the world, is at risk. Will our children and grandchildren be exposed to greater levels of indifference, violence and abuse? Are the experiences of the children of the ethnic hill-people in Taiwan, of whom around 100,000 have been pushed into child sex tourism to provide food for their families (as discussed in Chapter 6), destined to become increasingly common? Or will the currents of awareness and sensitivity which have been developed over previous decades be maintained and strengthened? The current cultural distortions of human sexuality make it harder for men to empathize but easier for them to impose their own normative constructions of adult male sexuality onto other people. Will these distortions continue, so that the level of rape experienced in the Congo, for example, spreads across other countries as resource-wars and 'ethnic cleansings' intensify in the face of population pressure, famine and drought? Or will humans emerge from this crisis with their humanity intact, able to shake off at last the abuses of the Axial Age and, even before that, the violent inheritance from our ancestral primate 'demonic males'?

There is a place for paedophiles within society. Adults sexually attracted to children seem to be part of the normal continuum of human sexuality. This is unlikely to change. Some paedophiles understand the harm caused by adult sexual contact with children and choose not to act on that attraction. We need to hear from them and learn about restraint and self-control. It is possible that such adults, predominantly men, can point us towards a gentler model of adult male sexuality. We need to learn more about this model and we need to learn from anyone who can teach us. There is a place for love within our communities. Love includes celebration, sweetness and passion. Love includes listening sensitively to the voices of others. Love includes feeling the pain and loneliness of others, of all of us. Love includes holding and healing the profound pain of vulnerable children, taking it seriously, finally recognizing that the wellbeing of children matters above any other consideration in our society. Society will be profoundly challenged over the coming decades as we move, globally, from the Industrial age into a hitherto unimagined future. The twenty-first century will challenge us more than any previous time in human history. Perhaps at last we can let go of the deadening inheritance of generations and move towards something new.

Finally, we know that there is no inscrutable or inexplicable 'Other': there is only us. We previously met the paedophile in the guise of the Big Bad Wolf in Nicole Kassell's (2005) Hollywood movie *The Woodsman* but, as Charles Dickens reminds us in his 1862 novel *The Haunted House*, 'the play is, really, not *all* Wolf and Red Riding Hood, but has other parts in it' (2009:16). Indeed, as the jazz musician Louis Jordan memorably phrased it, 'There ain't nobody here but us chickens.' And all of us chickens together had better take responsibility.

References

Allison, R. (2000) 'Doctor driven out of home by vigilantes'. *Guardian Unlimited.* Posted 30 August 2000. Available online at http://www.guardian.co.uk/child/story/0,7369,361031,00.html, last accessed 9 December 2009.

American Psychiatric Association (2000) (4th edn, revised) 'Paedophilia'. *Diagnostic and Statistical Manual for Mental Disorders DSM-IV-TR.* Arlington, VA: American Psychiatric Association.

Anderberg, A. (2007) *History of the Internet and Web.* Available online at http://www.anderbergfamily.net/ant/history/, last accessed 11 August 2009.

Arch Diocese of New York (2008) *Pope Benedict's Message.* Posted 16 April 2008. Available online at http://www.archny.org/pastoral/safe-environment-program/pope-benedicts-message/, last accessed 14 December 2009.

Arendt, H. (2006) *Eichmann in Jerusalem: A Report on the Banality of Evil.* London: Penguin Classics.

Armstrong, K. (2006) 'Karen Armstrong on the prophets who emerged in a great age of spiritual insight'. *The Sunday Times.* Posted 12 March 2006. Available online at http://entertainment.timesonline.co.uk/tol/arts_and_entertainment/books/article738686.ece, last accessed 2 June 2008.

Armstrong, L. (1978) *Kiss Daddy Goodnight: A Speakout on Incest.* New York: Hawthorn.

Arnow, P. (1977) 'Pomeroy on … Children: An Interview with Dr Wardell Pomeroy' [ellipses in original], *Multi Media Resource Center, Resource Guide, Human Sexuality*, 2 (1) (Fall): 4–5 and 53–4.

Atiya, N. (1984) *Khul-Khaal: Five Egyptian Women Tell Their Stories.* Cairo: The American University in Cairo Press. (Quotations from the women on circumcision are taken from various pages throughout the book.)

Baleta, A. (1998) 'Concern voiced over "dry sex" practices in South Africa'. *The Lancet*, 352 (17 October): 1292. Available online at http://www.cirp.org/library/disease/HIV/baleta1/, last accessed 17 June 2008.

Bancroft, J. (1998) 'Foreword' to the re-issued Kinsey's *Human Male* volume, published by Indiana University Press to mark the fiftieth anniversary of the Report.

Bancroft, J. (ed.) (2003) *Sexual Development in Childhood.* Bloomington, IN: Indiana University Press.

Barbaree, H. & Marshall, W. (1989) 'Erectile responses among heterosexual child molesters, father–daughter incest offenders, and matched non-offenders: Five distinct age preference profiles'. *Canadian Journal of Behavioral Science*, 21: 70–82 (cited in Hall *et al.*, 1995).

Bauserman, R. (1990) 'Objectivity and ideology: criticism of Theo Sandfort's research on man–boy sexual relations'. *Journal of Homosexuality*, 20, accessed via http://www.ipce.info/ipceweb/Library/bauserman_objectivity.htm, last accessed 1 April 2008.

Bauserman, R. (1997). 'Man–boy sexual relationships in a cross-cultural perspective'. In J. Geraci (ed.) *Dares to Speak: Historical and Contemporary Perspectives on Boy-love*. Norfolk, England: Gay Men's Press, pp. 120–37.

BBC (2003) 'Chinese foot binding'. Posted 22 October 2003. Available online at http://www.bbc.co.uk/dna/h2g2/A1155872, last accessed 20 June 2008.

Beck, U. (1992) *Risk Society: Towards a New Modernity*. London/Thousand Oaks, CA: Sage.

Becker-Blease, K., Friend, D. & Freyd, J. (2006) 'Child sex abuse perpetrators among male university students'. Poster presented at the 22nd Annual Meeting of the International Society for Traumatic Stress Studies, Hollywood, California, November 4th to 7th, 2006. Abstract available online at http://hdl.handle.net/1794/4318. Poster available online at http://dynamic.uoregon.edu/~jjf/istss06issd06/bbffISTSS06.pdf, last accessed 3 March 2008.

Beckett, A. (2009) 'The dark side of the internet'. *The Guardian*. Posted 26 November 2009. Available online at http://www.guardian.co.uk/technology/2009/nov/26/dark-side-internet-freenet, last accessed 26 November 2009.

Beksinska, M., Rees, H., Kleinschmidt, I. & McIntyre, J. (1999) 'The practice and prevalence of dry sex among men and women in South Africa: a risk factor for sexually transmitted infections'. *Sexually Transmitted Infections*, June 75(3): 178–80. Available online at http://www.ncbi.nlm.nih.gov/pubmed/10448396, last accessed 17 June 2008.

Bell, J. (2003), 'I cannot admit what I am to myself'. *The Guardian*, G2, 23 January, pp. 2–3, 8.

Bridcut, J. (2006) *Britten's Children*. London. Faber and Faber.

Briere, J. & Runtz, M. (1989) 'University males' sexual interest in children: Predicting potential indices of "pedophilia" in a non-forensic sample'. *Child Abuse and Neglect*, 13: 65–75.

British Psychological Society (2004) 'What is sexual grooming?' Press release. Posted 23 March 2004. Available online at http://www.bps.org.uk/media-centre/press-releases/releases$/division-of-forensic-psychology/what-is-sexual-grooming$.cfm, last accessed 20 April 2010.

Brock, R. Nakashima & Thistlethwaite, S. Brooks (1996) *Casting Stones: Prostitution and Liberation in Asia and the United States*. Minneapolis: Fortress Press.

Brongersma, E. (1986) *Loving Boys*, 2 vols. New York: Global Academic Publishing/SUNY.

Brook Clinic (undated), *Briefing on Consensual Sexual Activity and the Sexual Offences Bill*. Online. Available online at http://www.brook.org.uk/content/M6_1_1_sobbrief1.asp, last accessed 9 September 2008.

Brosnan, A, Maitrat, T., Colhoun, A. & MacArdle, B. (2002) 'P2P: Historical development'. Posted 6 December 2002. Available online at http://ntrg.cs.tcd.ie/undergrad/4ba2.02-03/p1.html, last accessed 12 February 2008.

Brown, K. (2005) 'Update on my son's seizure by the State'. Posted 15 March 2005. Available online at http://unkind.atspace.com/seizure.html, last accessed 23 April 2009.

Brown, M. (2004) 'The bedroom and beyond'. *The Age*. Posted 13 November 2004. Available online at http://www.theage.com.au/articles/2004/11/12/1100227565498.html, last accessed 9 December 2009.

Burba, V. (2006) 'Buddhist nuns seek hope for Nepali slaves'. *Dayton City Paper*. Posted 21 April 2006. Available online at http://www.bodhimandala.net/index. php?id=10,10,0,0,1,0, last accessed 13 June 2008.

Burnham, D. (1983) *The Rise of the Computer State: A Chilling Account of the Computer's Threat to Society*. London: Weidenfeld and Nicolson.

Cadman, C. & Halstead, C. (2007) *Michael Jackson: For the Record*. Sandy: Authors Online Ltd.

Califia, P. (2000) (2nd edn) 'No minor issues: age of consent, child pornography, and cross-generational relationships'. In P. Califia, *Public Sex: The Culture of Radical Sex*. San Francisco, CA: Cleis.

Campbell, D. & Connor, S. (1986) *On The Record: Surveillance, Computers and Privacy – The Inside Story ...* London: Michael Joseph.

CBS News (2008) 'War against women: The use of rape as a weapon in Congo's civil war'. Posted 17 August 2008. Available online at http://www.cbsnews.com/stories/2008/01/11/60minutes/main3701249.shtml, last accessed 23 September 2008.

Chandler, R. (2004) *All That Glitters: The Crime and The Cover-up*. Gurnee, IL: Windsong Press.

Chang, J. (1993) *Wild Swans: Three Daughters of China*. London: Flamingo.

Chi, Ching-Chi & Wang, Shu-Hui (2004) 'Inherited accessory nail of the fifth toe cured by surgical matricectomy'. *Dermatologic Surgery*, 30 (8): 1177–9. Available online at http://www3.interscience.wiley.com/journal/118800841/abstract?CRETRY=1&SRETRY=0, last accessed 2 July 2008.

Clarke, I. (2009) 'The Guardian writes about Freenet'. Hypergraphia Indulged: Ian Clarke's Blog. Posted 25 November 2009. Available online at http://blog.locut.us/main/2009/11/25/the-guardian-writes-about-freenet.html, last accessed 25 November 2009.

Clayboy (2006) Userpage. Posted date unknown. Previously available online at http://en.wikipedia.org/wiki/User:Clayboy, last accessed 4 June 2006. Taken down 7 March 2007. Now available online at http://www.fact-archive.com/encyclopedia/User:Clayboy, last accessed 5 December 2009.

Cohen, N. (2009) 'Why Roman Polanski just loves the English courts'. *The Guardian*. 4 October 2009. Available online at http://www.guardian.co.uk/commentisfree/2009/oct/04/roman-polanski-nick-cohen-law, last accessed 3 December 2009.

Cohen, S (2002) (3rd edn) *Folk Devils and Moral Panics*. London: Routledge.

Connell, R. (2002) *Gender*. Cambridge: Polity.

Constantine, L. & Martinson, F. (eds.) (1981) *Children and Sex: New Findings, New Perspectives*. New York: Little Brown and Company.

Cook, M. & Howells, K. (eds.) (1981) *Adult Sexual Interest in Children*. New York and London: Academic Press.

Corby, B. (2006) (3rd edn) *Child Abuse: Towards a Knowledge Base*. Maidenhead: Open University Press.

Cowburn, M. & Dominelli, L. (2001) 'Masking hegemonic masculinity: reconstructing the paedophile as the dangerous stranger'. *British Journal of Social Work*, 31: 399–415.

Cox, P., Kershaw, S. & Trotter, J. (eds.) (2000) *Child Sexual Assault: Feminist Perspectives*. Basingstoke and New York: Palgrave Macmillan.

Crawford, J., Geraci, J., Ianthe & Ogrine, W. (1997) 'Suggestions for further reading'. In J. Geraci (ed.) (1997) *Dares to Speak: Historical and Contemporary Perspectives on Boy-love*. Norfolk, England: Gay Men's Press, pp. 255–6.

Critcher, C. (2003) *Moral Panics and the Media*. Milton Keynes and Philadelphia: Open University Press.

Cummings, S. & Stone, K. (1997) 'Consequences of foot binding among older women in Beijing, China'. *American Journal of Public Health*, 87(10): 1677–9.

Danica, E. (1989) *Don't: A Woman's Word*. London: The Women's Press.

Davidson, J. (2008) *The Greeks and Greek Love: A Radical Reappraisal of Homosexuality in Ancient Greece*. London: Phoenix.

Diamond, M. (1990) 'Selected cross-generational sexual behavior in traditional Hawai'i: A sexological ethnography'. In J. Feierman (ed.) (1990) *Pedophilia: Biosocial Dimensions*. New York: Springer-Verlag.

Dickens, C. (2009; first published in 1862) *The Haunted House*. London: Oneworld Classics.

Dimond, D. (2005) *Be Careful Who You Love: Inside the Michael Jackson Case*. New York, NY: Atria Books.

Donath, J. S. (1999) 'Identity and deception in the virtual community'. In M. A. Smith and P. Kollock (eds.) *Communities in Cyberspace*. London and New York: Routledge.

Douglas, M. (1966) *Purity and Danger: An Analysis of Concepts of Pollution and Taboo*. London: Routledge and Kegan Paul.

Douglas, M. (1992) *Risk and Blame*. London: Routledge.

Duvert, A. (1973) *Good Sex Illustrated*. Reissued (2007) in a translation from the French by Bruce Benderson. Boston: Semiotext(e) / The MIT Press.

Driver, E. & Droisen, A. (eds.) (1989) *Child Sexual Abuse: Feminist Perspectives*. Basingstoke and New York: Palgrave Macmillan

Eichenwald, K. (2006) 'On the web, pedophiles extend their reach'. *New York Times*. Posted 21 August 2006. Available online at http://www.nytimes.com/2006/08/21/technology/21pedo.html, last accessed 9 January 2009.

Eisenstadt, S. (1978) *Revolution and the Transformation of Societies: A Comparative Study of Civilisations*. New York, NY: The Free Press.

Eisenstadt, S. (ed.) (1986) *The Origins and Diversity of Axial Age Civilizations*. New York, NY: Albany.

Elliott, C. (2008) 'Designer vaginas, anyone?' *The Guardian*. Posted 8 January 2008. Available online at http://www.guardian.co.uk/commentisfree/2008/jan/08/designervaginasanyone, last accessed 20 June 2008.

Evilvigilante (2007) The blog of Xavier von Erck. Notes from 'A symphony of motivational material in B minor'. Available online at http://www.evilvigilante.com/, last accessed 4 December 2009.

Fanning, D. (2007) 'Fanning speaks up on rape scene'. Anthony Breznican, *USA TODAY*. Posted 23 January 2007. Available online at http://www.usatoday.com/life/movies/news/2007-01-23-fanning-hounddog_x.htm, last accessed 26 November 2009.

Fedora, O, Reddon, J. R., Morrison, J. W., Fedora, S. K., Pascoe, H. & Yeudall, L. T. (1992) 'Sadism and other paraphilias in normal controls and aggressive and nonaggressive sex offenders'. *Archives of Sexual Behavior*, 21: 1–15.

Feierman, J. (ed.) (1990) *Pedophilia: Biosocial Dimensions*. New York: Springer-Verlag.

Ferwerda, R. (1986) 'The meaning of the word soma (body) in the Axial Age: an interpretation of Plato's Cratylus 400c'. In S. Eisenstadt (ed.) (1986) *The Origins and Diversity of Axial Age Civilizations*. New York, NY: Albany.

Finkelhor, D. (1991) 'Response to Bauserman'. In T. Sandfort, E. Brongersma & A. van Naerssen (eds.) (1991) *Male Intergenerational Intimacy: Historical, Socio-psychological and Legal Perspectives*. New York and London: Harrington Park Press.

Ford, C. & Beach, F. (1951) *Patterns of Sexual Behavior*. New York: Harper & Row (cited in numerous texts, for example Green, 2002; Levine, 2002).

Frenzel, R. & Lang, R. (1989) 'Identifying sexual preferences in intrafamilial and extrafamilial child sexual abusers'. *Annals of Sex Research*, 2: 255–75 (cited in Hall *et al.*,1995).

Freud, S. (2001) *The Standard Edition of the Complete Psychological Works of Sigmund Freud: Volume XIX (1923–25) The Ego and the Id and Other Works*. London: Vintage. [*The Ego and the Id* was first issued in English translation 1927.]

Freund, K. & Costell, R. (1970) 'The structure of erotic preference in the nondeviant male'. *Behaviour Research and Therapy*, 8: 15–20.

Freund, K. & Watson, R. J. (1991) 'Assessment of the sensitivity and specificity of a phallometric test: An update of phallometric diagnosis of pedophilia'. *Psychological Assessment*, 3: 254–60.

Garbarino, J. (1999) *Lost Boys: Why Our Sons Turn Violent And How We Can Save Them*. New York: Free Press.

Gardner, W. (2003) 'The Sexual Offences Bill: Progress and the future'. Keynote speech at Tackling Sexual Grooming Conference, Westminster, London, September 2003. Available online at http://www.childnet-int.org/downloads/online-grooming2.pdf. Last accessed 25th January 2011.

Gathorne-Hardy, J. (1998) *Alfred C. Kinsey: Sex the Measure of All Things*. London: Chatto and Windus. (Other editions published 1999, 2000, 2004.)

Gathorne-Hardy, J (2004) *Half An Arch: A Memoir*. London: Timewell Press.

Gebhard, P., Johnson, A. & Kinsey, A. (1979) *The Kinsey Data: Marginal Tabulations of the 1938–1963 Interviews Conducted by the Institute for Sex Research*, NIMH Grant. Indiana: Indiana University Press.

Geraci, J. (ed.) (1997) *Dares to Speak: Historical and Contemporary Perspectives on Boy-love*. Norfolk, England: Gay Men's Press.

Giddens, A. (1993) *The Transformation of Intimacy: Love, Sexuality and Eroticism in Modern Societies*. Cambridge: Polity.

Gilligan, J. (1999) *Violence: Reflections on our Deadliest Epidemic*. London: Jessica Kingsley.

'Ginni' (undated) 'Childlover testimonies: Ginni'. *Amaros*. Available online at http://www.amaros.info/childlover/childlover.amaros, last accessed 9 December 2009.

Gomez, L. (1997) *An Introduction to Object Relations Theory*. London: Free Association Press.

Goode, S. D. (2008a) 'Paedophiles in contemporary culture'. In N. Billias (ed.) *Territories of Evil*. Amsterdam and New York: Rodopi.

Goode, S. D. (2008b) ' "The Splendor of Little Girls": social constructions of paedophiles and child sexual abuse'. In N. Billias & A. Curry (eds.) *Framing Evil: Portraits of Terror and the Imagination*. Oxford: Inter-Disciplinary Press.

Goode, S. D. (2009) *Understanding and Addressing Adult Sexual Attraction to Children: A Study of Paedophiles in Contemporary Society*. London: Routledge.

Green, L. & Goode, S. D. (2008) 'The "Hollywood" treatment of paedophilia: comparing some cinematic and Australian press constructions of paedophilia between 2003 and 2006'. *Australian Journal of Communication*, 35 (2): 71–85.

Green, R. (2002) 'Is pedophilia a mental disorder?' *Archives of Sexual Behavior*, 31 (6): 467–71.

Greenwood Publishing Group (undated) Advertising blurb for Foyd Mansfield Martinson, *The Sexual Life of Children*. Posted date unknown. Available online at http://www.greenwood.com/catalog/H376.aspx, last accessed 10 December 2009.

Guest, L. (2006) *The Trials of Michael Jackson*. St Bride's Major, South Wales: Aureus Publishing.

Gutierrez, V. (1997) *Michael Jackson was my Lover: The Secret Diary of Jordie Chandler*. Tajique, NM: Alamo Square Dist Inc (now unavailable).

Hall, G. Nagayama; Hirschman, R. & Oliver, L. (1995) 'Sexual arousal and arousability to pedophilic stimuli in a community sample of normal men'. *Behavior Therapy*, 26: 681–94.

Haywood, T., Grossman, L. & Cavanaugh, J. (1990) 'Subjective versus objective measurements of deviant sexual arousal in clinical evaluations of alleged child molesters'. *Psychological Assessment*, 2: 269–75 (cited in Hall *et al.*, 1995).

Heinberg, R. (2007) *Peak Everything: Waking Up to the Century of Decline in Earth's Resources*. Forest Row, East Sussex: Clairview Books.

Herdt, G. (1999) *Sambia Sexual Culture: Essays from the Field*, Chicago: University of Chicago Press.

Hughes, G. (2004) *Redemption: The Truth Behind the Michael Jackson Child Molestation Allegation*. Radford, VA: Branch and Vine.

Human Rights Watch (2003): 'Traditional practices that increase HIV/AIDS risk to women and girls: Dry sex'. Section in *Policy Paralysis: A Call for Action on HIV/AIDS-Related Human Rights Abuses Against Women and Girls in Africa*. Policy report available online at http://www.hrw.org/reports/2003/africa1203/6.htm, last accessed 21 April 2010.

Inquistion21 (undated) 'His art became his life'. Editorial. Posted undated online. Web-page no longer in existence. Text available online at http://www.religiousforums.com/forum/current-events/19851-kevin-brown.html, last accessed 5 December 2009.

Internet World Stats (2009) 'Internet usage statistics: the internet big picture; world internet users and population stats.' Posted date unknown. Available online at http://www.internetworldstats.com/stats.htm, last accessed 3 December 2009.

Itzin, C. (ed.) (2000) *Home Truths about Child Sexual Abuse: Influencing Policy and Practice: A Reader*. London and New York: Routledge.

Jackson, B. (2000) *Splendid Slippers: A Thousand Years of an Erotic Tradition*. Berkeley, CA: Ten Speed Press.

Jayaram, V. (2007) 'Gender equality and status of women in Zoroastrianism'. Hindu Website. Posted exact date unknown, 2007. Available online at http://www.hinduwebsite.com/zoroastrianism/gender.asp, last accessed 13 June 2008.

Jefferson, M. (2007) *On Michael Jackson*. New York, NY: Vintage Books USA.

Jenkins, P. (1992) *Intimate Enemies: Moral Panics in Contemporary Great Britain*. Hawthorne, NY: Aldine de Gruyter.

Jenkins, P. (1998) *Moral Panic: Changing Concepts of the Child Molester in Modern America*. New Haven, CT: Yale University Press.

Jenkins, P. (2003) *Beyond Tolerance: Child Pornography Online*. New York and London: New York University Press.

Jenks, C. (1996) *Childhood*. London: Routledge.

Jones, A. (2007) *The Michael Jackson Conspiracy*. Bloomington, IN: Universe Inc.

Jones, G. (1991) 'The study of intergenerational intimacy in North America: Beyond politics and pedophilia'. In T. Sandfort, E. Brongersma & A. van Naerssen (eds.) *Male Intergenerational Intimacy: Historical, Socio-Psychological and Legal Perspectives*. New York and London: Harrington Park Press.

Jones, J. (1997) *Alfred C. Kinsey: A Life*. London: W. W. Norton and Co.

de Jonge, N. (2007) Extracts from *Child Love TV*. Posted 13 May 2007. Available online at http://www.clogo.org/Child_Love_TV_20070513_GIV1.html (now defunct), last accessed 29 June 2007.

Kampmeier, D. (2008) '"Hounddog" Director says Dakota Fanning rape scene was all technical'. Starpulse. Posted 30 September 2008. Available online at http://www.starpulse.com/news/index.php/2008/09/30/hounddog_director_says_dakota_fanning_ra., last accessed 26 November 2009.

Kelly, L. (1987) 'The continuum of sexual violence'. In J. Holmes & M. Maynard (eds.) *Women, Violence and Social Control*. London: Macmillan, pp. 46–60.

Kelly, L. (1996) 'Weasel words: paedophiles and the cycle of abuse'. *Trouble and Strife*, 33: 449.

Kincaid, J. (1998) *Erotic Innocence: The Culture of Child Molesting*. Durham, NC: Duke University Press.

Kinsey, A., Pomeroy, W. & Martin, C. (1948) *Sexual Behavior in the Human Male*. Philadelphia: W. B. Saunders and Co. (Many re-issues of the original text, the most recent being by Indiana University Press on 1 June 1998, to mark the book's 50th anniversary).

Kinsey, A., Pomeroy, W., Martin, C. & Gebhard, P. (1953) *Sexual Behavior in the Human Female*, Philadelphia: W.B. Saunders and Co. (As with *Sexual Behavior in the Human Male*, numerous re-issues.)

Kipling, R. (1902) *Just So Stories*. London: Macmillan and Co. (Numerous reprints and editions.)

Kitzinger, J. (2004) *Framing Abuse: Media Influence and Public Understanding of Sexual Violence against Children*. London: Pluto Press.

Kitzinger, S. (2008) (4th edn.) *The New Pregnancy and Childbirth: Choices and Challenges*. London and New York: Dorling Kindersley.

Knegt, P. (2009) 'Over 100 in film community sign Polanski petition', IndieWire. Posted 30 September 2009. Available at http://www.indiewire.com/article/over_100_in_film_community_sign_polanski_petition/. Accessed 3 December 2009.

Ko, D. (2002) *Every Step a Lotus: Shoes for Bound Feet*. Berkeley, CA: University of California Press.

Ko, D. (2007) *Cinderella's Sisters: A Revisionist History of Footbinding*. Berkeley, CA: University of California Press.

Kobrin, S. (2004) 'More women seek vaginal plastic surgery'. *Women's eNews*. Posted 14 November 2004. Available online at http://www.womensenews.org/article.cfm/dyn/aid/2067/context/archive, last accessed 20 June 2008.

Krafft-Ebing, R. (1998) *Psychopathia Sexualis*. Complete English language translation. New York: Time Warner.

Kreisler, H. (2000) 'The case of trauma and recovery: Conversation with Judith Herman'. Interview, 21 September 2000. Transcript posted online. Available online at http://globetrotter.berkeley.edu/people/Herman/herman-con2.html, last accessed 14 December 2009. (Quotation is on p. 2 of interview transcript.)

Kun, K. (1998) 'Vaginal drying agents and HIV transmission'. *International Family Planning Perspectives*, 24 (2), June. Available online at http://www.guttmacher. org/pubs/journals/2409398.html, last accessed 17 June 2008.

Kwan Um School of Zen (1997) *Sayings of Zen Master Kyong Ho: The Great Matter of Life and Death*. Posted exact date unknown, 1997. Available online at http://www.kwanumzen.com/primarypoint/v15n1-1997-spring-kyonghozm-thegreatmatter.html, last accessed 13 June 2008.

Lear, A. & Cantarella, E. (2008) *Images of Ancient Greek Pederasty: Boys were their Gods*, London: Routledge Classical Studies.

Leurs, K. (2005) Exploring Pedophilia: a Pragmatic Inventory of the Pedophilic Discourse Observed from a Digital Media Perspective. Utrecht University, Communication and Information Studies, unpublished bachelor thesis, 8 July 2005 (personal communication).

Levine, J. (2002) *Harmful to Minors: The Perils of Protecting Children from Sex*. Minneapolis/London, University of Minnesota Press.

Li, C., West, D. & Woodhouse, T. (1990) *Children's Sexual Encounters with Adults*. London: Duckworth.

Liedloff, J. (1986) *The Continuum Concept: In Search of Happiness Lost*. Cambridge, MA: Da Capo Press.

Lightfoot-Klein, H. (1989) *Prisoners of Ritual: An Odyssey into Female Genital Circumcision in Africa*. New York, NY: Haworth Press.

Lightfoot-Klein, H. (1991) 'Prisoners of ritual: some contemporary developments in the history of female genital mutilation'. Paper presented at the Second International Symposium on Circumcision in San Francisco, 30th April – 3rd May. Available online at http://www.fgmnetwork.org/Lightfoot-klein/prisonersofritual.htm, last accessed 19 June 2008.

MacIntyre, D. (2002) 'Base instincts'. *Time*. Posted 5 August 2002. Available online at http://www.time.com/time/magazine/article/0,9171,501020812-333899,00.html, last accessed 3 June 2008.

MacQuarrie, B. (2004) 'Man defends attacks on sex offenders'. *Boston.com*. Posted 5 December 2004. Available online at http://www.boston.com/news/local/articles/2004/12/05/man_defends_attacks_on_sex_offenders/, last accessed 3 December 2009.

Malone, A. & Allen, V. (2007) 'Why Portugal is a haven for paedophiles'. Originally posted online at *Daily Mail*, 20 October 2007. Now available online at http://www.redicecreations.com/article.php?id=2041, last accessed 3 December 2009.

Malinowski, B. (2001; first published in 1927) *Sex and Repression in Savage Society*. New York and London: Routledge Classics.

Markay, L. (2009) 'The view's Whoopi Goldberg on Polanski: "It wasn't rape-rape"'. *Newsbusters*. Posted 29 September 2009. Available online at http:// newsbusters.org/blogs/lachlan-markay/2009/ 09/29/views-whoopi-goldberg-polanski-it-wasnt-rape-rape, last accessed 8 December 2009.

Mars-Jones, A. (2006), 'Lie back and think of Britten'. *The Observer*. Posted 4 June 2006. Available online at http://observer.guardian.co.uk/review/story/0,,1789768,00.html, last accessed 4 June 2006.

Martens, J. (2004), 'Congo rape victims seek solace'. *BBC News Online*. Posted 24 January 2004. Available online at http://news.bbc.co.uk/1/hi/world/africa/3426273.stm, last accessed 1 December 2008.

Martinson, F. M. (1994) *The Sexual Life of Children*. Westport, CT: Bergin and Garvey/Greenwood Publishing Group.

Masson, J. (1985) *The Assault on Truth: Freud's Suppression of the Seduction Theory*. New York: Farrar, Straus, Giroux.

McGeary, J. (2001) 'Death stalks a continent'. *Time*, cover story. Available online at http://www.time.com/time/2001/aidsinafrica/cover.html, last accessed 17 June 2008.

McKenna, K. & Bargh, J. (1998) 'Coming out in the age of the internet: Identity 'demarginalization' through virtual group participation'. *Journal of Personality and Social Psychology*, 75 (3): 681–94.

Mead, M. (2001; first published 1928) *Coming of Age in Samoa: A Psychological Study of Primitive Youth for Western Civilisation*. New York: Harper Perennial.

Mead, M. (2002; first published in 1935) *Sex and Temperament in Three Primitive Societies*. New York: HarperCollins.

Meyer, A. (2007) *The Child at Risk: Paedophiles, Media Responses and Public Opinion*. Manchester: Manchester University Press.

Miller, F., Vandome, A. & McBrewster, J. (eds.) (2009) *Historical Pederastic Relationships*. Beau Bassin, Mauritius: Alphascript Publishing.

Mitchell, P. (2003) 'Arrest of Portugal's elite in paedophile scandal'. *World Socialist Web Site*. Posted 18 June 2003. Available online at http://www.wsws.org/articles/2003/jun2003/port-j18.shtml, last accessed 3 December 2009.

Mohr, R. D. (1999) 'The pedophilia of everyday life'. *The Guide*. Posted January 1999. Available online at http://www.guidemag.com/magcontent/invokemagcontent.cfm?ID=E6B2CF69-031D-11D4-AD990050DA7E046B, last accessed 2 December 2008.

MSNBC (2005) '2 jurors say they regret Jackson's acquittal'. Posted 9 August 2005. Available online at http://www.msnbc.msn.com/id/8880663/, last accessed 3 December 2009.

Newman, M. (2009) 'Paedophilia research riles and titillates the academy'. *Times Higher Education*. Posted 10 September 2009. Available online at http://www.timeshighereducation.co.uk/story.asp?storycode=408084, last accessed 14 December 2009.

New York Post (2009) 'Inside story of the night that Polanski raped a child', by Joe Mozingo. Posted 29 October. Available online at http://www.nypost.com/p/news/international/inside_story_of_the_night_that_polanski_uXANQuPlq2G8LgAl5b1b7O, last accessed 7 November 2009.

New York Times (2007) 'Rape epidemic raises trauma of Congo war', by Jeffrey Gettleman. Posted 7 October 2007. Available online at http://www.nytimes.com/2007/10/07/world/africa/07congo.html, last accessed 23 September 2008.

Niven, J. (2009) 'Michael Jackson: Bad! And very dangerous'. *The Independent*, 4 July 2009. Available online at http://www.independent.co.uk/news/world/americas/michael-jackson-bad-and-very-dangerous-1731258.html, last accessed 10 August 2009.

Norris, S. (2007) 'International Literacy Day: women, literacy and education'. *ESRC Society Today*. Posted exact date unknown, 2007. Available online at http://www.esrcsocietytoday.ac.uk/ESRCInfoCentre/about/CI/CP/Our_Society_Today/Spotlights_2005/literacy.aspx?ComponentId=12508&SourcePageId=11457, last accessed 12 June 2008.

O'Carroll, T. (1980) *Paedophilia: The Radical Case*. London: Peter Owen Ltd.

Oliver, D. (1974) *Ancient Tahitian Society*. Honolulu, HI: Honolulu University Press. Ethnography (2nd edn), Vol. 1 (cited in Green, R. 2002).

Percy, W. (1996) *Pederasty and Pedagogy in Archaic Greece*. Urbana and Chicago: University of Illinois Press.

Perel, D. & Ely, S. (2005) *FREAK! Inside the Twisted World of Michael Jackson*. New York: HarperEntertainment.

Perverted Justice (2005, online) 'Online encyclopaedia is a gathering for internet paedophiles'. Posted 12 December 2005. Available online at http://www.perverted-justice.com/opinions/?article=11, last accessed 5 December 2009.

Plummer, K. (1995) *Telling Sexual Stories: Power, Change and Social Worlds*. London and New York: Routledge.

Pomeroy, W. (1968) *Boys and Sex*. New York: Delacorte Press.

Pomeroy, W. (1971) *Girls and Sex*. New York: Delacorte Press.

Pomeroy, W. (1974) *Your Child and Sex: A Guide for Parents*. New York: Delacorte Press.

Popham, P. (2003) 'Ten charged in Portuguese paedophile ring scandal'. *The Independent*. Posted 31 December 2003. Available online at http://www.independent.co.uk/news/world/europe/ten-charged-in-portuguese-paedophile-ring-scandal-578119.html, last accessed 3 December 2009.

Porter, D. (2007) *Jacko, His Rise and Fall: The Social and Sexual History of Michael Jackson*. New York: Blood Moon Productions.

Pravda (English language version) (2006) 'Child prostitution becomes global problem, with Russia no exception'. Posted 10 November 2006. Available online at http://english.pravda.ru/society/stories/11-10-2006/84991-child_prostitution-0, last accessed 4 June 2008.

Primates World (1998) 'Sex-crazed bonobos may be more like humans than thought'. Posted 15 May 1998. Available online at http://www.primatesworld.com/BonobosLikeHumans.html, last accessed 19 May 2008.

Pritchard, C. (2004) *The Child Abusers: Research and Controversy*. Maidenhead: Open University Press.

Quinsey, V., Steinman, C., Bergersen, S. & Holmes, T. (1975) 'Penile circumference, skin conductance, and ranking responses of child molesters, and "normals" to sexual and nonsexual visual stimuli'. *Behavior Therapy*, 6: 213–19 (cited in Green, 2002).

Rashbaum, A. (2004) 'Michael Jackson accused of paying hush money to boy in 1990', *MTV* online. Posted 3 September 2004. Available online at http://www.mtv.com/news/articles/1490750/20040903/jackson_michael.jhtml, last accessed 3 December 2009.

Reavey, P. and Warner, S. (eds.) 2003 *New Feminist Stories of Child Sexual Abuse: Sexual Scripts and Dangerous Dialogues*. London and New York: Routledge.

Reisman, J., Eichel, E., Muir, J. & Court, J. (1990) *Kinsey, Sex and Fraud: The Indoctrination of a People*. Lafayette, LA: Huntington House Publishers.

Reisman, J. (1998) *Kinsey: Crimes and Consequences the Red Queen and the Grand Scheme*. Crestwood, KY: Institute for Media Education.

Reisman, J. (2010) *Sexual Sabotage: How One Mad Scientist Unleashed a Plague of Corruption and Contagion on America*. Washington, DC: World Ahead Media / WorldNetDaily Publishers.

Reiss, I. (2000) 'In memory of Floyd Martinson'. *The Journal of Sex Research*, 37 (4): 391. Available online at http://www.jstor.org/stable/3813142, last accessed 10 December 2009.

Rich, A. (1996; first written 1980, first published 1986) 'Compulsory heterosexuality and lesbian existence'. In *Blood, Bread and Poetry: Selected Prose 1979–1985*. New York: W. W. Norton and Co.

Robinson, K. (1996) 'Of mail order brides and "Boys' Own" tales: representations of Asian-Australian marriages'. In *Feminism in the Antipodes. Feminist Review*, 52 (*The World Upside Down*). Spring: 53–68.

Robinson, P. (1976) *The Modernization of Sex: Havelock Ellis, Alfred Kinsey, William Masters, and Virginia Johnson*. New York: Harper and Row.

Ross, J. (2002) 'The shoe man'. In *Formosan Odyssey: Taiwan Past and Present*. Taipei: Taiwan Adventure Publications. Posted exact date unknown, 2002. Available online at http://www.romanization.com/books/formosan_odyssey/footbinding.html, last accessed 26 June 2008.

Rubin, G. 1992 'Thinking sex: Notes for a radical theory of the politics of sexuality'. In C.Vance (ed.) *Pleasure and Danger: Exploring Female Sexuality*. London: Pandora Press.

Rush, F. (1980) *The Best Kept Secret: Sexual Abuse of Children*. Englewood Cliffs, NJ: Prentice Hall.

Salter, A. (2003) *Predators: Pedophiles, Rapists and other Sex Offenders*. New York: Basic Books.

Sandfort, T. (1987) *Boys on their Contacts with Men: A Study of Sexually Expressed Friendship*. New York: Global Academic Publishers.

Sandfort, T., Brongersma, E. & Naerssen, A. van (eds.) (1991) *Male Intergenerational Intimacy: Historical, Socio-psychological and Legal Perspectives*. New York and London: Harrington Park Press.

Sandfort, T. & Rademakers, J. (eds.) (2001) *Childhood Sexuality: Normal Sexual Behaviour and Development*. London: Routledge. Schultz, P. (2005) *Not Monsters: Analyzing the Stories of Child Molesters*. Lanham, MD and Oxford, UK: Rowman and Littlefield.

Seisay, M. (2008) 'Gender violence in Sierra Leone: female genital mutilation makes a comeback'. *Suite 101*. Posted 31 January 2008. Available online at http://sierra-leone.suite101.com/article.cfm/the_resurgence_of_female_circumcis, last accessed 26 June 2008.

Silverman, J. & Wilson, D. (2002) *Innocence Betrayed: Paedophilia, the Media and Society*. Cambridge: Polity

Sinclair, M. (1988) *Hollywood Lolita: The Nymphet Syndrome in the Movies*. New York: Henry Holt and Company. (Cited in Kincaid, 1998).

Smiljanich, K. & Briere, J. (1996) 'Self-reported sexual interest in children: sex differences and psychosocial correlates in a university sample'. *Violence and Victims*, 11 (1): 39–50.

Stoltenberg, J. (2000a) (rev. edn) *Refusing to be a Man: Essays on Sex and Justice*, London: UCL Press.

Stoltenberg, J. (2000b) (rev. edn) *The End of Manhood: Parables on Sex and Selfhood*, London: UCL Press.

Swedien, B. (2009) *In the Studio with Michael Jackson*. Milwaukee, WI: Hal Leonard Publishing Corporation.

Tarvainen, S. (2004) 'Portugal in paedophile "hell"'. *News 24*. Posted 7 January 2004. Available online at http://www.news24.com/Content/World/News/1073/0952d1e3989b4d6d9f767a9d3d3be0d5/07-01-2004-07-20/Portugal_in_paedophile_hell, last accessed 11 December 2009.

Tatchell, P. (2002) 'Why the age of consent in Britain should be lowered to fourteen'. *Legal Notes 38*. London. Libertarian Alliance. (Cited in Waites, M. (2005) *The Age of Consent: Young People, Sexuality and Citizenship*. Basingstoke. Palgrave Macmillan.)

Taylor, Y. (2008) 'Interview: Professor Ken Plummer'. In *Network: Newsletter of British Sociological Association*, Autumn: 6–8.

Telegraph (2007) 'Paedophile abducted Madeleine, police say'. Posted 5 May 2007. Available online at http://www.telegraph.co.uk/news/main.jhtml?xml=/news/2007/05/06/nmaddy06.xml, last accessed 12 June 2008.

The Smoking Gun (2003) 'Polanski the predator: recently unsealed grand jury minutes detail 1977 sex assault'. Posted 11 March. Available online at http://www.thesmokinggun.com/archive/polanskicover1.html, last accessed 7 November 2009.

The Smoking Gun (2005) 'The case against Michael Jackson: the predator'. Posted 1 June 2005. Available online at http://www.thesmokinggun.com/archive/010605jackson.html, last accessed 3 December 2009.

Thomas, T. (2005) (2nd edn) *Sex Crime: Sex Offending and Society*. Cullompton: Willan.

Times (2007) 'Paedophile ring focus to Madeleine hunt'. Posted 9 May 2007. Available online at http://www.timesonline.co.uk/tol/news/uk/crime/article1769019.ece, last accessed 12 June 2008.

Thompson, D. (undated) 'Gary Glitter biography'. *AOL All Music Guide*. Available online at http://www.allmusic.com/artist/gary-glitter-p17891/biography. Last accessed 25 January, 2011.

Tremblay, P. (2002) 'Social interactions among paedophiles'. PDF format. Available online at www.sp2.upenn.edu/~restes/CSEC_Files/Tremblay_R2_020523.pdf, last accessed 8 December 2009.

Tremlett, G. (2002) 'Portugal's elite linked to paedophile ring'. *The Guardian*. Posted 27 November 2002. Available online at http://www.prisonplanet.com/portugals_elite_linked_to_paedophile_ring.html, accessed 3 December 2009.

Tremlett, G. (2004) 'Portugal rocked by child abuse scandal'. *The Guardian*. Posted 21 November 2004. Available online at http://www.guardian.co.uk/world/2004/nov/21/childprotection.uk, accessed 3 December 2009.

Turkle, S. (1997) *Life On The Screen: Identity In the Age of the Internet*. London: Phoenix.

Unicef (2006) *Child Protection Information Sheet: Female Genital Mutilation / Cutting*. United Nations Children's Fund. PDF file posted May 2006. Available online at http://www.unicef.org/protection/files/FGM.pdf, last accessed 16 June 2008.

USA Today (2006) 'Deadline blog discussion on gay marriage'. Available online at http://blogs.usatoday.com/ondeadline/2006/07/mass_court_oks_.html, last accessed 29 June 2007.

Usborne, D. (2006) 'UN report uncovers global child abuse'. *The Independent.* Posted 12 October 2006. Available online at http://www.independent.co.uk/ news/world/politics/un-report-uncovers-global-child-abuse-419700.html, last accessed 10 December 2009.

Vergnani, L. (2003) '"Uterine fury" – now sold in chemists'. *Times Higher Education.* Posted 9 May 2003. Available online at http://www. timeshighereducation.co.uk/story.asp?storyCode=176539&sectioncode=26, last accessed 11 August 2009.

Verstraete, B. & Provencal, V. (2006) *Same-Sex Desire and Love in Greco-Roman Antiquity and in the Classical Tradition of the West.* New York: Haworth Press.

Vincent, N. (2006) *Self-Made Man: My Year Disguised as a Man.* London: Atlantic.

Vineyard, J. (2004) 'Jackson says $25M settlement is not an admission of guilt'. *MTV* online. Posted 17 June 2004. Available online at http: //www.mtv.com/news/articles/1488501/20040617/jackson_michael.jhtml, last accessed 3 December 2009.

de Waal, F. (1995) 'Bonobo sex and society: the behaviour of a close relative challenges assumptions about male supremacy in human evolution'. *Scientific American* (March): 82–8.

de Waal, F. (1997) *Bonobo: the Forgotten Ape.* Berkeley, CA: University of California Press.

Waites, M. (2005) *The Age of Consent: Young People, Sexuality and Citizenship.* Basingstoke and New York: Palgrave Macmillan.

Wallechinsky, D. & Wallace, I. (1981) 'History of sex surveys: *Kinsey Report on Male Sexual Behavior.* Part 7: Conclusions. Available online at http://www.trivia-library.com/a/ history-of-sex-surveys-kinsey-report- on-male-sexual-behavior-part-7-conclusions.htm, last accessed 8 September 2008.

Ward, T; Polaschek, D. & Beech, A. (2006) Theories of Sexual Offending. Chichester, John Wiley and Sons

Wattenburg, B. (2000) Interview with Paul Gebhard. A New River Media interview. *The First Measured Century.* Available online at http://www.pbs.org/fmc/ interviews/gebhard.htm, last accessed 21 August 2008.

Weeks, J. (1989) (2nd edn) *Sex, Politics and Society: The Regulation of Sexuality since 1800.* London and New York: Longman.

Weeks, J. (2007) 'Wolfenden and beyond: The making of homosexual history'. History and Policy Paper. Posted February 2007. Available online at http://www.historyandpolicy.org/papers/policy-paper-51.html, last accessed 10 December 2009.

Wellings, K., Field, J., Johnson, A. & Wadsworth, J. (1994) *Sexual Behaviour in Britain: The National Survey of Sexual Attitudes and Lifestyles.* London: Penguin.

Wiker, B. (2001) 'Do you bonobo? Meet our make-love-not-war primates'. *Discovery Institute Center for Science and Culture.* Posted 10 November 2001. Available online at http://www.discovery.org/a/1066, last accessed 20 May 2008.

Wikipedia (2005) 'User: Linuxbeak / angry letter'. Posted 13 December 2005. Available online at http://en.wikipedia.org/wiki/User:Linuxbeak/Angry_letter, last accessed 20 April 2010.

Wikisposure (2009) 'Wikipedia campaign'. Last updated 29 November 2009. Available online at http://www.wikisposure.com/Wikipedia_Campaign, accessed 3 December 2009.

Williams, D. (2006) *The Warren Cup (Objects in Focus)*. London: British Museum Press.

Woodiwiss, J. (2009) *Contesting Stories of Childhood Sexual Abuse*. Basingstoke and New York: Palgrave Macmillan.

Wrangham, R. & Peterson, D. (1996) *Demonic Males: Apes and the Origin of Human Violence*. Boston, MA: Houghton Mifflin.

Yates, A. (1978) *Sex Without Shame: Encouraging the Child's Healthy Sexual Development*. New York: Morrow. (Text now out of print but available online.)

Yoshimi, Y. (2000) *Comfort Women: Sexual Slavery in the Japanese Military during World War II*. New York: Columbia University Press. (Original edition 1995, English translation by Suzanne O'Brien.)

Index

CPSIA information can be obtained at www.ICGtesting.com
Printed in the USA
LVOW07*1717040813

346202LV00009B/138/P